Becoming a Brother

Becoming a Brother

A Child Learns About Life, Family, and Self

Morton J. Mendelson

A Bradford Book
The MIT Press
Cambridge, Massachusetts
London, England

155./443
Men Bec
1990

Library of Congress Cataloging-in-Publication Data

Mendelson, Morton J.
  Becoming a brother : a child learns about life, family, and self /
Morton J. Mendelson.
    p.   cm.
  "A Bradford Book."
  Includes bibliographical references (p.   ).
  ISBN 0-262-13260-5
  1. Brothers and sisters—Case studies. 2. Brothers—Psychology—
Case studies. 3. Childbirth—Psychological aspects—Case studies.
I. Title.
BF723.S43M46   1990
155.44'3—dc20   90-5905
                                                              CIP

To Beverley with deepest friendship and abounding love and to
Simon, Asher, and Dana—our treasures, our delight

Contents

Acknowledgments

When I started, I had no idea that this study would take five years to complete. Yet I thoroughly enjoyed every step, partly because I was extraordinarily lucky to be helped by many good people. I thank them here:

Most important, Bev, for letting me tell what is, after all, her story too, for advising me from start to finish, for participating as an observer, for reading and rereading the manuscript, for constant encouragement, and for sharing my joy. I could not have done this without her.

Laurie Gottlieb, for first prompting me to ask questions about brothers and sisters; for unselfishly sharing her insights about siblings, attachment, and role acquisition; for thoughtful, challenging comments; and for many suggestions that improved the book.

Debbie Moskowitz, for advising me throughout the project, for willingly discussing anything from organizing themes to figures, and for her constructive criticism of the manuscript.

Laura Petitto, for her enthusiasm about my case study when it was still just an idea, for her advice about collecting language protocols, and for her perceptive comments on the book.

Frances Aboud, Kurt Fischer, Nina Howe, and Peter LaFrenière, for carefully reading the manuscript and pointing out many ways to improve it.

Betty Stanton, who believed in my proposal, and the other fine professionals at the MIT Press, for doing their part to gently guide me and the manuscript through publication.

Judy Todd, for "interviewing" Simon, transcribing audiotapes, coding daily diaries, and scoring behavioral questionnaires.

Josée Garneau and Sandra Gordon-Loiello, for filling out biweekly questionnaires from October to April and for giving Simon a supportive and stable daycare experience.

The McGill University Faculty of Graduate Studies and Research, for providing seed money for the project.

Finally, Simon, Asher, and Dana, for teaching me so much about life and love.

Parts of the study were presented at the International Conference on Infant Studies, Washington, D.C. (Mendelson, 1988a), at the Quebec Developmental Psychologists Consortium, Montreal, Quebec (Mendelson 1988b), and at the International Conference on Infant Studies, Montreal, Quebec (Mendelson 1990).

Introduction

Bev was pregnant toward the end of our sabbatical year in Jerusalem, and we opted to share the exciting news with Israeli friends before returning to Montreal. We told our son, Simon, too—earlier than we might have under other circumstances—so he would hear about the baby directly from us rather than inadvertently from someone else. Telling him early would also give him time to adjust to the potentially stressful prospect of a new sibling before our trip home, a move that would undoubtedly present its own challenges.

"Listen, Simon," I began one evening at supper, "Mommy and Daddy have something to tell you. There's a baby inside Mommy, in Mommy's uterus. The baby's very small now, so that's why Mommy doesn't look big, but the baby will grow, and then Mommy will start getting bigger. We expect the baby to come out of Mommy by December, in the winter, maybe a few days after your birthday" (3,4,21).[1] Simon immediately reacted with wonderment. Smiling broadly, he told Bev, "Mommy, you know what? There's a baby inside you!" He was apparently unaware that Bev would already know either on her own or even from my announcement.

We mentioned that Simon would be a big brother when the baby was born. Although we purposefully avoided any reference to the baby's sex, Simon drew his own conclusion and referred to a baby brother. Consequently we explained that we did not know whether the baby would be a boy or a girl, but no matter which, that Simon would still be a brother. Simon then indicated his limited understanding of family relationships by confusing unrelated dimensions; he

---

1. Simon's age in years, months, and days is indicated after every comment or observation; Asher is 4 years and 3 days younger than Simon. Where it is implied by the text, references should be understood as representing several possible examples. Comments that I recorded from memory are referenced simply with Simon's age: I often report them as indirect speech, retaining as much of the original language as possible. But for clarity, I sometimes present them as direct quotations. Conversations that were transcribed from audiotapes are indicated as such and are typically presented as dialogue.

was concerned that if the baby were a girl he would not be the big brother but rather the little brother. We assured him, much to his pleasure, that he would be the big brother no matter what the baby's sex. Three important issues had been raised: a baby was growing inside Bev, the baby would come out, and Simon would be a big brother. Simon grappled with these issues before Asher was born, just as he grappled with a variety of other concerns during the ensuing months.

I was finishing up a sabbatical year in Jerusalem, so I could not possibly have initiated a new project, especially a case study with daily commitments. Yet I was soon struck by Simon's reaction to the prospect of a new sibling, by the psychological "work" that he undertook. He wondered about biology, discussed plans for the baby, and spontaneously raised a variety of other relevant topics. I casually noted the questions, comments, and anecdotes. At the very least, I could use them to enliven my undergraduate lectures. But I became increasingly curious about the cognitive, social, and emotional implications of the transition to older sibling. I also realized how valuable it would be to construct an intensive account of how a preschooler adapts to the arrival of a new baby.

Why a Case Study?

By conducting a case study, I significantly departed from typical research in social development. The case method has enjoyed a long tradition in child psychology—dating back at least to Charles Darwin's account of his son Doddy in 1877—and has proved useful for investigating children's literacy, language, motor skills, and thinking (Bissex 1980, Brown 1973, McGraw 1935, Piaget 1952/1963). Despite such notable successes, case studies are generally seen as deficient; at best, they are considered merely a basis for subsequent research with traditional methods and relatively large groups of subjects. Yet there is growing appreciation that psychology can benefit from alternative approaches, including case methods and qualitative designs (Bromley 1986, Glaser and Strauss 1971, Packer 1985, Yin 1984). Like traditional research, case studies are useful for exploration—revealing previously unrecognized or rare phenomena (Darwin 1877)—for description—formulating theory and providing a heuristic for further investigation (Piaget 1952/1963)—and for explanation—testing specific hypotheses (McGraw 1935). They are also appropriate for capturing holistic and meaningful characteristics of real-life events, especially when event-context boundaries are unclear, as when a child is faced with family change.

There were many advantages to conducting a case study of my son. I was not an outsider, so my presence did not influence events by artificially changing the context. And I could delve more deeply than would be possible in a conventional study involving thirty or forty children. I had access to privileged information because I was intimately familiar with the participants and because I observed private situations such as Simon's bathtime and bedtime. I did not have to restrict myself to a few relatively brief observations but could garner information from daily encounters. I therefore witnessed relevant events, even if they were rare, and I could trace the development of issues over extended time periods.

As a second departure from conventional research, I did not restrict myself to preconceived constructs and measures. A legitimate case study must be a true-to-life account of a particular individual in a particular context (Bromley 1986). Thus I tried to understand Simon's experience as much as possible by remaining open to emerging issues and unfolding events. Yet I must admit that I had some preconceived ideas: for example, that a sibling's birth is potentially stressful and that a baby brother or sister might affect a preschooler's self-concept (Dunn and Kendrick 1982a). I must also acknowledge my role as participant-observer. I did not passively record events from a distance; when appropriate, I pursued issues by asking Simon questions or by getting information from others. As Simon's father, I was a fellow traveler on his journey to brotherhood—at times a companion, at times a guide—and I would not have sacrificed that experience even if it might have benefited my research.

At the outset, I should address what is probably the primary objection to case research: how can one generalize on the basis of a single instance? The criticism is apparently supported by a common result in the sibling literature: considerable variability both across pairs and within pairs across time in many aspects of the early sibling relationship (Dunn and Kendrick 1982a, Gottlieb and Mendelson 1990, R. B. Stewart 1983). Only some children are distressed by the arrival of a new brother or sister, and even their reactions vary in form and intensity. Children also differ in their behavior toward an infant sibling and in the amount of their involvement. Finally, sibling relationships vary in their overall affective tone and in the functions they serve, such as play, caregiving, and protection.

Researchers have begun to identify some sources of variability. Age differences influence preschoolers' interactions with a younger sibling. For example, firstborns older than 3 are more nurturing toward a newborn brother or sister than younger firstborns (Gottlieb and Mendelson 1990). Differences in preschoolers' competency may also affect their interactions with a baby brother or sister. Thus, perspective taking in young children is associated with a positive sibling relationship and may also predict nurturance to a baby brother or sister in distress (Howe and Ross 1990, Light 1979, R. B. Stewart and Marvin 1984). Sex differences may exist in early sibling relationships. Firstborn girls may be more prosocial toward an infant sibling than firstborn boys (Abramovitch et al. 1979, 1980, Lamb 1978b). And although the existing evidence is contradictory, the sex combination of the pair may be a factor (Dunn and Kendrick 1982a, Lamb 1978b).

The sibling relationship is also affected by mothers and fathers in a variety of ways. Children's relationships with parents provide the foundation for other social encounters (Bretherton and Waters 1985), so it is not surprising that preschoolers' interactions with a newborn sibling are related to mothers' and fathers' responsiveness to the firstborn (Gottlieb and Mendelson 1990). Children's interactions with an infant sibling may also be affected by parents' interactions with the baby; firstborns whose mothers are highly involved with an 8-month-old brother or sister tend to be less friendly toward the sibling six months later (Dunn and Kendrick 1982a). And parents may directly influence the sibling relationship; indeed negative interactions between siblings increase when mothers are merely present (Corter et al. 1983, Dunn and Munn 1986, Lamb 1978a).

Single cases cannot possibly represent typical families and children, but neither can samples in traditional studies. At best, researchers select families from a limited geographic area based on specific criteria about social class, language, and so on. Yet criticisms about external validity are based on mistaken analogies with survey research where results from properly selected samples are statistically generalized to a population. But case studies, just like traditional experiments, are analytically generalized to theory (Yin 1984). I am using the experience of one boy to identify the types of issues and explanations that may be relevant to understand what happens when a child becomes a brother or sister.

Goals and Procedures

My study was guided by three broad goals: to examine issues that a preschooler might confront during the period surrounding the birth of a sibling, to describe the preschooler's developmental tasks, and, if at all possible, to explain the basis for a preschooler's relationship with a new sibling. I began collecting data in earnest six weeks after returning from sabbatical (3,7,8), and I continued for ten months;

thus, with one or two exceptions, this book concerns the period of time from five months before to five months after Asher's birth.

I attempted to safeguard the validity of my findings and avoid the danger of possible emotional bias by using multiple measures from a variety of sources (Bromley 1986, Yin 1984). The time lines for my sources of data are shown in figure I.1. Most of the information presented in this book was derived from over 750 pages of qualitative observations and language protocols. The material included not only a daily log of my observations of Simon's actions and comments but also transcripts of taped conversations with Simon, taped dialogues between Simon and an undergraduate student, and taped interactions between Simon and Asher. These qualitative sources of information are described in appendix A (Qualitative Methods). The study also included quantitative methods that are described in appendix B (Behavioral Ratings of Adjustment) and appendix C (Daily Diaries).

Plan of the Book

This book addresses a variety of social, emotional, and cognitive issues related to becoming a brother. In chapter 1 I introduce three central themes relevant to understanding a child's adaptation to a

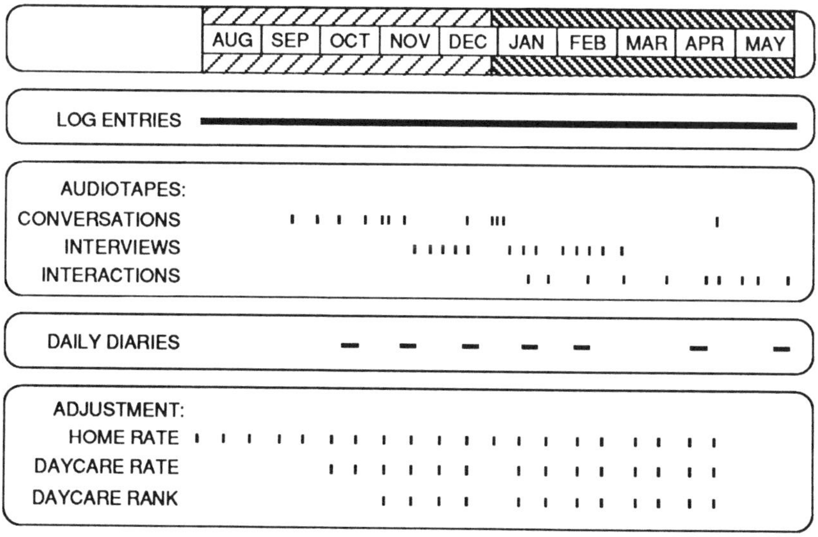

Figure I.1
Time lines for sources of data.

new sibling: family systems theory, life changes as role transitions, and personal narratives.

Chapters 2 and 3 focus on some of the psychological work that Simon initiated before Asher's birth. In chapter 2 I explore Simon's understanding of conception, gestation, and birth. The issues were conceptual puzzles for him, but they were also much more. I discuss Simon's anticipation of Asher's birth and his emotional reaction to the prospect of our going to the hospital without him. And I suggest how understanding biological origins is relevant to self-knowledge.

In chapter 3 I show that even before Asher's arrival Simon began to construct a concept of the baby and to alter his own self-concept. I start by elaborating how Simon's view of biological issues influenced his self-concept; specifically, Simon accepted the reality of his unborn sibling, which had implications for his understanding of his own role as brother. I also discuss Simon's expectations for the baby after birth and for fulfilling his brotherly role. Last, I examine how Simon strove to differentiate himself from the baby.

Chapter 4 is a narrative account of Simon's perspective on the events surrounding Bev's confinement and Asher's first few days at home. Initially I outline Simon's previous experience with babies; in addition to psychological work, Simon unknowingly prepared himself for the new baby in practical terms by gaining experience with other infants. I discuss Simon's previous separations from Bev and me, which possibly prepared him for Bev's stay in the hospital. Finally I examine Simon's initial adaptation to the stresses and strains of a new baby and a new family constellation.

The next two chapters deal with Simon's psychological adjustment to his new brother. In chapter 5 I attempt to construct a coherent account of Simon's reactions to Asher's arrival. To set the scene, I describe both continuity and change in Simon's daily routines from before to after Asher's birth. I then present background information relevant to Simon's adjustment before Asher was born and I examine signs of distress afterward. Finally I discuss three relevant issues: sources of stress, reactions to stress, and coping with stress.

In chapter 6 I address the popularly held misconception that preschoolers with a new sibling are necessarily consumed by jealousy. I examine instances, however rare, that might be taken as examples of Simon's rivalry and hostility. But I propose alternative explanations for Simon's apparently negative feelings and seemingly antagonistic behavior.

Chapters 7 to 9 concern positive aspects of Simon's relationship with his baby brother. In chapter 7 I examine Simon's attitudes toward Asher. For heuristic purposes, I organize the material in terms of five qualities or functions: acceptance of the baby as a family member, identification with the baby, brotherly affection, a desire to help by sharing, and protectiveness. I show how Simon's attitudes reflected his social understanding of roles, babies, himself, and the family.

In chapter 8 I discuss Simon's early interactions with his baby brother in terms of his responsiveness to Asher's signals. I explore Simon's reaction to Asher's crying and fretting and Simon's own initiatives to be involved with his brother. I then discuss Simon's response to Asher's smiles and laughter. In chapter 9 I examine Simon's speech to his baby brother and his emerging ability to sustain interactions. I discuss how the boys' interactions were gradually supported by both strategies that Simon acquired and social skills that Asher developed.

Last, in chapter 10 I explore several implications of my findings. I propose a general model to account for the early interactions and emerging relationship between a child and a new sibling. I focus on a young child's self-concept, interactive skills, and motivation to interact with a baby brother or sister and examine how the preschool child may be influenced by family members and family relationships. I then demonstrate how the model can account for the transition to the role of big brother or sister as a specific instance of role acquisition.

Chapter 1

Theoretical Themes

Strictly speaking, Simon became a brother when Asher was born at 8:16 A.M. on December 27 (4,0,3). Yet role transitions take time. Simon began the psychological process of becoming a brother many months earlier, when he first learned that we were expecting a baby, and he continued developing his new family role long after Asher came home from the hospital.

This book concerns Simon's emotional, cognitive, and social adaptation to his baby brother. But before presenting Simon's story, I outline three theoretical themes that I weave through the book and ultimately draw together in a model of the early sibling relationship: In this chapter, I briefly examine family systems theory to highlight the reciprocal influences of family roles and to show how the arrival of a second child dramatically increases the structural complexity of a family. I then propose that the birth of a brother or sister—like any other life transition—can be viewed as an instance of role acquisition; the suggestion is hardly radical, but, surprisingly, its implications have not been explored in the literature. Finally I advocate that a personal-narrative approach to self-concept is useful for describing a preschooler's transition from only child to big brother or sister.

Family Systems Theory

While conducting this case study, I tried to observe Simon and his emerging relationship with Asher in as realistic a light as possible. I could have seriously biased my observations if I had adopted a strict theoretical orientation. Yet one framework—family systems theory—actually enhanced my view of possible influences on Simon and his new role. The nuclear family is a social system nested within broader systems such as the extended family, a circle of friends and acquaintances, and the community, each of which is reciprocally related to the nuclear family; for example, changes in the nuclear family can affect the extended family and vice versa (Bronfenbrenner 1979). The family itself consists of members in different positions: wife/mother, husband/father, daughter/sister, and son/brother. And they participate in various subsystems, based not only on their positions—husband-wife, parent-child, or sibling-sibling—but also on other criteria such as gender—the boys or the girls—and interest—the skiers, the musicians, and so on. Finally, family members and subsystems reciprocally influence other members, other subsystems, and the total family system (Feiring and Lewis 1978).

Figure 1.1 diagrammatically shows a three-member family: a wife/mother (WM), a husband/father (HF), and a child (C). Actually two diagrams are possible—one for a son and one for a daughter—but possible differences between them are irrelevant here. All the lines in this and subsequent system diagrams should be understood as double-ended arrows. The heavy black lines stand for reciprocal influences between pairs of individuals; for example, a mother and child both affect each other. The hatched lines stand for reciprocal influences between individuals and relationships. These may be second-order effects in which individuals influence the relationship between two other parties; for example, the father's presence reduces interactions between the mother and baby (reviewed by Belsky 1981). But individuals also reciprocally affect relationships in which they participate (D. M. Klein et al. 1978); for example, a mother's self-esteem may influence and be influenced by how well she interacts with her baby (Goldberg 1977). The thin black lines designate reciprocal influences between relationships, for example, between parenting (M-C or F-C) and the marriage (W-H) (Belsky 1981, Hinde and Stevenson-Hinde 1988).

The arrival of a second child alters the family structure and conse-

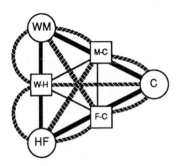

Figure 1.1
System diagram of a three-member family (WM = wife/mother; HF = husband/father; C = child).

quently affects existing interactional patterns (Kreppner et al. 1982). The baby establishes two parent-infant subsystems, places the first-born in a sibling relationship, modifies the parent-firstborn relationships, and probably disrupts the marriage. Like every other system, the family responds to new demands to maintain a steady state. Specifically, it regulates itself through three spheres of activity: access to space, time, and energy (Kantor and Lehr 1976). But a baby may disturb all three, and a new equilibrium will have to be established: living space may have to be rearranged, schedules will have to accommodate the baby's needs, and parents will have less energy until they learn to care for two children (LaRossa 1983).

A system diagram of a four-member family is extremely complex (figure 1.2). Adding a second child increases the number of relationships from three to six, and each individual is reciprocally influenced by the three other individuals and by the six relationships. A

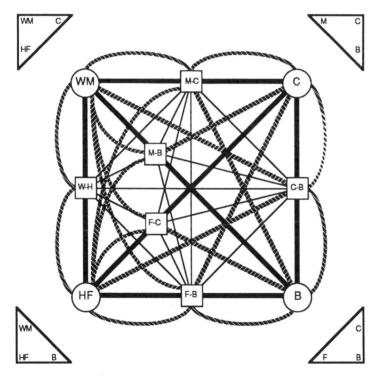

Figure 1.2
System diagram of a four-member family (WM = wife/mother; HF = husband/father; C = child/sibling; B = baby/sibling).

family of four also includes four triads, each reciprocally influencing the other triads, the six relationships, and the four members.
Although the triads are shown in the figure, their reciprocal influences are not. Yet the figure is probably still too complicated to be
useful.

   Figure 1.2 can be simplified for my purposes by ignoring the triadic
subsystems, disregarding the marriage, and combining the parents
into one node. Thus, figure 1.3 (top) shows the family members—
parents, child/sibling, and baby/sibling—and the subsystems—
parent-child, parent-baby, and child-baby—all reciprocally related.
Although the diagram graphically illustrates the context of the child
and the sibling relationship, it can be simplified further to highlight
my main concerns: figure 1.3 (bottom) emphasizes the two most relevant nodes—child and child-baby—and retains only the reciprocal
influences that I found to be most important.

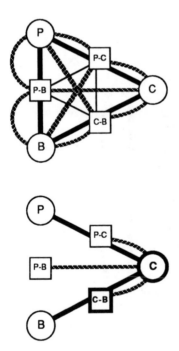

Figure 1.3
System diagrams of a four-member family (P = parents; C = child/sibling; B =
baby/sibling). The top diagram is complete; the bottom diagram is a simplified version that retains the elements most relevant to a discussion of the child and the
child-baby relationship.

Life Changes as Role Transitions

The birth of a brother or sister is a common yet significant transition that shares structural features with other life changes (A. J. Stewart 1982). It may transform the firstborn's everyday routine, and it demands new behavioral, cognitive, and emotional responses, including symbolic shifts in the child's conception of family and self (Dunn and Kendrick 1982a). Generally a life change can be characterized as a crisis, a stressor, or a role transition (A. J. Stewart et al. 1986), but psychologists who have discussed preschoolers' reactions to the birth of a brother or sister have focused primarily on crisis and stress.

Psychodynamic theorists have forcefully argued that the transition to sibling status is a crisis in the sense of a traumatic event because it necessarily involves dethronement or displacement within the family (Freud 1909/1955, Levy 1937). But the facts belie such a one-sided view; many children respond quite positively to a new sibling, and those who do not show considerable variability in the intensity of their reactions. Thus, the arrival of a sibling may herald a crisis in the sense of a turning point when development must move one way or another (Erikson 1968). Regardless, virtually all researchers have viewed the transition to sibling status as a stressful life change that may or may not elicit coping (Dunn and Kendrick 1982a, Field and Reite 1984, Feiring et al. 1983, Gottlieb and Mendelson 1990, Kramer 1989, Legg et al. 1974, Nadelman and Begun 1982, R. B. Stewart et al. 1987, Thomas et al. 1961, Trause et al. 1981).

As a whole, investigators have asked what aspects of the transition might be stressful and what personal or social resources might account for differences in children's coping. Certainly they have acknowledged that the changes in family roles associated with the birth of a brother or sister are potentially stressful, especially for firstborns. But no one has actually examined the transition to sibling status as an instance of role acquisition; no one has attempted to understand the processes whereby children adopt the sibling role.

When I started my study, I did not envision the value of role theory for explaining either a firstborn's reaction to the birth of a sibling or the initial relationship with the baby. But analyzing my data drew me inexorably to just that conclusion. My primary theoretical goal in this book is to elaborate how processes of role acquisition are central for understanding the transition to sibling status.

Before proceeding, I should define some essential terms from role theory (Shaw and Costanzo 1982). A role consists of behaviors associated with a position in a social context, and, as in the family, it may be paired with a reciprocal or complementary role of another position. Behavioral norms, which are prescribed expectations about the functions, obligations, and rights associated with the role, are defined by a social group and are presumably internalized by individuals; for example, the role of big brother may be understood in terms of companionship, teaching, being admired, and so on. Enactment of the role consists of the behaviors actually performed by an individual; a given brother may provide companionship by engaging in fantasy play or by roughhousing. And based on experience, individuals acquire predictive expectations about how others will respond to them or to particular situations; a child may expect a sister to enjoy playing house or learn that a baby brother enjoys being tickled. Last, an individual's role enactment may be evaluated either by others with reference to social norms or by the individual with reference to internalized values; a brother who disrupts his sister's tea party may be sanctioned by their mother, while a brother who successfully amuses the baby may be pleased about his own role performance.

It is probably impossible to fully define a role, like brother or sister, that not only varies across families and cultures but also changes with time. Yet even if the functions served by the relationship and its overall affective tone differ across sibling pairs, the relationship between brothers and sisters may have several positive qualities (Bank and Kahn 1982, Dunn 1983, Goetting 1986). Table 1.1, which partly defines the roles in a sibling relationship, presents nine such qualities

Table 1.1
Qualities of a Sibling Relationship with Corresponding Attitudes, Feelings, and Behaviors

Quality	Attitudes, Feelings, and Behaviors
Friendliness	not rivalrous, not jealous, not competitive
Getting along	not hurting, not domineering, not fighting, not teasing, not quarreling
Acceptance	inclusion, interest, pride
Identification	want to be similar, try to do similar things, imitate
Affection	love, warmth, admiration
Help	assist, share, teach, encourage
Protection	provide security, look out for, stick up for
Nurturance	comfort, show kindness, caregive
Companionship	want to be together, enjoy each other's company, cooperate

Source: Adapted from Furman and Buhrmester (1985), Mendelson et al. (1988), and Mendelson and Gottlieb (1988).

along with attitudes, feelings, or behaviors associated with each. Two of the qualities—friendliness and getting along—are construed here as the absence of rivalry and conflict. But the remaining qualities are defined positively. Some of them refer predominantly to feelings (friendliness, affection, approval, and identification), some to the general quality of interaction (getting along and companionship), and some to specific functions that may be served by the sibling relationship (help, nurturance, and protection). The list is not exhaustive; for example, loyalty and intimacy are missing, two qualities that are relevant in middle childhood and beyond. Yet the list does characterize the potential richness of a preschooler's role as brother or sister.

But how does a young child acquire the role? Fortunately the literature on maternal role acquisition provides an appropriate model for an answer. Mercer (1981) framed a description of maternal role attainment (R. Rubin 1967) within a general theory that proposed four phases of role acquisition: anticipatory, formal, informal, and personal (Thornton and Nardi 1975). The foundations for the maternal role are likely established during childhood (Ricks 1985). Yet pregnancy serves as a more immediate anticipatory phase. A pregnant woman begins to adjust socially and psychologically by learning role expectations. She mimics appropriate models—perhaps her mother or her friends—and she may role play with someone else's child. More significant, she fantasizes about being a mother and relates to her unborn baby, especially when she starts feeling fetal movement. Finally, she seeks information not only about pregnancy and childbirth but also about motherhood (Deutsch et al. 1988).

The formal phase of maternal role acquisition is initiated by the baby's arrival. A woman begins to identify her baby and to assume maternal tasks (Gottlieb 1975). Yet her role performance is mainly influenced by the prescribed expectations of a variety of experts: her mother, doctor, nurses, friends, books, and so on. Thus, she seeks information about motherhood more during her baby's first month than at other times (Deutsch et al. 1988). Gradually a new mother enters an informal phase, during which she begins to perform her role in her own way. She acquires predictive expectations that are relevant to her baby, so she no longer rigidly follows the prescribed expectations or advice of others, and she can evaluate the extent to which a recommendation or a model is appropriate for her and her baby.

During the personal phase of role acquisition, a new mother establishes her own enactment style that is generally accepted by others. She gains a sense of identity within the maternal role, a sense of where she has been and where she is going. Yet adopting a new role involves giving up competing aspects of previous roles; for example, a first-time mother must let go of her role of bride. In relinquishing prior identities, a woman reviews associated attachments and events—"grief work" that presumably loosens ties with her former self (R. Rubin 1967). Second-time mothers often find this quite difficult since they must also disengage from their firstborn to some extent (Walz and Rich 1983).

The model of maternal role acquisition is useful for considering the transition to big brother or sister. In becoming a brother, Simon experienced anticipatory, formal, informal, and personal phases of the transition. Within this framework, I will explore a number of relevant issues: Simon's understanding of the new baby and the baby's role; Simon's concept of his own role as big brother; relinquishing his earlier role as only child; acquiring the behavioral skills associated with his new role; and finally, changing his own self-concept, a topic that requires some elaboration.

Personal Narratives

A child's self-concept develops in a social context. Self-identity is tied to social identity (Sarbin and Scheibe 1983), and knowledge about the self is acquired concurrently with knowledge gained about others through social interaction (J. M. Baldwin 1897, M. Lewis and Brooks-Gunn 1979). Therefore a firstborn's self-concept should be influenced by the birth of a baby brother or sister, a life change that creates a new role, establishes a new relationship, and modifies existing relationships. And as the two children develop, their identities may become more and more intertwined (Bank and Kahn 1982).

Theorists have distinguished between two aspects of the self-system, between the *I* and the *Me* (reviewed by Harter 1983). The I is the self as subject—the active observer-knower or the structure of its defining cognitive processes; the Me is the self as object—the product of the observing process or the content of the self-system (James 1890/1963, M. Lewis and Brooks-Gunn 1979). Most research on children's self-concept has concerned the Me, and the scant work with 3- to 5-year-olds has usually involved self-descriptions (Keller et al. 1978, Mendelson et al. 1987), although there are notable exceptions in which self-understanding has been cast in a social-cognitive framework (Fischer et al. 1984, Pipp et al. 1987).

When I started my case study, I suspected that Simon's understanding of himself and his family might be relevant, and I initially focused on the content of his self-knowledge. But it soon became clear that a number of issues—not only those related to self-concept—were best understood in terms of self-narratives. The narrative is a root metaphor. People think, perceive, imagine, and dream in narrative structures—meaningful patterns that organize otherwise chaotic meaningless input. As a result, storytelling, oral traditions, fables, and myths are universal, present even in the earliest cultures. The narrative metaphor can also be applied to the self-concept; the I can be conceived as the storyteller and various Me's as roles within the story (Mancuso and Sarbin 1983).

The term *self-narrative* has been used to refer to individuals' accounts of self-relevant events across time (Gergen and Gergen 1983). According to this view, individuals actively construct and reconstruct their self-concept and understand themselves as historically emerging beings. Their identity is therefore not a sudden and mysterious event but a sensible result of a life story. Self-narratives are social; they emerge from social events, not from intrapsychic processes. Finally, they reflect social connectedness because an individual's life story is necessarily related to the life story of important others.

It is useful to distinguish between macronarratives—about extended sequences of events such as a lifetime or a nation's history—and micronarratives—about short-lived events such as social encounters (Gergen and Gergen 1983). A life story is an example of a macronarrative. It reflects an individual's attempt to represent the past, present, and future as a coherent narrative. It may begin generations back, perhaps with a famous, or notorious, ancestor or with great-grandparents who emigrated from the old country. Even if it lacks an extended history, a personal narrative still includes information about the past—about parents and childhood circumstances. And it is also projected into the future through goals and expectations or even beyond death through a will and through expectations for children and grandchildren.

Narratives are embedded in narratives. A life story includes narratives of each relationship, which include narratives of different aspects of the relationship, which include micronarratives of specific encounters. Narratives about relationships are not simply retrospective accounts; they contain information and predictive expectations about both role partners. And like event schemas or scripts, micronarratives represent the dynamic frameworks of experienced events (Mandler 1983, Nelson and Gruendel 1981, Schank and Abelson 1977). Thus, narratives about relationships enable individuals to plan, anticipate trends, and conduct themselves in social encounters.

The narrative approach is certainly consistent with previous theorizing about the self-concept: It distinguishes between the I and the Me, it stresses the importance of the self in relation to others, and it provides a constructivist account of the development of the self-system (Harter 1983). The narrative approach is also apt for considering young children. It is consistent with preschoolers' knowledge both about scripts (Nelson 1981) and about roles in fantasy play (Bretherton 1984, P. Miller and Garvey 1984); it can be used to explain their knowledge about other people; and it is compatible with recent theorizing about young children's relationships with family members (Bretherton 1985).[1]

As I discovered, a new brother or sister may prompt a child to revise or construct personal narratives. The baby's arrival highlights the child's own biological origins and infancy; it also creates a new present by dividing social time between a past without the baby and a future tied to expected developmental change. Modifications to the family and to existing family roles may require the child to revise narratives about family routines and relationships. And in adopting the role of big brother or sister, the child will probably acquire scripts for interacting with the baby and construct narratives that include the newcomer.

1. Discussing attachment to parents, Bretherton (1985) linked the notion of internal working models to scripts and to a scientific-theory metaphor of the self (Epstein 1973, Epstein 1980). The narrative metaphor shares many of the advantages of the scientific-theory metaphor for self-concept. Most notably, both provide a means for organizing and interpreting self-relevant information, but the narrative metaphor accommodates social roles more directly and is more plausible for preschoolers' self-concept. Young children's scientific theories are probably more akin to stories or myths than to systems of postulates and deductions. And children have considerable experience comprehending and generating narrative forms before they understand even the most basic hypothetico-deductive argument.

Chapter 2
Biological Issues

Preschoolers have sorely limited understanding of biology, perhaps especially about where babies come from. They lack not only the essential facts about reproduction (Goldman and Goldman 1982) but also an intuitive biological theory to organize the facts (Carey 1985). The impending arrival of a new sibling affords a curious child an opportunity to learn at least the rudiments of conception, pregnancy, prenatal development, and birth.

Children's Explanations of Reproduction

Interviewers who have asked children from preschool to adolescence about the origin of babies have obtained answers that typically take one of six forms (table 2.1) (Bernstein and Cowan 1975, Goldman and Goldman 1982). Although youngsters' explanations are apparently correlated with Piagetian measures of cognitive development, the correlations could very well be spurious reflections of common improvement with age. Indeed there is no evidence that the six explanations of reproduction form an invariant developmental sequence as presumably would be the case if cognitive status were critical. There are, more tellingly, systematic national differences in children's understanding of reproduction that correspond to national attitudes about the human body, sexuality, and sex education. Thus, immature accounts of reproduction might be eliminated or reduced by sensitive, sensible explanations from uninhibited adults.

Most preschoolers are geographers or manufacturers (table 2.1), including 90 percent of the 3- and 4-year-old children of highly educated, middle-class families in Berkeley, California (Bernstein and Cowan 1975). Ronald and Juliette Goldman (1982) interviewed more representative samples of children from North America, England, Australia, and Sweden. Approximately 85 percent of English-speaking 5-year-olds responded at the first two levels, and the remaining responded as agriculturalists. But only 54 percent of Swedish 5-year-

Table 2.1
Six Types of Explanations of Reproduction

Level	Type of Reasoning	Explanation
1. Geographer	spatial causality	Babies are not really made but have always been in a specific place—like "heaven" or "Mommy's tummy"—preexisting even the mother.
2. Manufacturer	artificialism	Babies are made from materials manufactured by God, medical workers, or fathers, perhaps in a factory attached to a hospital; the manufactured baby is inserted into the mother nonsexually, perhaps by a doctor who performs an operation (Caesarean conception).
3. Agriculturalist	semiphysical, semiartificial, semipsychological	A baby comes from a seed, perhaps bought by the father at a gardening shop, from an egg, possibly obtained by the mother with her groceries, or from another critical ingredient, like milk or fish. The agricultural theory is then combined with the digestive fallacy: the seed, egg, or other ingredient is swallowed and grows into a baby in the mother's stomach, literally as a seed grows into a flower in the soil.
4. Reporter	physical, technically realistic	Babies result from a vaguely understood biological process that occurs during a little understood type of physical or sexual joining at, for example, the navel.
5. Miniaturist	animalculism or ovism	Babies are formed during a procreative act that involves the joining of the sexual organs but does not include complementary roles of egg and sperm; the baby exists in miniature form either in the sperm, in which case the egg provides a suitable environment for growth, or in the egg, in which case the sperm triggers growth.
6. Realist	physicalism freed from precausality	Babies are the result of sexual union that involves the passing of sperm from the man to the woman and subsequent fertilization, which entails the fusion of the sperm and ovum to create a new individual.

Sources: Bernstein and Cowan (1975), Goldman and Goldman (1982).

olds answered at the lowest two levels, and the rest were evenly divided between agriculturalists and reporters. By 7 years of age, almost no English-speaking children achieved even reporter status, yet 56 percent of Swedish children responded at this level or better. The difference between the English-speaking and Swedish children was attributed to the latter having freer access to relevant information.

Children who do not have access to honest answers about reproduction presumably construct their own explanations. Young children are hampered particularly by partial information, by poor understanding of even basic biological concepts (Carey 1985), and by unintentionally misleading analogies and metaphors (Goldman and Goldman 1982). Consequently they explain reproduction with narratives that include inappropriate elements and irrelevant causal principles.

Bev and I were not familiar with the relevant literature at the time of this case study. We did know what child-care books advise (Spock and Rothenberg 1985): wait for questions and answer them as forthrightly as possible, using accurate terms but replying simply enough for the child to understand. Regardless, Bev and I made many of the same errors committed by countless other parents, so Simon's experience was fairly typical in this regard.

Simon's ideas about conception, pregnancy, and birth were similar to the opinions expressed by children in previous studies. The narrative that follows is not meant to be a report of how much a preschooler learns about the facts of life. Rather, it illustrates how the impending arrival of a new sibling raises biological questions for a curious preschooler and how difficult it may be for the child to grapple with the answers.

Where Is the Baby?

Stomachs, Tummies, and Uteruses
Like all other modern-day preschoolers, Simon discerned that babies grow inside their mother (Goldman and Goldman 1982). Listening to a Cabbage Patch book (McQueen 1984), he knowingly agreed it was silly that Cabbage Patch kids grow in cabbages and confidently offered that they grow "inside their mommies" (3,7,17). Simon realized that he had once been inside Bev, a fact supported by pictures of Bev when she was pregnant and by many conversations. Trying to persuade Simon to drink his milk, I might observe, "You know that Mommy also drinks a lot of milk. That's so the baby's bones will grow. When you were inside Mommy, she used to drink a lot of milk

so your bones would grow, but now you have to drink the milk your-self" (taped 3,7,30). Thus, when Simon's grandfather mentioned to Bev that she looked big, it was no surprise that Simon could explain, "That's because she has a baby inside her" (3,8,7).

But exactly where inside creates a critical misconception for chil-dren, who almost universally believe that babies grow in their mother's stomach (Goldman and Goldman 1982). This apparently in-nocuous error is unfortunately consistent with several other childish misconceptions: that babies are conceived by swallowing a seed or by eating special food and that babies are born through the anus or mouth. A preschooler uses an initial premise, however wrong, and constructs a fairly coherent explanation in the form of a narrative that is consistent with it.

It is easy to imagine reasons for the misconception that babies grow in their mother's stomach. Young children understand the body's in-terior, which they refer to as *stomach* or *tummy*, only in global terms and do not distinguish among the various organs (Crider 1981). Con-sequently a preschooler might spontaneously assume that a baby was in a woman's tummy, and adults often support this piece of misin-formation. An adult talking to a preschooler chooses *tummy* as the most obvious word to refer to the unborn baby's location because *tummy* is the adult's infantile version of *abdomen*. However misleading it may be to a young child, *tummy* seems to be the appropriate term, especially for the external manifestation of pregnancy. Simon once pointed out a pregnant woman and appropriately used *tummy*, at least to my ear. When Bev asked him how he knew she was pregnant, he responded, "Because her tummy sticks out. I think she has a baby inside her" (3,8,2). Even if Simon meant *tummy* to refer to *stomach*, most adults would have understood it as *abdomen*. And I doubt that any adult native speaker would have said, "Because her *uterus* sticks out."

Simon may have known slightly more than many other preschool-ers about the stomach, specifically about its role in digestion. For al-most a year he had continually requested the "story about what happens when we eat food," which was appropriately a favorite when he was moving his bowels. I typically reviewed each process and organ in the sequence from chewing through elimination. Si-mon's unflagging fascination with the story probably reflected both curiosity about his body and difficulty in understanding such an ab-stract account. Even before he knew about the baby, Simon could accurately recite the digestion story, which included vigorous hand movements to indicate how the stomach grinds up food. He also oc-casionally illustrated how hungry or full he was by drawing a line in a circle to represent the level of food in his stomach. Yet the stomach's role in digestion does not necessarily exclude it from a role in reproduction.

However much Simon appeared to know about digestion and however acceptable *tummy* may be in certain circumstances, Bev and I tried to avoid using it when talking about the unborn baby. On first telling Simon that Bev was pregnant, I said that there was a baby "inside Mommy, in Mommy's uterus" (3,4,21). Simon had rarely, if ever, heard *uterus* before then. We had possibly used the term without explanation when discussing other pregnant women or as an extension to the statement, "Boys have a penis, and girls have a vagina." Even so, Simon certainly did not know what a uterus is or where it is located, yet he did not ask what it meant, and we unfortunately did not offer an explanation.

By telling Simon that the baby was growing in Mommy's uterus, we hoped to demystify the process of conception, pregnancy, and birth. We did not succeed, mainly because we failed to distinguish between appropriately using the term and understanding the concept. We had provided an undefined alternative to *tummy*, so Simon was actually left to his own devices, and he solved the problem as virtually every other child does. Despite our repeated efforts to set the terminology right, Simon had trouble remembering that an unborn baby is not in its mother's stomach. Simon and I were discussing cars one day, and I mentioned that we had a Maverick when he was a baby. Trying to specify the time exactly, Simon asked, "When I was in Mommy's stomach?" I corrected him, "Babies are in their mommy's uterus, not in their mommy's stomach," whereupon he claimed that he knew but had just forgotten (3,7,13).

Notwithstanding his claim, Simon and I repeated the conversation the very next day. I mentioned that a local street was built a very long time ago, and again Simon sought clarification by asking, "When I was in Mommy's stomach?" I first dealt with the time issue; I explained through recursion that it was much longer ago than Simon thought, that it was before Simon "was in Mommy's stomach, before Mommy was in Bubby's [Grandma's] stomach, even before Bubby was in her mommy's stomach." Simon giggled, presumably at the thought of his grandmother inside her mother. But I then realized the problem with *stomach* and reminded Simon that babies are not in their mommy's stomach but in their uterus. Simon acknowledged the correction and changed the subject (3,7,14).

Seven weeks later Simon still occasionally mentioned that the baby was in "Mommy's tummy" (3,8,24), but he sometimes used *uterus* correctly and eventually did so not only when talking to Bev or me. Simon's aunt once jokingly traced his age back from 3 and asked how old he was before he was 1; Simon replied, "I was in my Mommy's uterus" (3,10,11). Another time, Simon's daycare teacher asked if he had felt Mommy's tummy; Simon corrected, "No, her uterus" (3,11,3). Here, *tummy* was more apt, but Simon had finally learned a poor lesson: to use *uterus* without understanding what it meant.

In time Simon was even amused by the inappropriate use of *tummy*. Two weeks before he became a brother, he intently listened to a book that depicted various baby issues (Althea 1973) and genuinely laughed when I read, "The baby is in the Mommy's tummy" (3,11,19). Two days later I read, "Your mother will go to the doctor quite often. He listens to make sure the baby is comfortable in her tummy." Simon immediately objected, "Not tummy!" and, when asked, he explained, "the uterus" (taped 3,11,21). A preschool book had it wrong, but Simon had it right, at least verbally.

After Asher was born, Simon still occasionally mentioned stomachs and tummies. He sometimes corrected himself—"Babies are inside their mommy's stomach . . . I mean uterus" (4,1,3)—but not always— "And that [photo] is when I was in my Mommy's tummy" (taped 4,1,11). Yet Simon could still use the appropriate term. He once referred to a pregnant woman as a "lady with a baby." When I asked where the baby was, he responded in a distinctly why-are-you-asking tone of voice, "In her uterus" (4,3,0).

What Is a Uterus Anyway?
Simply knowing the term *uterus* was not enough. Although we tried to keep Simon on track by avoiding *tummy*, we were remiss in not providing relevant details. Therefore many pieces were missing from Simon's puzzle, and he was confused for quite a while about where an unborn baby is and where it can be. Early on Simon wondered about alternative places for a baby to grow. He asked about animals having babies, and I explained among other things that baby animals grow inside their mommy. When Simon inquired why animals cannot grow in their daddy, I responded that daddies do not have uteruses, so they do not have any place for babies to grow. Exploring another possibility, Simon suggested that they can grow in their daddy's mouth, but when I stated that babies do not grow in mouths, Simon chuckled and claimed that he knew, that he was just kidding (3,7,23).

Another day Simon was still grappling with alternatives and revealed his animistic thinking about the problem. Rather than ascribe biological causes, he, like other young children, thought in terms of psychological explanations. "Where does a boy grow," Simon asked haltingly, "if he doesn't want to grow . . . uh . . . inside . . . uh . . . his mommy's . . . uh . . . tummy?" I mentioned once again that all babies grow inside their mommy's uterus. Yet Simon persevered: "What if the boy didn't *want* to?" Simon not only attributed a mind to the unborn baby but also implied that the baby's psychological state could influence its location, presumably just as his own desires might determine his location. Bev simply stated, without explanation, that there was no choice (3,8,20).

Within the next weeks Simon appeared convinced that babies grow only inside mothers. We were talking about a drawing of a daddy dog, a mommy dog, and a puppy, shown X-ray fashion inside the mommy dog (figure 2.1). To test Simon, I suggested that the baby begins to grow inside the daddy. Simon objected, and his answers to further questioning suggested that he knew babies always grow inside mommies, never inside daddies (3,9,5) (but note Simon's confusion in the fairly long conversation cited below from 3,10,20).

Simon was, of course, confronted with ample evidence that our baby was inside Bev. He took obvious delight looking at Bev's tummy, often noting how "fat" it was. And he realized it was big due to the baby, perhaps because he felt the baby move (first on 3,7,18). Noticing Bev's tummy when she was dressing, Simon asked why the baby (not her tummy) was so big (3,9,4). But seeing and feeling did not necessarily clear up the mystery about where inside.

One evening Simon was sitting next to Bev and patted her tummy. He mentioned that he felt the baby push him and added that the baby was trying to get into Bev's back. He continued that the baby was "here and here and here," pointing all over Bev's abdomen. Finally,

Figure 2.1
A dog family: The couple is expecting a first child.

using the appropriate term, he asked Bev where her uterus was. She pointed to her abdomen. "But that's your tummy," he said, revealing the preschooler's problem. He then pointed to her breast and asked if her uterus was there. "No, those are my *tsitses*," Bev replied, using a Yiddishism. "I thought they were your *polkes*," Simon said, confusing the Yiddishisms for breasts and thighs (3,9,4). Simon had trouble remembering the names of some external body parts—perhaps because we occasionally referred to them with Yiddish terms—so it is unsurprising that he was puzzled about parts unseen, which we referred to with terms that could just as well have been Yiddish.

The details of the uterine environment were also puzzling to Simon. One day the topic of amniotic fluid arose in a discussion about a newborn who had dry skin. Simon had trouble understanding that babies "swim" in water in their mother's uterus. Unfortunately the term *swim* probably elicited an image for Simon of the activity in our apartment swimming pool. Simon did mention that our baby was in a basket, possibly drawing on the story of baby Moses in the Nile; if Moses needed a basket because he could not swim, surely our baby needed one too (3,8,5).

Simon again referred to a basket several months later.

> Simon: But how do daddies get born? I thought mommies got born from daddies.
>
> Father: No. What do you mean "mommies got born from daddies"?
>
> Simon: Daddy was there, and then . . . Daddy was there, and then a baby came out.
>
> Father: The baby was inside the daddy? Is that possible? No.
>
> Simon: How come?
>
> Father: Because babies grow only inside mommies.
>
> Simon: How come?
>
> Father: Because mommies have uteruses and daddies don't.
>
> Simon: *How come? Then this . . . there can be the basket and just . . . and then the baby can lie there.*
>
> Father: But that's not the way it works. Because ladies and men don't always have the same things. You know daddies have a penis and mommies have a vagina and a uterus. So they're different (taped 3,10,20).

Simon's last statement was halting and ungrammatical. His confusion was apparent, as was my difficulty in setting the record straight. We may have avoided one set of misconceptions by stressing that the baby was in Bev's uterus, not in her stomach. But Simon was faced

with an alternate problem because he lacked complete information—
for example, that babies do not need to breathe before birth—so he
fabricated his own solution in the form of a narrative explanation.

Even if Simon did not know the anatomical details, his understanding that the baby was inside Bev was eventually concrete enough for
him to imagine the baby's position. Asher briefly turned to a breach
position about a month before he was born. Bev discussed the situation with several people, and Simon could easily have heard her conversations. About a week later Simon remarked that the baby was
facing Bev's right and that his feet were up and his head was down.
(3,11,21). Asher was standing on his head inside Bev in a place called
a uterus.

Whether or not Simon understood exactly where the baby was, the
fact that there was a baby inside Bev raised other obvious concerns:
how the baby got there and, more important to Simon, when and
how it was going to get out.

How Does a Mommy Get Another Baby in Her Tummy?

Simon's book *Mousekin's Birth* described the birth of various reptiles,
birds, and mammals (E. Miller 1974). Like so many other children's
books on the subject, it used examples from the animal kingdom to
explain biological origins. But although animals are interesting in
their own right, preschoolers do not readily generalize biological facts
about animals to people (Carey 1985). Thus books such as *Mousekin's
Birth* may actually confuse young children (Goldman and Goldman
1988).

Simon was particularly intrigued by the story about turtles. Even
when we were not reading, he often asked about how turtles grow
in eggs. I typically responded with the facts. The daddy turtle "puts
a seed on the eggs"; the mommy turtle buries the eggs in the sand;
the eggs incubate; the baby turtles dig their way out of the sand and
scamper to the water; and some of the baby turtles grow up to be
mommy and daddy turtles themselves. One day Simon asked about
horses after hearing about turtles. I told him that a "seed" from the
daddy horse joins an "egg" from the mommy horse; the baby grows
in the mommy horse's uterus; the baby horse comes out and is able
to stand up right away. Still intrigued, Simon asked about "all animals," and I repeated the basic ideas about the seed, the egg, and the
uterus (3,7,23).

Simon was clearly curious about the topic. For several weeks he
had repeatedly asked for the story about turtles and had always lis-

tened intently. Now he wanted me to extend the account to horses and all other animals. He obviously could not be expected to generalize the explanation himself; since the concrete details of reproduction are quite different in reptiles and mammals, the generalizations can be made only at a very abstract level.

My explanation of reproduction in turtles demonstrates the pitfalls of sex education by analogy. Analogies may highlight solutions to problems but only for individuals who are sufficiently familiar with the domain to analyze causally relevant aspects of the analogy and the target (Holyoak 1985). Thus, even young children can solve physical problems by analogy (Holyoak et al. 1984), partly because they adeptly manipulate physical objects and grasp principles of physical causality (Shultz 1982). But preschoolers are unlikely to benefit from analogical explanations of reproduction because they are usually unfamiliar with biological processes.

Although Bev and I were particular about correctly labeling the uterus, we—like many other parents and most children's books—did not use *sperm* and *ovum*. By an incorrect analogy I called the sperm a *seed* (*pollen* would have been more apt), perhaps thereby sowing an agriculturalist view of conception. Using *egg* for *ovum* no doubt elicited an image of a hen's egg, a problem compounded by the analogy with turtles' eggs. The agricultural fallacy may have been further nurtured by the true information that baby turtles grow in eggs buried in sand. Even if *sperm* and *ovum* would not have clarified the issue any more than did *uterus*, the correct terms would have at least avoided such obvious misconceptions. The analogy between reptile and mammal or between egg and ovum would probably have been useful only if Simon had already understood the process of fertilization.

My account of reproduction lacked at least one critical piece of information: how the daddy's seed gets to the mommy's egg. I waited for the question, fully expecting to give a forthright answer that would satisfy Simon's curiosity. Simon did eventually ask, but I was not as forthright as I should have been. The topic arose while Bev, Simon, and I were driving on the highway. Simon asked where he was when we were children, and I replied that part of him was in Bev and part of him was in me. My response amused Simon but did not satisfy him since it was inconsistent with his own information about reproduction. He countered that he could not have grown in me because I did not have a uterus. I reiterated my standard explanation that a baby starts as a seed in the daddy and an egg in the mommy and that, when the seed joins the egg, the baby starts to grow in the mommy. Simon then asked the critical question, and I told him through the mommy's vagina, which is attached to her uterus. Trying to grapple with this new piece of information, Simon challenged, "But you're not attached to Mommy." Like others before me, I was embarrassed and opted for evasion. "No," I replied, "but we were for a little bit." Bev also opted for evasion and changed the subject (3,8,22).

Simon had asked a geographer's question about his existence in the past—about where he had been. Quite possibly young children's preformist views about the origins of babies reflect their inability to imagine their own nonexistence. My cryptic response to Simon's initial question was inconsistent with Simon's partial understanding, so I elaborated, but Bev and I avoided the issue when actually confronted with an opportunity to discuss sexual intercourse with our 3-year-old.

We had left Simon with the enigma of how the seed reaches the egg, and he returned to the issue eight days later. Simon wondered if a friend of ours who had recently given birth to her first child was going to have two or three babies. I said that he would have to ask her to find out. Then, turning to what was still a problem, he inquired, "How does a mommy get another baby in her tummy . . . uh . . . uterus after the baby comes out?" Although I changed one of the terms, I did not fill in the details; I explained that "a sperm from the daddy goes into the mommy, and if the sperm meets an egg in the mommy, a baby may start to grow." "Hm. Very interesting," Simon commented. Unlike the week before, he did not ask for clarification (3,9,4).

Simon had asked about conception, but my reply, however straightforward, could not have possibly resolved the mystery. Yet he did not return to the topic until six months after Asher was born when he spontaneously asked how the seed from the daddy reaches the egg from the mommy, at last giving me the chance to correct my previous evasions. I explained sexual intercourse in simple terms. Simon was convinced I was "being silly," but I assured him I was not. He finally asked if it felt good. I told him it did. And this time *he* changed the subject (about 4,5,22).

Despite misconceptions and gaps in his knowledge, Simon grasped that human life begins as a seed. Perhaps more important, he generalized the concept from the baby to others and even to himself. Asked when a person starts to become a baby brother, Simon answered, "In a seed, in a shell and a seed" (taped 3,11,17). The shell probably referred to an eggshell, yet another misunderstanding based on *egg* as an analogy for *ovum*. Simon also realized that the seeds are very small. Indeed the issue of the original seed was often raised in conversations about size. I once joked that I was as big as an elephant. "No, but you're bigger than a seed," Simon said, ". . . but once you were only a seed. Did you know that?" (3,9,17). Another time, I measured Simon on his growth chart and commented how much he had grown.

> Simon: Show me how tall I was when I was 1 year.
> Father: (indicating heights on the chart) This tall. And when you were born, you were this tall.
> Simon: (pointing to approximately 15 inches) When I was a real little baby I was this tall, right?
> Father: Well, when you were born, you were this tall. And before that you were this and this and this tall, when you were inside Mommy.
> Simon: (pointing at the carpet) Then I was this small, when I was an itsy-bitsy seed (3,8,29).

When Will the Baby Come Out?

In fact, Simon was only passingly interested in the problem of conception, but he was thoroughly enthralled by two problems related to the baby's birth: when and how. Waiting for a new baby highlights the flow of time—at least the countdown to the expected date of birth, if not the seemingly eternal cycle of life. The due date has several meanings for family members. For parents, it is a deadline for making arrangements; for a preschooler, it is a puzzle about numbers, calendars, and time. And for Simon, it also raised questions about age.

Simon already knew the order of the seasons and the month of his birthday when we first told him about the baby, so I said, "We expect the baby to come out of Mommy by December, in the winter, maybe a few days after your birthday" (3,4,21). In the ensuing weeks Simon often heard us tell people we were expecting a baby around his birthday. But even if he seemingly learned this piece of information, he did not fully understand it and returned to the topic on a number of occasions. He once apparently wanted to verify that the baby would come out after he turned 4, so I tried to communicate that the due date was only approximate. I explained that we were expecting the baby then but did not know exactly when the baby would come out, that the baby might be born a little after, a little before, or even right on his birthday when he turned 4. "Or," Simon added, apparently testing the limits of uncertainty, "when I turn 5, right?" But I assured him that the baby would be born around the time he turned 4 (3,6,7).

In the Goldmans' research (1982), approximately 1 percent of English-speaking and 10 percent of Swedish 5-year-olds estimated the length of gestation between 8 and 10 months; for 7-year-olds, the proportions were, respectively, only 9 and 33 percent. It is therefore not surprising Simon did not understand that the due date was biologically constrained. Unfortunately we did not explain, and by stressing the uncertainty we may have actually confused Simon about the due date. In any event, he often asked when the baby would "come out," and we typically said "in December" or "around your birthday" (3,8,5; 3,8,26).

Simon's many questions about the baby's arrival were consistent with his general interest in time (3,8–3,9). He often asked about the timing of anticipated events, such as a visit by a friend or an excursion to the movies. After we told him a particular time—for example, on Tuesday or next week—he usually requested specific information about how many days that was. He already knew that there are seven days in a week and 30 days in a month, and he could count to twenty-nine without prompting. But he was still trying to figure out many temporal terms; phrases such as *this morning, this afternoon,* and *tomorrow* had to be translated into *before lunch, after your nap,* and *when you get up in the morning.*

Simon often overheard Bev and me discuss the baby's age and the time until delivery; he occasionally even saw me count the weeks on a calendar in the pantry. If he joined in, the conversation inevitably shifted to a discussion about numbers. One morning, Bev wondered when the baby would be 24 weeks. Simon asked how many weeks it was until the baby came out, but he was puzzled by my response of 16½, so we continued about whether 16½ is more than 17 (3,8,11). In other instances, Simon spontaneously inquired how many weeks were left. After Bev answered, "15," Simon rhetorically asked how many that was and immediately counted to it (3,8,19). Again, the situation afforded Simon the opportunity to think about numbers— but it was more than just that. When Simon finished counting, he was quite excited and sought me out to report enthusiastically that the baby would come out in 15 weeks. Simon was indeed genuinely anticipating the baby. The day before, he voiced his impatience: "I want to see the baby right now!" (3,8,18). And he similarly verbalized his excitement 7 weeks later. "The baby's going to come out in 8 weeks," he announced to me right after a count led by Bev. "That's soon. I'm excited. Are you excited?" (3,10,6).

At least for short time periods, Simon remembered some of the information about how far off the due date was. The day after he counted 15 weeks, he asked when our apartment pool would be heated. My reply of 2 weeks prompted his usual request for clarification, so I translated, "in about 14 or 15 days." Simon observed that it was "the same as the baby." I explained that the pool would be open in 15 days, and the baby would arrive in 15 weeks, adding that weeks are longer than days. He agreed but said that it was the same number (3,8,18). Here a question about time turned into a discussion about when the baby would be born.

As the due date approached, we stressed the possibility that the baby might not arrive when we expected. A month before he became a brother, Simon asked when the baby was "going to come." Again my reply—"in about 4½ weeks"—led to a discussion about how long that was. But this time Bev and I emphasized that we were not sure when the baby would be born. By way of explanation, we told Simon that he was born just when the doctor said he would be but that babies are sometimes early or sometimes late (3,11,2).

Two days later I was more specific about how early or late. Simon's interest was caught by the calendar in the pantry, and he asked when the baby would come. Using the calendar, I showed him the day's date and the date of his birthday, December 24. I also indicated that the baby would probably be born between December 27 and December 29 but possibly earlier or later. When Simon suggested that the baby might come as early as December 1, I explained probably not before December 15. And when he suggested the baby might come as late as January 31, I explained probably not after January 11 (3,11,4).

The excitement in our house mounted. Simon heard more and more conversations about babies, the upcoming birth, and the countdown, conversations that could only reinforce his own anticipation. Bev told a friend that there were two more weeks until the baby and that we were excited; Simon wholeheartedly agreed (3,11,15). Simon's daycare teacher asked me how Bev was feeling, and Simon listened to the ensuing discussion about the baby's due date and about Simon's being born on time (3,11,16). I mentioned to a friend that the baby could arrive any day (3,11,19). And Bev spoke to a friend about when she expected to go to the hospital (3,11,24).

A week before Asher's birth I sat down to breakfast singing, "Any day now, any day now . . ." Bev said it could be ten days, and I observed it could even be longer. Simon knew we were talking about the baby though we had not directly said so. "I know when the baby is going to come," he offered, ". . . the day after my birthday . . . or even on my birthday." I observed how exciting that would be, and Simon agreed, adding that we should get a cake without a lot of sugar, so the baby could eat some (3,11,25). The following week was filled with excitement. Relatives arrived from out of town. Simon had his birthday and a party. He no longer asked when the baby would be born.

How Does the Baby Come Out?

When young children are asked where the baby gets out of the mother's body, they are likely to mention any of the openings in the body—mouth, ears, nose, eyes, anus, and vagina—as well as what appears to be a semiclosed opening—the navel (Goldman and Goldman 1982). Many children who cannot imagine an exit or who have overheard discussions about Caesarean sections assume the only possibility is cutting open the mother. At 5 years of age, only 13 percent of children in English-speaking countries but 37 percent of Swedish children correctly answer the question; by 7 years of age, the percentages are, respectively, 24 and 40.

Simon knew that he had a penis and that a vagina is located in the same anatomical area, yet he never heard about the vagina's functions or its relation to the uterus. Thus, fully aware that the baby was inside Bev, he continually wondered how it was going to get out. We tried to answer his questions but apparently did not succeed. When I first began my log, Simon spontaneously asked Bev, "How does the baby get out?" "Through the vagina," she replied. "You know that" (3,7,12). Even as early as then, he had asked the question often enough for her to assume that he already knew the answer, but as often as he was told the simple answer, he did not understand it or possibly did not believe it. It is certainly not surprising that a verbal explanation would fail to satisfy a 3- or 4-year-old's curiosity about birth. Even though I have witnessed the delivery of our three children, I am still struck with disbelief when I contemplate the process.

Eleven weeks before Asher's arrival, Simon spontaneously started a conversation that exemplified not only his confusion about birth but also our difficulty explaining it. He asked how the baby comes out, and I told him "through Mommy's vagina." When he sought clarification, Bev explained that the vagina is closed at first, but opens, and the baby can fit through. I offered that the vagina is like a tube, and the baby gets through. Bev added that "the baby comes out near where the pee comes out," and Simon, pursuing the issue, asked if the baby "comes out where poo comes out." I tried to explain that Bev has a vagina where Simon has a penis and that she pushes the baby out through her vagina. But each explanation raised another problem, and Simon expressed his concern that pushing might hurt the baby. Trying to clarify, I said, "I meant push as in squeeze, like when you squeeze out poo," another unfortunate analogy that probably only confused him (3,9,17).

We tried to provide a reasonably coherent explanation but soon discovered the depth of Simon's puzzlement. He was clearly struggling with the problem of how the baby comes out. "Well, I always thought voices and words go into your stomach," he explained cryptically. When I asked what he meant, he expanded, "Voices and words into your . . . and still will enter your stomach and out of your ear." Then Simon suggested alternatives for where the baby comes out, suggestions I had not heard before. He had obviously imagined possible alternatives but expressed them as rejected hypotheses: "I always, always, always thought babies come out of the back. . . . Then I always, always said it came out of your head. . . . And then I thought, hmm, maybe a baby comes out of your eyes. . . . And then I thought, hmm, maybe a baby climbs up to your nose and sneaks out. . . . And then I always thought a baby climbs up through the hole, out of the mouth." When Bev suggested that he now knew and asked where the baby really comes, Simon asked her to turn around while he guessed because he wanted to look and see (taped 3,9,17). Perhaps we had disabused Simon of the obvious childlike solutions, but Simon still could not—or would not—tell us where the baby comes out.

Construing a medical model of birth, Simon assumed that someone would "take the baby out." I first realized this from a conversation that we had walking home from daycare. I mentioned that Bev was not yet home because she had lost her bracelet and was retracing her steps to the hospital. Hearing *hospital*, Simon suddenly looked worried, so I started to explain that she had been there for a meeting, not . . . But a relieved Simon finished my phrase, "Not for the ladies to pull out the baby" (3,10,14).

A week later Simon raised the issue about birth once more.

Simon: But who . . . who's going to take [the baby] out?
Father: Well, the baby comes out, it sort of comes out itself, and Mommy has to . . . Mommy has to push it out.
Simon: How do you push it out?
Father: To squeeze it out.
Simon: How?

Father: Because Mommy . . . when the baby's ready to be
           born, Mommy's uterus starts to push the baby out.

We discussed some further details, perhaps confusing Simon again
with our analogies.

Father: When it's time for the baby to be born, Mommy starts
           to feel it, that the baby is ready to be born.
Simon: How?
Mother: . . . You know what it feels like? . . . Like you have a
           tummy ache . . . like, you know, when you have to
           go to the bathroom to make a poo sometimes?
Simon: Yeah.
Mother: That's the feeling, almost. All of a sudden you feel
           like you have to . . .
Father: Have the baby!
Mother: Push. And then you start to push. Enggh! (groaning)
Simon: (giggles)
Mother: And then the uterus starts to push. Enggh! And then
           all of a sudden, the baby comes . . .
Simon: Out of . . . out of the back or the front?
Mother: The front.
Father: Out of the front.
Mother: Near where Mommy makes pee.
Father: Not where Mommy makes pee.
Mother: Near where mommy makes pee. And then you start
           to push.
Simon: That's where the poo comes out of!
Mother: No, the poo comes out of where your tuss is.
Father: It comes out of the back.
Simon: (worried) Oh! This is not the back. It's the middle!
Father: It's the middle. The poo comes out of the middle.
           And the baby comes out of the front, out of the va-
           gina, which is the front (taped 3,10,20).

Simon soon returned to the question he was trying to answer:
"How do they take the baby out?" This time he objected when I mentioned the uterus pushing, and he insisted that "the nurse does it,
not the mommy." "No, the mommy does it," I corrected. "Not even
mommies. The mommy's uterus does it. The baby's . . . in the uterus,
and then when the baby's ready to come out, the uterus . . . starts
getting smaller. And then the baby goes, 'Oy! There's not enough
room in here.' The mommy's uterus gets smaller, and it pushes the

baby out." But Simon still asked how, and, not answering his concern, I simply said, "That's the way it does" (taped 3,10,20).

Simon never satisfied his curiosity about the obvious problem of how a baby is born. On our way to the hospital the day Asher arrived, Simon asked how the baby came out. I reviewed as simply as I could that the uterus is attached to the vagina and that the baby is pushed out, yet Simon still seemed confused. On our way home, he raised the topic again.

Simon: Daddy, can you tell me how he was born?
Father: . . . Well, Mommy's uterus pushed Asher out. OK?
         And Mommy had to help too.
Simon: How did Mommy have to help?
Father: Mommy had to squeeze, help squeeze Asher out. And
         Asher came out. All babies come out of their mommy's vagina.
Simon: You mean uterus.
Father: Well, uterus. They come out of the uterus, and the
         uterus is connected to the vagina. The vagina is like a
         little tunnel from the uterus to the outside. So the
         baby comes out of the uterus. And then it goes
         through the tunnel, through the vagina, to the
         outside.
Simon: Right.
Father: And the first thing that comes out is the head.
Simon: Right.
Father: And then . . .
Simon: And then you have to see how he's coming out.
Father: That's right. And then the shoulders, and then the
         rest of his body! And then he came out, and he went,
         "Waah, waah!" Started to cry. Babies sometimes start
         to cry when they're first born.
Simon: Yeah. I know.
Father: And that was that (taped 4,0,3).

That was indeed that. Simon did not ask about how a baby is born even once during the five months after Asher's birth, but he probably never really understood the explanation, which, after all, was about an abstract process involving unseen body parts.

How Long Will Mommy Stay in the Hospital?

Separation from mother while she gives birth is presumably stressful for firstborns (Field and Reite 1984, Trause 1978, Trause et al. 1981).

Anticipating the separation may be stressful as well. Indeed Simon's concern about when and how the baby would arrive were at least partly related to his worry about Bev's leaving for the hospital.

Simon was so intent on discovering how a baby is born that he wanted to see the birth. "When it's time for the baby to come out and for Mommy to go to the hospital, I'm going to go too," he announced early on (3,6,21). Initially I thought he was worried about being left alone, so I sidestepped the issue and said that we would see what happens when the time comes, adding that he would definitely visit Bev and the baby in the hospital. Two months later Simon again asked what I would do when Bev was in the hospital. I said that Bev and the baby would be there for a few days and that Simon and I would live at home but that we would visit them. "I want to go on the first day," Simon said, "because I want to see how the baby comes out." I explained that watching a baby born was not something for children to do (3,8,19).

Other issues were also raised in that conversation. When Simon asked why Bev and the baby had to stay at the hospital, I tried to give him a sense of what would happen. I explained that a mommy needs rest after she has a baby and that the hospital is a good place for it because the nurses can do things for her. I also told him that the baby had to be in the hospital for a few days to make sure it was all right and that Bev had to stay there to help care for the baby. Simon wondered why the nurses could not take care of the baby, and I explained that Bev had to breast-feed the baby (3,8,19).

My explanations did not settle the issue. One evening we were talking about Simon's friend Jeff and his new baby sister. Bev mentioned that Carla and the baby were still in the hospital. Simon was obviously worried and asked what was going to happen when Bev gave birth; he wondered if he and I would go to the hospital when our baby was born. Still thinking that Simon was concerned about separation, I explained that we would visit the hospital to see Bev and the baby. But Simon, raising what was really on his mind, asked, "How come they don't let children to see how they take babies out?" I reiterated my previous explanation: it was for grown-ups—not for children—to see how babies are born. Simon asked why, but I did not answer. Rather I explained that I had to go to the hospital with Bev because she would need help and that one of his grandparents would stay with him. Simon cried that he wanted to come too, and I assured him that I would take him to the hospital as soon as the baby was born (taped 3,10,20).

Simon returned to the issue of seeing the birth and pleaded to accompany us.

Simon:	(to Father) Are you going to see how the baby is born?
Father:	I'm going to help. I'm going to help Mommy. If Mommy needs help, then I'm going to be there so I can help Mommy.
Simon:	(crying) How come I can't help Mommy?
Father:	(sighs) I know, you're such a sweet boy!
Simon:	. . . How come I can't help Mommy?
Mother:	You know what, sweetie? . . . They don't let children come in there and do it. . . . You know what? I'm going to tell you a secret. They usually don't let children in the hospital at all. But just because a mommy gives birth to a baby, they always let the brother or the sister, whoever's at home, come and visit the mommy. It's a special thing.
Father:	Yeah. So brothers are allowed to come and see the baby, but only . . . after the baby is born.

Simon, crying by now, continued the conversation and finally raised the issue of separation, inquiring when I would come back.

Father:	Right away! . . . It doesn't take long. It doesn't take long.
Simon:	(crying) But when?
Father:	Well, we're not going right away. It's not the time now for the baby to be born. . . . It's not time now. When is the baby going to be born? Do you know how many weeks?
Simon:	(crying) It's a long time.
Father:	Six weeks. It's six weeks.

Simon pleaded, proposing a way to prevent me at least from going to the hospital with Bev.

Simon:	But how come they don't want little brothers seeing? Or big brothers and big sisters?
Father:	. . . This is in the hospital. And they let the doctors and the nurses. And Mommy has to be there because Mommy's the one that's having the baby. And they let one other person besides the mommy. They let the daddy come, too.
Simon:	How come?
Father:	To help the mommy if the mommy needs any help.
Simon:	But . . . but ask Mommy to say yes or no.
Father:	To say yes or no about what?

Simon: About the baby, if she needs help. Ask Mommy.
Father: . . . A woman usually needs help. . . . Now, when you were born, Mommy went to the hospital. And you know who else was there with Mommy? I was. I helped Mommy when you were born. And I was right there when you were born. . . . I was right there (taped 3,10,20).

Simon continued questioning why big brothers and sisters cannot come to the hospital. I said that was just the way it was. And Bev explained that no brothers and sisters could come, even if they were much older than Simon. "But the ones that won't touch can come," he countered, still obviously upset. Bev said that it was not a matter of touching and reiterated that the hospital did not want children there. I explained that it was not so much fun to watch, that children could not help, and that children are not allowed there in the hospital. Jumping at an apparent discrepancy, Simon said that he was once at the hospital to see the doctor, but I explained that he was not in the place where the babies are born (taped 3,10,20).

I tried to assure Simon that I would not stay at the hospital for long.

Father: . . . But then you'll come to the hospital and you will visit Mommy. . . . Even when Mommy's in the hospital, I'm not going to stay in the hospital all the time. I'm going to be coming home. I'm going to be sleeping at home. And just as soon as the baby is born, I'm going to be staying with you.
Simon: But how . . . how much are we going to stay there?
Father: How long are we going to stay? . . . We're going to visit. And Mommy isn't going to be in the hospital very long with the baby. Just a few days.
Simon: How come?
Father: Because Mommy's going to have to rest.
Simon: But she can come home and rest.
Father: And she'll come home as soon, as soon, as possible.
Simon: (whining, almost crying) When is she going to come home?
Father: . . . Maybe in two days or three days. Something like that probably.
Simon: (protesting) No (taped 3,10,20).

Simon was obviously worried about Bev's going to the hospital. He was genuinely concerned when he heard she had gone there to look for her bracelet and when she was reviewing a list of things to bring to the delivery room (3,10,14; 3,11,1). As the big day approached, we tried to prepare him for what would happen. About two weeks before the due date, we drove past the hospital to show Simon where Bev would give birth. I told him it was where he was born and where our baby would be born. Simon asked why there. I replied that it was a nice hospital and that they took good care of him and Bev when he was born. Bev added that her doctor worked there. Simon verified that I would take him to see the baby as soon as it was born, and I assured him that we would see the baby the very day but maybe not right away because we would have to wait for visiting hours (3,11,21).

Simon raised his various concerns—about when and how the baby would be born and about our going to the hospital—during our drive home from visiting Bev the day Asher arrived.

Simon: Why did Mommy . . . have to . . . get the baby out in the middle of the night?

Father: Because that was the time that Asher was ready to come out. . . . A mommy doesn't get to choose the time.

Simon: Asher gets to choose the time?!

Father: That's right! Whenever the baby was ready to come out, whenever Asher was ready to come out, he had to come out!

Simon: Well, how did Mommy know Asher was ready to come out?

Father: Because Mommy started to feel . . . her uterus starting to push Asher out. And that's what happens. The uterus starts to push the baby out, and that's it. So Mommy had to go to the hospital.

Simon: The baby didn't come out in the cold, did he?

Father: No, no, no. The baby didn't come out in the cold. (Explained that babies are born in a hospital in case there are problems that need to be taken care of by a doctor or a nurse.) . . . Well that's why we had to go. And you were sleeping. We didn't want to disturb your sleep, because you needed to have a good night's sleep. Because today was going to be such an exciting and big day . . . (taped 4,0,3).

Confusion and Clarification

Reproduction
Previous work with hundreds of youngsters has detailed the range of children's opinions on reproduction, sex, and related topics (Gold-

man and Goldman 1982,1988). It has been suggested that reasoning about reproduction is somehow related to the child's stage of cognitive development (Bernstein and Cowan 1975), but such an argument generally suffers as an explanation (Carey 1985). Contrary to Piaget's claim, children's thinking appears to be domain specific (Carey 1983, Fischer 1980, Gelman and Baillargeon 1983). Yet cognitive status may constrain the explanations of reproduction that children construct from limited or misleading information furnished by adults.

The literature does not adequately account for young children's understanding of reproduction; at best it describes what they do not know. Perhaps attempts to discover the nature of preschoolers' biological concepts will prove more fruitful, especially as first steps toward a full account (Carey 1985, Gelman 1988, Keil 1986). But such attempts do not address how young children use even poorly understood concepts in their explanations, and the available research raises at least one important question: how are children's ideas about reproduction influenced by parents or by events such as the birth of a sibling?

I propose that young children's biological explanations are essentially stories, related more closely to myths than to scientific theories. Children presumably organize biological facts as they understand them into narratives consistent with their experience. But young children may base their explanations on irrelevant details, partial information, or misunderstood concepts; they may also include causal links that are less appropriate for biological processes than for descriptions of familiar physical, psychological, or social events. Still, children's explanations may be as internally logical and coherent as any of their narratives, and initial myths are presumably revised and eventually transformed into theories when children gain more information, clarify their concepts, and realize what causal links are appropriate for different types of explanations.

It is probably unwise to wait for queries from young children before offering explanations about reproduction; sometimes children may not realize that there is a question or know how to ask it. Yet it is difficult teaching them about complex processes such as conception, pregnancy, and birth, especially given the problems they have learning about internal body parts (Vessey 1988). Biological facts are often confusing without an overall structure, but individual facts must be understood before the structure is discernible.

For example, the most concrete statement about reproduction—the baby is growing inside Mommy—seems simple enough, but only because an adult understands it in relation to an intuitive biological theory that includes information about conception, pregnancy, female anatomy, and so on (Carey 1985). A preschooler in contrast lacks an intuitive biological explanation of where the unborn baby is and how it got there. Without such an organizing theory, even children who superficially understand simple biological statements will not appropriately constrain them. Although Simon knew that babies grow inside their mother, he still explored other possibilities—that they grow inside their father or float in baskets. And Simon, like other children who have not yet constrained permissible causal links, entertained a psychological explanation—that babies could grow somewhere else if they wanted to.

Thus a statement about the baby's location—even one consisting of only familiar words—is potentially puzzling to a preschooler, so a new term such as *uterus* should not be expected to clarify the issue. Yet without explicit information to the contrary, a preschooler has every reason to believe an unborn baby is in its mother's tummy (stomach). The mother's tummy (abdomen) does stick out, and most adults, including those who write children's books, refer to the baby's location as *Mommy's tummy*. To compound the difficulty, a young child typically does not think of the body interior in terms of differentiated organs, and the stomach's role in digestion does not logically exclude its involvement in reproduction.

It is not surprising that Simon had trouble learning the correct term for the baby's location, even if Bev and I typically said *uterus*. He often referred to *tummy* or *stomach*, eventually substituting the appropriate term only after many corrections. But merely using the right word—essentially an abstraction since it refers to an unseen body part—is not sufficient for a preschooler to abandon what appear to be reasonable assumptions about the baby's location. I suspect Simon would have benefited from an explanation of what the uterus is, where it is located, what it is attached to, what function it serves, why only women have one, and what it is like for the baby inside. Without such information, Simon had to construct the concept on his own and the result—likely an incorrect guess—could hardly be expected to further his understanding of other aspects of conception, pregnancy, and birth.

Simon did raise the topic of conception, even if he did not dwell on it. We tried to explain the facts but committed several common errors that were predictably confusing. We used analogies—*seed* for *sperm* and *egg* for *ovum*—that Simon understood quite literally and we provided incomplete information about intercourse. Not yet 4, Simon was very likely too young to understand conception; indeed only 23 percent of Swedish 5-year-olds know the basic facts, and they cannot really explain them (Goldman and Goldman 1982). But we might have confused Simon less by using correct terms and offering fuller explanations beyond his questions.

The real puzzle for Simon was how the baby would come out. Although we told him, he had trouble grasping that a baby is born through the mother's vagina. He lacked the anatomical details, and, even if I had explained them fully, he may not have been able to imagine unseen body parts. Perhaps pictures typically found in books for expectant parents might have helped. Regardless, Simon's effort to solve the problem and his list of rejected hypotheses concretely support the suggestion that children construct successive biological explanations (Carey 1985).

At the time, Simon was interested in reproductive biology mainly because Bev's pregnancy raised a number of intellectual problems that he tried to solve (Nadelman and Begun 1982). (Expectant women are also interested in pregnancy and birth and seek information from relatives, friends, experts, and books [Deutsch et al. 1988].) Once Asher was born, Simon virtually stopped asking questions about conception, gestation, and birth, only to resume three years later when we were expecting Dana. But even if a sibling's birth affords a special opportunity to explore biological questions, Simon had many other chances to do so. He often joined discussions about friends who were pregnant. Some of his books raised biological issues, and we probably should have found something for him specifically about reproduction. Finally, he looked at his own baby pictures and listened to stories about events in his infancy or before he was born. Thus, any parent can find natural situations to discuss biological origins with a curious preschooler.

Anticipating the Arrival

We told Simon we were expecting a baby over seven months before the due date, an exceptionally long time for a preschooler. In the ensuing months, he continually asked, "How long is it until the baby comes out?" The question—akin to "When will we get there?" or "How much farther?"—demonstrated the same impatience all young children show on family excursions. But pregnancy involves seasons, months, and weeks, considerably longer time periods, which Simon was just beginning to understand.

I suggested that Simon had difficulty understanding biological explanations because he lacked essential details and a theory to organize the facts. Similarly, he may have had trouble with the due date because the time intervals were unfamiliar and, much to my surprise now, because we never explained that pregnancy lasts nine months. Young children obviously have to be told the typical length of pregnancy; it is not information that they can garner from experience. But even if they are told, they may not remember. Indeed virtually no 5-year-olds accurately identify the length of gestation within one month (Goldman and Goldman 1982).

Simon may have benefited from a simple explanation but perhaps not without better understanding of mathematical concepts and biological processes. As it happened, conversations about the baby's due date afforded what have been called socially organized numerical activities (Saxe et al. 1987). And Simon's questions about when the baby would come led more naturally—and perhaps less embarrassingly—to mathematical discussions of numbers, temporal terms, and calendars than to biological explanations of conception, gestation, and birth.

Simon's questions had emotional implications as well. His curiosity about the due date probably reflected his enthusiastic anticipation of the baby; he not only said he was excited but also appeared so. At the same time, his countdown possibly reflected negative feelings: worry about our leaving for the hospital, concern about Bev's stay there, and frustration about not seeing how a baby is born.

There were parallels between Simon's mathematical and biological interests. Both were aroused quite spontaneously by Asher's impending birth; Simon typically raised questions on his own, although he occasionally did so upon overhearing discussions between Bev and me. But both interests reflected general concerns. In addition to reproduction, Simon's biological interests included digestion, respiration, and blood circulation. His mathematical interests included counting coins as well as months, weeks, and days, playing various games involving dice and numbers, and discussing clocks and temporal terms. Bev and I encouraged Simon's interests as much as possible. We tried to answer his questions fully, but we succeeded more for mathematics than for biology.

The Beginning of a Personal Narrative
Although a personal narrative is probably based mainly on experience, background information is necessarily obtained from others. Bev's pregnancy and Asher's arrival prompted Simon to learn about the first part of his own personal narrative. For example, discussions about conception, gestation, and birth led Simon to consider his own biological origins. He realized that he began as a seed and had grown inside Bev. Simon also apparently grasped the recursiveness of the life cycle. He understood that Bev and I were once children—albeit

in the distant past before he was "in Mommy's uterus"—and he wondered where he was at the time (3,8,22). He even wondered where he was when I was in my mother's uterus, something we failed to explain adequately (3,9,25).

For Simon, questions about life before conception were perhaps more philosophical or scientific than autobiographical. But stories of events surrounding his birth, certainly highlighted because of Asher's impending arrival, were relevant to his personal narrative. In telling Simon about the arrangements for the baby's birth, we often drew comparisons with his own. When Simon pleaded to come to the hospital, I tried to explain why fathers help and indicated that I had attended his birth (3,10,20). When talking about relatives' plans to come to Montreal after the baby was born, we mentioned who had come when Simon was born (3,10,18). When I showed Simon the hospital, I naturally told him that he had been born there too (3,11,21). Similarly, discussions about Asher's name led to conversations about the origin of Simon's (4,0,3), and preparations for the baby evoked conversations about Simon's old clothes and baby supplies (3,9 to 4,0).

Simon also sought information on his own. Given his general interest in numbers, calendars, and clocks, it is not surprising that he asked what time he was born—if it was during the night. We told him that it was early in the morning, and he wondered why we were up. Bev explained we were at the hospital waiting for him to be born. The conversation continued about Simon's birth. For example, Bev told him he did not cry when he was born. Simon asked why, and I replied, "Because you were such a good boy" (3,10,18).

Discussions and comments about Simon as a baby were common during the months before Asher was born. Asher's impending arrival affected Simon's self-concept by providing a context for elaborating his own personal narrative. It also affected his self-concept by prompting a role change.

Chapter 3
Anticipatory Role Changes

Parents expecting their first child typically experience the psychological impact of their new role before the baby's birth, a process that may be associated with adjustment afterward (Deutsch et al. 1988, Leifer 1980, Mercer 1981, R. Rubin 1967). Women not only start to redefine their marital and occupational roles but also fantasize about the maternal role. They seek relevant information from a variety of sources, possibly role play with babies whom they know, and start forging a relationship with their unborn baby.

As the pregnancy progresses, expectant parents increasingly think about their unborn baby as a person (Gloger-Tippelt 1988). Initially they view the child as an undifferentiated biological entity; somewhat later, as an independent human being with a human form and with a personality consisting of rudimentary intentions, perceptions, and feelings; and near birth, as an individual who looks like a member of the family with a personality consisting of concrete attributes—a specific temperament and particular traits. Since every family role is reciprocally paired with another, parents' changing ideas about the baby might foster changes in their own role identity. Indeed both are promoted by evidence of the baby's existence: by feeling fetal movement, observing ultrasonography, and obtaining information about the baby's sex.

But it is impossible to foresee fully the impact of a new family member or the demands of a new role, so any anticipatory role changes must be incomplete. Pregnant women certainly differ in how much they identify with the maternal role (Olioff 1982). And if some women have trouble imagining themselves as a mother, how could young children be expected to envision themselves as a brother or sister?

Of course, preschoolers are not left to their own imagination. Even before the baby is born, parents impart certain expectations about the new role of older brother or sister. Part of that role is simply being a big boy or girl, an expectation that parents may communicate by a variety of maturity demands, such as higher standards for behavior and encouragement for independence (A. L. Baldwin 1947, Walz and Rich 1983). Parents may also explicitly foster two potentially misleading myths. The playmate myth—that the firstborn will play with the baby—is problematic because a young child who expects a playmate will likely be disappointed by the reality of a newborn. The helping myth—that the firstborn will help care for the baby—is also problematic. Although most preschoolers can certainly help the parent, for example, by getting a diaper, they cannot help directly with the baby, especially with a young baby. The myths nonetheless provide young children concrete ideas about what big brothers or sisters do, at least eventually. But no one has asked if young children begin to adopt the sibling role before their baby brother or sister is born. I address this question by exploring several related issues.

The Baby before Birth

Even before Bev looked obviously pregnant, Simon thought about the baby as a human being with needs and wants, which is really not surprising. Most youngsters, even adolescents, do not understand prenatal development (Goldman and Goldman 1982), and Simon certainly lacked the scientific knowledge to think of the baby as simply a biological entity. Besides, Bev and I never distinguished embryo, fetus, and baby, and we often told him specifically that there was a baby inside Bev (3,4,21). Since babies are people, Simon had every reason to assume that our unborn baby was also a person.

How Does the Baby Get Food?

Throughout Bev's pregnancy, we had many discussions about the baby's size, growth, and nourishment. We mentioned at the outset that the baby was very small but growing (3,4,21). As Bev grew larger, we often returned to the topic. Simon asked two possibly related questions that implicitly ascribed human—or at least animal—functions to the unborn baby: he wondered how the baby "gets food" and how the baby "can cry inside." Simon already knew about the digestive system, so we told him that the baby gets the "good things" in the food that Bev eats. We also told him the baby does not have to cry because the baby gets everything he or she needs, which seemed to baffle Simon (3,6,7).

Simon once asked about babies' food preferences, indicating that he believed babies have personal tastes, another human quality. Bev's response illustrated how we typically tried to explain fetal nourishment and how simplifications can be misleading.

Simon: Daddy, what do babies don't like to eat?
Father: I don't know. Babies, when they're inside their mom-
            mies, don't eat anything. They get all the food from
            their mommy.
Mother: . . . Mommy eats food, and it goes down to my
            stomach and gets shhhh all mashed up. And then it
            goes . . . into another tube. And it feeds the baby. In-
            side. So the baby eats anything that I eat. After the
            baby comes out, then the baby likes certain things or
            doesn't like certain things. But right now, the baby
            will eat anything that I eat (taped 3,9,17).

By the end of Bev's pregnancy, Simon grasped some of the essen-
tials. Simon understood that Bev's food also provided the baby nourishment. I had told him once that Bev had to drink milk so the baby's
bones would grow (3,7,30). Three months later Simon tried to avoid
drinking more milk by using the same information. Bev poured some
milk from her glass into his. "I don't want more," Simon protested.
"If you don't have enough milk, then the baby won't have enough,
you know" (3,11,5). And Simon also understood that Bev's food en-
ergized the baby; he once said that the baby "moves a lot around after
dinner, because he's just had his dinner" (taped 3,11,17).

Do You Feel It, Mommy?
Fetal movement is probably the most dramatic proof that a woman is
carrying a new life, so the first time she senses the baby's quickening
is a momentous event (R. Rubin 1975). As the baby grows, its movements become more noticeable, and the woman can gradually distinguish rolls, pokes, and kicks. She may eventually discern cycles of
activity and rest, recurring reminders of her baby's existence. Not surprisingly, fetal movement is often evidence enough for a pregnant
woman that the baby is a person and she is a mother (Blum 1980, R.
Rubin 1967, Shereshefsky and Yarrow 1973). In time she can invite
other people to feel the baby by placing their hands on her tummy,
and mothers expecting a second child typically encourage their firstborn to do just that, assuming it will encourage acceptance of the new
brother or sister (Walz and Rich 1983). Such concrete proof of the
baby might indeed be important for young children, who know very
little about gestation and pregnancy.

Bev first sensed quickening at about 16 weeks, and Simon knew
about it soon after that (3,7). Sometimes she prompted him to feel the
baby; at other times he asked. Yet he was disappointed for several
weeks even if he would not admit it. He once said he felt the baby's

head, but his hand was on Bev's breast (3,7,6). When he finally did feel the baby move, there was no mistake: he beamed from understandable pleasure (3,7,18).

In the ensuing months, Simon often felt the baby move, usually when Bev told him to, but sometimes when he asked to try or when I suggested it or by accident when he was leaning on Bev. Regardless, we discussed many topics—like the baby's sex and size or Simon's relationships to the baby—which suggested that fetal movement reified the baby for Simon, just as it does for parents (3,7,18; 3,8,30; 3,9,3). Simon even assumed that the baby was a person independent of Bev. One day she put his hand on her tummy; he laughed with pleasure each time the baby kicked and finally asked, "Do you feel it, Mommy?" (3,8,18). His excitement about feeling the baby never diminished. Other situations—reading books, interacting with babies, or preparing baby supplies—also prompted Simon to think about our baby, but none with an immediacy that engendered the same enthusiasm as actually feeling his brother move.

The baby was small but growing. The baby "got food." The baby moved, kicked, rolled, and poked. The baby was independent of Bev. Surely there was something else. Or was there?

> Father: So what else are you confused about?
> Simon: Well, I'm confused because I . . . I wanna know . . . how . . . how . . . This is very hard to say like . . . but how does it . . . how does it . . . where does it do . . . where does it play?
> Father: . . . The baby doesn't play when it's inside Mommy.
> Simon: How come?
> Father: Because the baby is just inside Mommy growing. It's almost as if the baby sleeps. Most of the time it's like the baby was sleeping. . . . But it moves a little bit.
> Simon: Some babies sleep and move at the same time.
> Father: That's right! It's like it's sleeping a lot. And sometimes it moves.
> Simon: You know. Sometimes it's . . . it's . . . babies sleep . . . sleep while we're still up.
> Father: That's right.
> Simon: (using a rare reference to the baby as a girl) And then when you . . . when she wants to have something, the baby gets it even when it's sleeping (taped 3,9,17).

He or She, Brother or Sister
Gender, an important social category, organizes our understanding of ourselves and others (Maccoby 1988). Thus, it is not surprising that

parents' concepts of their unborn child are influenced by information about the baby's sex (Gloger-Tippelt 1988). Children as young as 3 years old label themselves correctly as boy or girl and know cultural sex stereotypes for toys, clothing, tools, household objects, games, and work (Huston 1983). Perhaps information—or even guesses and suppositions—about the baby's sex also colors preschoolers' concepts of their unborn brother or sister.

When we first told Simon that we were expecting, we consciously avoided any reference to the baby's sex (3,4,21). In the ensuing months we referred simply to "the baby" or "he or she," and we typically corrected Simon when he specified a sex even inadvertently by using only one pronoun. We also explicitly told Simon that one of the surprises about a baby is whether it is a boy or girl (3,6,7). (Actually Bev and I did learn that the baby was a boy, but we decided to keep the information a secret, even from Simon [3,7,20]. Afterward we still did not specify the baby's sex but probably were not as consistent about correcting Simon when he did.)

Simon clearly believed that we did not know the baby's sex. I once suggested that he and I play a game with Fisher-Price people as "Mommy, Daddy, Simon, and the baby." Simon went to his room for the figures and returned with two for the baby, explaining that we did not know yet if it was a boy or a girl (3,8,12). But Simon did not typically specify both possibilities; with only a few exceptions (3,9,17), he always referred to the baby as a boy.

There may have been several reasons that Simon implicitly insisted the baby was a boy. Although he could tell the difference between boys and girls, he did not actually know the critical distinction between them. Like most other preschoolers, he focused on hair length (Thompson and Bentler 1971).

Mother:	(holding Simon's hand to her tummy) Feel that.
Simon:	(pleased) I feel his foot coming at me.
Mother:	Maybe it's her foot. When will we know if it's a girl or a boy?
Simon:	I don't know.
Mother:	How do we know you're a boy? What do boys have?
Simon:	(knowingly) Short hair!
Mother:	And girls?
Simon:	Long hair!
Mother:	What else do boys have? (pointing) Here?
Simon:	A penis.
Mother:	And girls?
Simon:	Polkes. (Simon often referred to breasts incorrectly as polkes [thighs].)

Mother: (chuckling) No, girls have a vagina, and these are
tsitses. Mommies have tsitses (3,7,18).

Although we often tried to correct his misconception, Simon did
not change his criterion. Thus he said an imaginary turtle that had
just "hatched" was a girl because it had long hair; then, changing his
mind, he said it was a boy but that it needed a haircut. I unsuccessfully tried to elicit the real distinction from him, so I told him that a
boy has a penis and a girl has a vagina (3,9,17). Two months later
Simon still had it wrong. Talking about a stray kitten in a story, he
said, "I could tell [if it's a boy or a girl] from the hair. Because I see if
it's short hair, it must be a boy. If it's long hair, it must be a girl"
(taped 4,2,1).

Thus Simon lacked basic biological knowledge about what determined the baby's sex. He also presumably did not understand how
and when it was determined. And before he was 4 he was probably
unaware that it would not change (Aboud and Ruble 1987). In fact,
Simon's appropriate use of gender terms belied his incomplete understanding of various basic categories and their connections with
each other—brother or sister, boy or girl, long hair or short hair—all
very confusing. Simon apparently needed at least nominally to specify the role he and the baby would play in their new relationship. He
was concerned that he would be a little brother, not a big brother, if
the baby were a girl (3,4,21). And he wondered, "It doesn't matter if
the baby is a boy or a girl. Right? It's still a baby" (3,8,17).

Even if Simon did not completely understand the basic categories,
he probably could not conceive of a genderless baby. But why did he
refer to the baby as a boy rather than a girl? He may have simply
assumed that it would be a boy. One day Simon said something about
a "baby brother," so I reminded him that it might be a brother or a
sister. "Well," he replied quite seriously, "*I'm* expecting a brother"
(3,6,13). He had often heard us tell people that we were "expecting a
new baby" and apparently used the expression to serve his own argument. About six weeks later, I saw what looked like two brothers
walking together. "Aw, I never had a brother," I joked. "I'm expecting a brother," said Simon. "What are you expecting?" I answered,
"We don't usually know until the baby is born whether it's a boy or
a girl" (3,7,24).

Simon may have really wanted a brother and may have expressed
his preference by assuming it to be true. Alternatively he may have
wanted the baby to be like him. Or, despite our assurances, he may
have doubted that he really would be a big brother if the baby were
a girl. Regardless, I never heard him actually say he wanted a brother

before Asher was born, and he certainly was given the chance to do so; virtually everyone who knew about the baby asked Simon if he wanted a brother or a sister. Simon occasionally avoided the question but usually said that he wanted "both" (3,8,14). His answer amused most adults, which I suspect encouraged him to use it again and again.

I tried to find out what Simon wanted and what he meant by "both." Once, he and I were talking about a picture of a dog family (figure 3.1).

Father: Is [the baby inside the mommy dog] a baby sister or a baby brother?
Simon: (emphatically) You can't tell!
Father: You can't tell? Well [the big brother] may know. What do you think he would like? Do you think he would like a baby brother or a baby sister?
Simon: (immediately) Both!
Father: What do you mean both?
Simon: He . . . I like both.
Father: He would like both? He would like either a brother *or* a sister?
Simon: Yeah.
Father: Or he wants a brother *and* a sister.
Simon: He wants a brother and a sister (taped 3,9,5).

A month later we were talking about Simon's friend whose family was also expecting a baby. I asked if Jeff wanted a brother or a sister. "Both," Simon said. "I want both, and he wants both." He explained that "both" meant a brother and a sister, so I told him that Jeff's mother, like Bev, was going to have only one baby. "But I like both!"

Figure 3.1
A dog family: The couple is expecting a second child.

he protested. Then, following my lead, he said that he meant he did not care (taped 3,9,29).

Simon said he was expecting a brother and almost always referred to the baby with masculine pronouns. Yet before Asher was born, Simon refused to say what he wanted or even to guess what Jeff or a dog in a picture wanted. At last, the day after Asher was born, Simon did express a preference. His aunt Esta asked him if he was happy now that he had the brother he wanted. Simon replied that he actually always wanted a baby sister (4,0,4). But later that day someone told Simon how lucky he was to have a baby brother, and Simon said that he got a baby brother because that was what he wanted—sex determination by preference.

The Unborn Baby's Big Brother
Simon had a fairly concrete idea about his unborn sibling. He attributed the baby with the form, functions, and psychological attributes of a person. Indeed he never even suggested that his unborn sibling was anything but a small human baby. And given that he accepted the baby's existence, it makes sense that he identified himself as a brother. He explicitly said so during a self-concept game that we played before Asher was born. One by one, I showed Simon a series of cards, each containing a printed descriptor—*happy, sad, nice,* and so on. I read each descriptor and asked if it applied to him, if it belonged in his pile. Simon accurately ascribed several roles to himself—*boy, cousin, friend,* and *son*—and excluded others—*aunt, bubby* (grandmother), *daughter, girl, lady, mommy, sister, uncle,* and *zaide* (grandfather). He also excluded *daddy* but said he would be one, perhaps more because he expected to grow up than because he foresaw having children and adopting a new role. Regardless Simon might have made a similar prediction about *brother,* but he did not. No; he already was the baby's brother (3,8,12; 3,8,24).

I was somewhat surprised that Simon identified himself as a brother before Asher was born. It was something he apparently figured out for himself. When we first told him about the baby, we specifically said that he would be a big brother when the baby was born (3,4,21). In the ensuing weeks, we made a point of calling him a big boy or big cousin. But we reminded him that he would be a big brother, typically adding *good, wonderful, terrific, the best,* and so on. For example, Simon said the baby could touch his toys, and I told Simon he was "going to be a terrific big brother" (3,7,22). Similarly he said he would try to make the baby feel better, and Bev told him he was "going to be the best big brother anyone ever had" (3,8,18).

Simon did once say that the unborn baby was going to have a brother in the future. He thought about our baby after a visit to our friend Fran and her newborn.

Simon: Our baby is luckier than Fran's . . . because he's going to have an older brother. (Earlier Fran had praised Simon, telling him that Charles would be lucky to have a brother like him.)

Mother: Yes, you're going to be his older brother. . . . You're going to be a good older brother.

Simon: After the baby's born, I'm going to do whatever you tell me.

Mother: It's very nice of you to say that. I'm sure you're going to be a terrific older brother (3,8,5).

Yet three weeks later, Simon already identified himself as the baby's brother (3,8,18) and in time specifically said that the unborn baby had a brother. Feeling the baby move may have reinforced Simon's idea that he was already its big brother. Several comments about the baby saying hello support this suggestion. In the first, Bev talked about the future. Simon was feeling the baby kick. Bev said, "The baby's saying, 'Hi. Are you going to be a good big brother?'" (3,9,3). Another time he was feeling the baby, Simon talked about the present, "He's saying hello to his big brother." And kissing Simon, Bev continued in the present, "You're a wonderful big brother" (3,10,30). A few days later Simon also used the present when he said, "Daddy, I just felt the baby kick his big brother's hand" (3,11,2). The baby moved, so he was real, so Simon was obviously a big brother.

The Baby Brother's Role

During an interview about family relationships, Simon observed that a person starts to become a baby brother "in a seed, in a shell and a seed." This was certainly consistent with the idea that he was a big brother months before Asher was born. Simon also said not all little boys are baby brothers, that there had to be a big boy there to make him a brother; in other words, baby brothers are little boys with big brothers. Finally he observed that baby brothers "cry and throw food on the floor and spit"—typical baby behaviors—but there was not anything special a person had to do when he was a baby brother (taped 3,11,16; based on Watson and Amgott-Kwan 1983). Yet Simon actually had more detailed expectations about the baby, and it is useful to explore these because his own role expectations were tied to his ideas about his role partner.

Babies Do Only Four Things: Eat, Sleep, Cry, and Poo

Before he ever saw Asher, Simon knew what other preschoolers know about babies: that they are small, need special care, and have limited abilities (Melson, Fogel, and Toda 1986). Such qualities are definitionally associated with babies, especially in the mind of a young child who is acquiring many new skills and trying to become a "big boy." Simon accurately knew that babies cannot do a variety of activities: reach high, walk, play with a complicated toy, dive or skate or participate in other sports, and read a book (3,7,9; 3,8,10; 3,8,19; 3,9,14; 3,11,14). And although he could reasonably imitate a variety of baby noises—like babbling, squeaking, and wailing—he knew that babies do not talk (3,8,8; 3,11,0).

Simon had more trouble understanding what babies can do than what they cannot do. And, unexpectedly, one characterization of a baby that amused him reinforced his impression that young babies have many limitations. When we were in Israel, we posted a picture of Simon's new cousin Michael with other family pictures (about 3,1,0). We often showed the photos to Simon, reviewing everyone's name, so he would remember them while we were away. Bev invariably made Simon laugh when she talked about Michael. "Michael only does four things," she joked, with appropriate sound effects, "eat, sleep, cry, and poo."

When we knew we were expecting, we tried to avoid the playmate myth by specifically telling Simon that newborns do not do much. Simon once commented how small an 11-day-old baby was. "And he doesn't do very much," Bev observed. "Small babies generally don't do much" (3,8,5). Another time Simon expressed his impatience about seeing the baby. "Well, the baby isn't ready yet," Bev said. "You know, when he or she comes out, it will be little. Babies do four things—eat, sleep, poo, and cry" (3,8,18).

Simon learned the lesson. He was watching "Sesame Street" with my father and me. A 4-year-old boy was visiting the hospital to see his mother and the new baby. During a scene of the nursery, my father asked Simon what the babies were doing. "Babies don't do anything," Simon responded. But my father said they do some things, and Simon admitted that they eat and drink and sleep (3,8,29).

Simon was more emphatic when I suggested that babies actually do more than he assumed. He found me reading a research report.

Simon: What are you reading?
Father: An article that says newborn babies can tell the difference between their mommy and a stranger.

Simon: (very forcefully) No! Babies can't do anything!
Father: Why not?
Simon: All they can do is eat and sleep and drink milk and cry.
Mother: You haven't seen Charles lately. He can smile now. Babies soon do a lot.
Father: They have to learn who their mommy is and their daddy and their big brother (3,9,14).

But Simon assumed that babies know very little. Michael, who was 10 months old, refused the bottle. I asked Simon why.

Simon: (laughs) I don't know! If I were his mommy or his daddy, I would know.
Father: Do you think he knew why he wasn't drinking, or just his mommy and his daddy?
Simon: Just his mommy and his daddy.
Father: . . . How come not him?
Simon: He's too little to know.
Father: Well, he must know something. Do you think he knows anything?
Simon: (pause) Well, he's a teensie one. Babies know nothing, right?
Father: (laughs) That's right, they know nothing. . . . Maybe they know what makes them happy or what makes them sad.
Simon: Or angry (taped 3,9,5).

The idea that babies know very little arose several times after that. Michael once pulled a radio off a bureau, scraping his cheek. Simon asked why he did it, and we explained that babies do not always know that they are not supposed to do things (3,9,13). In the ensuing days, Simon repeatedly asked about the accident and each time received a similar explanation—that babies do not know very much.

Four days before Asher was born, Bev admonished Simon about misbehaving, and Simon attributed an emotion to his unborn sibling.

Mother: It doesn't make anyone happy when you don't cooperate. I'm not happy. Daddy's not happy. And then you're not happy.
Simon: The baby's happy.
Mother: The baby doesn't know anything about anything (3,11,30).

Later that day Simon generalized limited knowledge to pets. We visited Fran, and Simon found a piece of a broken ornament near her Christmas tree.

Simon: Why is this broken?
Fran: The cat broke the ornament.
Simon: Why?
Fran: Because cats make mistakes too.
Simon: Cats don't know anything about anything.
Father: Who else doesn't know anything about anything?
Simon: Babies . . . and dogs (3,11,30).

Life Is More Than Eating and Sleeping
Yet Simon did understand that babies do more than four things. We often talked about babies looking and listening, partly because even newborns do them and partly because of my own research interests (Mendelson and Haith 1976). When we first visited Fran's 11-day-old baby, I showed Simon how Charles oriented to the sound of jingling keys and, much to Simon's pleasure, how to attract Charles's attention by calling him. A bit later Simon noticed that Charles was looking at the light, but he mistakenly thought Charles was also watching the rain outside (3,8,5). And on other occasions I demonstrated how to attract Charles's attention by showing him objects (3,8,5; 3,8,24). It is therefore not surprising that Simon thought Charles could listen to a story and look at the pictures (3,8,24).

Given that Simon thought the baby played inside Bev (3,9,17), he clearly expected his brother or sister to play on the outside. After all, we prepared Simon's old toys for the baby. He once asked for a puzzle to help him count to 100 and suggested we also get one for the baby. I proposed that it would be good to share, but Simon countered that the baby should have his own toys (3,8,18). At other times Simon was more generous. "When the baby comes," Simon announced, "I'm going to give him one of my cars to play with" (3,7,13). And he also suggested that the baby have some of the toys he no longer used—his Cabbage Patch doll, a rattle, an old teething ring that happened to be among his bath toys, and his old mobile (3,10,6).

Simon knew the difference between appropriate and inappropriate toys for a baby. From his own perspective, he had clear preferences; he once complained about visiting Michael because he did not like to play with Michael's baby toys (3,10,10). Simon also understood a baby's perspective: some toys are too complicated (3,8,19), and others are dangerous because they have small pieces or because the baby may "push [them] down his throat" (3,7,22). We often talked about safety—specifically about the baby reaching for things, throwing them, mouthing them, chewing them up, and swallowing them or about the baby touching the stove and other hot objects. Simon's concern about these behaviors belied the claim that babies do only four things.

But the apparent contradiction evaporates if we assume that Simon had some understanding of developmental change. He did know that babies physically change in a variety of ways; for example, they grow bigger and sprout teeth. He also realized that they develop skills; babies eventually walk, talk, count, play, and so forth. We tried to pinpoint when a baby understands language during one conversation about what our baby should not play with.

> Simon: (jokingly about his favorite stuffed toy) Not Blossom, because then the baby might think that that pretend skunk is a real skunk.
> Father: Oh! Then what do you think will happen?
> Simon: She'll say yuck! . . . (giggles) I'll have to tell her that he's a friendly skunk. . . . Except she won't understand.
> Father: When do you think babies begin to understand?
> Simon: About when they're 3.

In the rest of our conversation I challenged Simon that babies begin to understand before 3 by asking him about babies he knew. Simon did not think Michael, who was 1 year, even understood his own name. But he realized that Adrian, who was only 2¾, understood language. And he hesitantly said that Daniel, 20 months, understood "just a few words." "You see," I said. "So babies begin to understand some things before they're 2 years old" (taped 3,10,19).

The Big Brother's Role

Before Asher was born, Simon began to think of himself as a brother and imagined what the baby would be like. Not surprisingly, he also began thinking what being a big brother meant and how he expected to fulfill that role. And there is a related issue: how Simon strove to define himself as a big boy.

A Little Boy . . . a Big Boy

Big is an important self-descriptor for a preschooler, perhaps as important as any other. And the shift from *little* to *big* is an issue that must be dealt with by every 3- or 4-year-old, even if the child does not expect a new sibling. By about 3 years of age, some children become defensive about referring to themselves as a baby (Pipp et al. 1987). Yet a young child must resolve the conflict between a fervent desire to be big and abundant evidence to the contrary. Being a big boy was both important and emotionally powerful for Simon. During our self-concept game, he experienced considerable internal conflict when he referred to himself as little.

Father: *Little.* Are you little?
Simon: Not that little!
Father: Not that little. So do you take it or do I take it?
Simon: I'm not as little as baby.
Father: No.
Simon: Though I'm still little.
Father: So who's going to take it?
Simon: I am.
Father: OK.
Simon: (apparently unable to abandon the idea) I'm not *that* little!
Father: Not *that* little but . . .
Simon: I'm still little (taped 3,8,24).

Similarly Simon only grudgingly admitted that he was young. "I'm not very young," he explained (3,8,12). He also adamantly objected to being called a little boy or, worse, a baby. For example, he once referred to an exceptionally small Cheerio as "a baby Cheerio." Bev jokingly asked, "A baby Cheerio for a baby?" "I'm *not* a baby," insisted Simon, definitely not amused (3,9,14). In addition to rejecting labels such as *little, young,* and *baby,* he actively sought the label *big.* He directed our self-concept game to ensure that it verified his own understanding of himself. He suggested that I ask him about *big,* which he put in his pile. And after saying he was a brother, he added, "Anywhere does it say *big* brother?" (3,8,24).

Simon was often explicit about how he was a big boy. He sometimes distinguished himself from the baby. He said that we could give his carseat to the baby. "If you stop suddenly," he explained "[the baby] needs these straps, but I don't because I'm a big boy" (3,8,10). Alternatively, he established himself as big by comparing himself to grown-ups. "Big boys and big girls and Mommies and Daddies can stay close to the baby when they're sick," he said. "Right?" (3,11,2).

A preschooler's intrinsic desire to be big is supported by the prospect of a new sibling for at least three reasons: to be a big brother or sister, to be different from the baby, and to live up to parents' maturity demands. In other words, becoming a sibling can affirm a child as as big boy or girl, just as becoming a parent can affirm a grown-up's personal sense of adult status (Breen 1975, Leifer 1980, C. Lewis 1986, Shereshefsky et al. 1973). But at the same time, expecting a baby may create conflict within a young child by providing at least three reasons for remaining small: to feel secure with parents, to resist an externally imposed role change, and to be similar to the baby. Resolving the conflict is part of the psychological work of growing up and becoming a big brother or sister.

A Big Brother Helps Give the Baby a Bath
Simon was interviewed about family relationships to assess his understanding of roles (taped 3,10,26 and 3,11,2; based on Watson and Amgott-Kwan 1983). His ideas about the two parental roles were quite similar: real grown-ups are mothers or fathers, although "some [grown-up men] are just big boys . . . and they're not men yet" and "some [grown up women] are girls." For someone to be a mother or father, the other parent has to be there—but a child has to be there as well. Mothers and fathers do things that only adults can do—like "light a match"—and that involve caregiving—like "take [children] in a taxi to the doctor to check their ears." Finally, mothers and fathers have to do one thing special for someone else: love.

Unfortunately Simon did not want to be interviewed about big brothers—he insisted on talking about baby brothers instead—so I must infer what he thought about his future role from other sources. As it happened, his ideas about big brothers were quite like his ideas about parents and involved similar actions and feelings. One topic is particularly relevant: Simon's intention to help care for the baby. Simon knew before Asher was born that the baby would have to be cared for and that caregiving would entail some effort. One evening he balked at bedtime and made several unnecessary demands on Bev. Bev initiated the following conversation with a rhetorical comment.

Mother: (exasperated) I don't know what people do with nine kids.
Simon: What did you say?
Mother: It isn't important.
Simon: (after a short silence) Mommy, it's going to be very busy when we have the baby.
Mother: What do you mean?
Simon: Going back and forth and back and forth and back and forth . . .
Mother: Doing what?
Simon: You tell me.

> Mother: Giving the baby a bath . . .
> Simon: I'll help give the baby a bath and feeding the baby
>   (3,8,4).

We often returned to the topic of what had to be done for the baby. Simon once remarked that people can have babies only if they are married. I explained that people usually do that because it is too hard to take care of a baby if they are not married. We then listed caregiving tasks—diapering, feeding, bathing, and so on (3,9,25). But Simon did not think of these tasks as exclusively part of the parental role. Rather he believed that helping with the baby was also an important part of the big brother's role. One day I asked him if a baby dog in a picture had any brothers and sisters. "He has a mother and a daddy," Simon answered, "except that he was born first. And he's gonna have another baby, so he's gonna be the big brother. At first he's goona be a baby. And then he's gonna be a big brother. And he's gonna take care of another baby with his mommy and daddy" (taped 3,9,29). Thus, Simon recited what was his personal narrative from the past—as a baby—projected into the future—as a big brother who helps his parents with another baby.

Simon hoped to help with a variety of tasks—bathing and feeding were obvious candidates (3,8,4)—but he also intended to make sure the baby would not touch what became a longer and longer list of forbidden objects: first pills, then books, things on the shelves, and the stove, then mushrooms and glass, and last fire and a light bulb (3,7,20; 3,7,22; 3,10,10; 3,11,10). Simon also offered to show Israel to the baby, to make him feel better, and to watch him when he eats because "he may throw food on the floor or in your face" (3,7,27; 3,8,18; 3,11,10). Simon even volunteered to wake up at night if we wanted him to help the baby (3,10,19).

By making these offers, Simon implicitly contrasted himself to the baby and favorably compared himself to Bev and me. But evaluating his own ability to fill the role of big brother, he did realize that he would not be able to help with everything. One day Simon offered to help put the baby's crib together. I asked what other things he was going to help with. "I'll help whatever it needs," he replied. "But . . . but some things I can do by myself with the baby, and some things . . . like . . . I can't. Like changing a diaper I can't do" (taped 3,9,29).

Although Bev and I consciously avoided the playmate myth, we both fostered the helping myth, occasionally by instructing Simon about what would happen.

> Mother: When you were born, [Bubby] gave us the bathtub.
>   We used to bathe you in the kitchen on the counter.

Simon: (surprised) I don't remember that!
Mother: I know. Because you were still little. . . . Are you
             going to help when we bathe the baby in the
             kitchen?
Simon: Yeah. It'll have to be over there.
Mother: We'll take everything off the counter, . . . take a little
             wash cloth . . . a little bit of soap. . . . Then the baby
             lies in the water. We have some warm water to wash
             with. Then we help the baby sit up (taped 3,10,19).

Thus, we supported Simon's expectation that he would help care
for his brother or sister and, by doing so, differentiated between him
and the baby. The helping myth was particularly useful for placating
Simon. In the following example, Simon and Bev were talking about
the baby's needs. Simon suddenly realized that there would be a
problem if he and the baby needed attention at the same time. At first
Bev solved the problem by depicting Simon and the baby in parallel
roles—each receiving a bath from one of us. But she then "graduated" Simon into the role of big brother.

Simon: I want to talk about the baby again.
Mother: What do you want to talk about?
Simon: What the baby needs—like clothes, toys. I could give
             the baby a bath. What happens if we both have a
             bath at the same time?
Mother: When the baby is small, we'll give the baby a bath in
             a small bathtub in the kitchen.
Simon: What if Daddy has to bathe both of us?
Mother: Well, one of us will bathe you, and one of us will
             bathe the baby. Or we'll bathe you first, and then
             you'll help with the baby (3,10,6).

Don't Touch the Stove!
Simon expected to help prevent the baby from touching dangerous
objects. His concern for the baby's safety demonstrated not only that
he wanted to help but also how he felt about his unborn brother or
sister.

Simon was interested in the baby's physical safety, even if Bev and
I rarely discussed the precautions necessary around the house when
the baby would be mobile. We have always been safety conscious.
When Simon was an infant, we baby-proofed the house by putting
guards on electrical outlets, installing latches on drawers, locking
cupboards, and so on. We also talked about the importance of physical safety as soon as Simon could understand. By the time Simon

was 3, he knew many safety rules and was appropriately wary of fire, sharp knives, and our busy downtown traffic.

Simon occasionally expressed his concern about the baby inside Bev. He was worried that pushing during delivery would hurt the baby (3,9,17) and warned Bev not to get stuck in the elevator door since that might hurt the baby too (3,7,22). Another time he asked to go swimming with me rather than Bev; he liked someone to catch him from the side of the pool and imagined he might hurt the baby if he jumped to Bev (3,7,22). Simon's reasoning was actually confirmed the next day when he did go swimming with Bev. "Mommy didn't want to catch me," he explained, "because it would hurt the baby" (3,7,23).

Simon also thought about the baby's safety outside Bev. "Right, a baby could eat all these books?" he rhetorically asked. "We'll have to put them up [on the higher shelves]. I can reach up." Bev and I agreed, saying that he was a big boy—again differentiating him from the baby (3,7,9). When he was helping Bev in the kitchen ten days later, he offered the first of several creative solutions to the problem of the stove, a problem he spontaneously raised himself.

Simon: (referring to the stove's on-off indicator) It's a good thing that the stove has a red light on it.
Mother: Why?
Simon: Because the baby will know not to touch it.
Mother: But what if the baby doesn't understand what the red light is about?
Simon: Then we'll have to put a big sign around the stove: "Don't touch the stove" (3,7,19).

Simon raised the topic again the next morning. He was watching me take a vitamin pill. I repeated a standard explanation that medicine was very dangerous and that, of course, he would not touch anyone else's medicine. "I'll make sure the baby doesn't touch your pills," he said and, presumably pursuing the topic of safety, added, "I think we have to put a sign up on the oven to make sure the baby doesn't touch it." I asked if he thought the baby will know how to read. "No," he replied laughing. "I was just kidding" (3,7,20).

A rather long discussion two days later showed how much Simon had generalized the topic of safety: he wanted me to put his silver cup on the top shelf of our bookcase so no one would touch it. I asked who he did not want to touch the cup. "Just anyone," he replied, "or a baby." At first he denied having any particular baby in mind, but after a brief pause added that he would make sure "our baby" did not touch books (he might chew them), things on the shelves, the stove, the television, toys with little things (he could swallow them), and Simon's new toys like his felt pen (the baby might push it down his throat). Simon said he would teach the baby what not to touch, whereupon I offered to teach the baby what Simon did not know. I then fostered the helping myth and implicitly confirmed that teaching is part of a big brother's role; I said I could teach Simon, and Simon could teach the baby. "That's a good idea," Simon complimented me, smiling (3,7,22).

Simon's continual interest in safety was partly related to privilege and status since they provide access to places and things. Simon proposed the ultimate solution to the stove problem: put up a sign and don't let the baby in the kitchen (3,8,4). In the following exchange, Simon differentiated himself from the baby and verified that his own status was not jeopardized.

Simon: Right, only I can touch your books?
Father: Right. But sometimes even you can't touch them.
Simon: Right. But babies can't touch your books. They might chew them, especially your special books (3,8,1).

A few weeks later Simon looked at our books and spontaneously rehearsed his safety rules: "Babies aren't allowed to touch your books. . . . But I am sometimes . . . unless you don't let me. . . . The baby can't touch the oven. . . . We shouldn't let the baby go in the kitchen" (3,8,21). But Simon again evaluated his own ability to fill the role of big brother, and acknowledging that he did not know how to prevent the baby from touching the stove, he seriously sought relevant information, just as pregnant women do in anticipation of their new role (Deutsch et al. 1988, R. Rubin 1967). The topic of safety led to a discussion about the baby's abilities, parenting techniques, and a comparison between Simon and the baby.

Simon: Well, how would we stop the baby from touching the oven?
Father: . . . When the baby first comes home, when the baby's first born, do you think the baby's going to be walking yet?
Simon: No.
Father: Do you think the baby's going to be crawling yet?
Simon: No.
Father: No. So at first the baby isn't going to be able to go near the stove. Right?
Simon: But when he starts to walk, he is going to touch it.
Father: And what will we say if the baby . . . if we see that

Simon: the baby is going to touch the stove? What do you think we'd say?

Simon: Don't!

Father: That's right! We'd say (adopting a stern voice), *"Don't touch the stove. No! No! Never, never touch the stove."*

Simon: And what . . . we . . . we could shut the [kitchen doors] so the baby doesn't even walk in.

Father: That's right. But some of the time the baby may walk into the kitchen. Don't you think?

Simon: Yeah.

Father: . . . [So] the baby has to learn not to touch the stove. Did you learn not to touch the stove?

Simon: Yes.

The conversation continued, and I raised the helping myth once more.

Simon: But even if you bump the stove, you touch it.

Father: Yeah. Well that's sort of an accident. But when the stove is turned on, do you go near the stove?

Simon: No.

Father: No, of course not.

Simon: Only if Mommy's there.

Father: Yeah. Well, the baby's going to have to learn the same thing. Don't you think?

Simon: Yeah.

Father: Just the same way. But you know what?

Simon: What?

Father: This time the baby will have you to help learn.

Simon: Right! And you too.

Father: That's right!

Simon: And you and Mommy to help learn.

Father: Yeah. And we'll help teach him. That's right.

Simon: We'll both be very busy.

And Simon really believed that he would help.

Simon: So we better keep away from [mushrooms and glass]. If we keep away from them, the baby would keep away from them.

Father: That's right! That's right!

Simon: Whatever we do, the baby would do.

Father: That's right (taped 3,10,10).

Yet Simon did not change his mind about how he would help solve the stove problem. "Well, the thing is, we have to not let the baby go into . . . the kitchen," he proposed another day," . . . because then, if he's in the kitchen, the stove might be on, and he might touch it. . . . So we have to make sure we shut the door" (taped 3,10,19).

What Prompted Anticipatory Role Changes?

Judy Dunn and Carol Kendrick (1982a, 156) speculated that a sibling's birth must "involve a major shift of a symbolic kind—a change in the child's conception of himself within the family and indeed of himself as a person." Certainly the birth of a second child creates a new family role for the first—as big brother or sister—and modifies existing roles. Yet the changes in self-concept associated with role changes do not necessarily occur just when the baby is born. As in Simon's case, they may actually begin long before.

Simon received a message from family and friends: you're going to be the big brother; you're not a baby anymore; you're a big boy now. The message was not only explicit but often implicit when, for example, we recruited Simon's help or prepared his old toys and clothes for the baby. And Simon eagerly believed the message. He wanted to think of himself as big and at least three months before Asher was born willingly assumed his new role as the baby's brother.

Simon's early description of himself as a brother was also consistent with his concept of the unborn baby. Simon knew virtually nothing about prenatal development, and we never suggested that the fetus was anything less than a little baby who happened to be inside Bev. But like most other preschoolers, Simon knew quite a lot about babies (Melson, Fogel, and Toda 1986)—general knowledge that he presumably transferred directly to the newest baby in his life. He endowed the unborn baby with various characteristics: a human form including body parts, biological functions such as eating and sleeping, infantile behaviors such as crying, childlike activities such as playing, and even mental states associated with communication, emotions, desires, and food preferences. Simon was also quite specific on one point: the baby was a *brother*.

Expectant parents are often convinced by fetal movement, ultrasonography, and amniocentesis that their unborn baby is real, that their child is an individual with personality traits, mental states, and even a particular appearance (Gloger-Tippelt 1988). Similarly Simon had proof that the baby was real: he had heard on the best authority—from his parents—that there was a *baby* inside Bev, and he often talked about the baby with us. He also delighted that Bev was growing larger and larger. Last and the best possible proof, he felt the baby move. If the baby was real, then surely Simon was already a brother.

Firstborns whose mothers talk about the newborn as a person are likely to have a friendly sibling relationship when the baby is a toddler (Dunn and Kendrick 1982a). But preschoolers, like Simon, may endow an unborn baby with human qualities, which possibly explains why they so readily believe that the baby will be a playmate. Simon not only thought that the baby inside Bev was a person, he projected the baby into the future. In an attempt to avoid the playmate myth, we stressed how few things young babies can do. Perhaps as a result, Simon did understand that the baby would at first have limitations, yet eventually grow and learn.

Simon projected his own role into the future, he sincerely believed that he would help care for the baby. Aligning himself with Bev and me, he defined his role in terms of ours. But he could not have accurately foreseen how he would help and, given his age, would not really be able to do much. He even admitted that there were some caregiving tasks that he could not do by himself. Yet he already did help around the house—vacuuming and cutting the salad, for example—so caring for the baby may have simply been another adult task he thought he could try. Simon was also concerned with the baby's safety, but not simply because it was something else for him to do. Even if his interest was sometimes self-serving, it was usually unselfish, as when he warned Bev about the elevator doors or worried about the baby being pushed during delivery. His brotherly protection often reflected the same concerns that parents have for the health of their unborn baby (Shereshefsky and Yarrow 1973).

Before Asher was born, Simon's changing concept of himself was closely related to his concept of the baby. Simon was a brother because the baby was real; Simon would help because the baby had limitations. Simon also compared himself directly to his unborn sibling just as firstborns compare themselves to a baby brother or sister (Dunn and Kendrick 1982a). When Simon talked about safety, he always drew at least implicit comparisons, especially about privileges and abilities, which confirmed his superiority.

Changes in Simon's understanding of himself and his brother were not limited to attributes. More important, Simon experienced the anticipatory phase of role acquisition (Thornton and Nardi 1975). His expectations for the future—about being a brother—were now tied to the baby's development. And Simon began to incorporate the baby into his own self-narrative. He was, in fact, making strides toward forging a relationship with his baby brother.

Chapter 4

First Encounters

Bev awoke with mild contractions at 4:30 A.M. and remained awake the rest of the night (4,0,2), but she did not change her plans for the day. Simon was oblivious to her condition, and we kept it a secret to avoid worrying him. Although Simon expected one of his grandparents to stay with him when we had to go to the hospital, my sister Roz was available that evening. As it happened, Bev's water broke about an hour after we went to bed. Since Simon needed his sleep, we left without telling him good-bye. We arrived at the hospital at midnight and were overjoyed eight hours later by a healthy baby (4,0,3).

When Simon awakened slightly before seven, as usual, he was unperturbed to learn that we were at the hospital. "My daddy is helping the baby come out," he explained to Roz. According to her, Simon was typically himself: he asked to help prepare breakfast, he wanted to play with her, and he was generally in a good mood. But when I telephoned at nine, he was quite subdued:

Father: Do you know where Mommy and Daddy are?
Simon: At the hospital.
Father: Guess what we have for you.
Simon: (obviously pleased) A baby!
Father: Can you guess what kind of baby? A boy or a girl?
Simon: (no response)
Father: It's a baby brother.
Simon: Oh.
Father: His name is Asher. Can you say that?
Simon: Asher.
Father: . . . Mommy and I love you very much.
Simon: (plaintively) When are you coming home?
Father: I'll be home in an hour (4,0,3).

When I returned home, I took Simon to see my parents, who gave him the first of many "big-brother" presents.

Prior Experience

Babies before Asher

Simon had plenty of experience interacting with familiar toddlers and babies. He started his Montreal daycare at 14 months. The groups were segregated by age, but they played outside in a common yard, and the children often visited other classes inside, even spending time with the babies. In Jerusalem Simon attended daycare with about twelve toddlers and preschoolers (about 2,8,15–3,5,15). He spent most of his time playing with the older children but also interacted with the younger ones in both group activities and one on one.

Yet Simon had only limited experience with very young infants. We once visited our friend Fran and her 11-day-old baby (3,8,5). Simon was struck that Charles was so tiny and had almost no hair, but he was far more interested in Fran's cat. He interacted with Charles very little and, when he did, was certainly not adept. Still, he treated Charles gently, talked to him appropriately with a modulated tone of voice, and responded well to directions. Simon, apparently upset when Charles started to cry, tried to soothe him by rocking his cradle. When that did not work, I prompted Simon to say "Charles" softly over and over, but that helped only for a few seconds.

Before Asher was born, Simon had other chances to spend an hour or two with Charles. Fran and Charles visited us when he was 4 weeks old and dropped him off when he was 11 and 18 weeks (3,8,24; 3,10,13; 3,11,18). Simon looked forward to seeing the baby and spent more time with him than he had at Fran's. These times Simon was not distracted by the cat, and both boys were more socially adept— Simon because he had learned a few rudimentary skills and Charles because he was older.

Simon usually wanted his turn holding Charles and usually as soon as possible. Charles was hungry when he and Fran arrived for their first visit, and he started to cry in Simon's lap. Simon was upset by the crying, so he was faced with a dilemma. I took Charles to calm him down; then Simon wanted him back in his lap, but Charles cried again. As a result we passed the baby back and forth several times (3,8,24). The first time we babysat, I had to hold Charles during supper to keep him calm, so I ate with him in one hand. Simon was upset that we would not let him have a turn doing exactly what I did. Since Charles would not settle down, I walked with him over my shoulder. Again Simon immediately wanted a turn, and this time I helped him hold the baby. Bev eventually took Charles, so that Simon and I could eat, but Simon preferred helping her amuse the baby (3,10,13).

Simon was also interested in Charles when we were not interacting with him. Bev offered to read a story to Simon and 4-week-old Charles. Simon eagerly got some books and insisted that Fran sit on the couch so that Charles could see the pictures. But Simon himself did not attend to the story; he watched Charles and repeatedly touched him (3,8,24). Seven weeks later Charles was sleeping on Simon's bed when Simon and I arrived home. Simon wanted to awaken him, but Bev and I explained that a baby must sleep until he gets up by himself. We still went to look at Charles, and despite our warnings about disturbing the baby, we had to restrain Simon from climbing onto the bed (3,10,13).

Simon used a variety of rudimentary skills to interact with Charles and willingly accepted advice to learn more. Simon happily sat with 4-week-old Charles facing out between his legs. Simon stroked him gently, kissed him, and started patting his head just as he had patted his back to burp him. We told him he had to stroke a baby's head gently, and he complied. Later Simon asked why Charles held his hands closed, and Fran said babies just do that. She then showed Simon how to get Charles to clutch his finger by stroking the side of his hand. Still later we prompted Simon to show Charles a small box, and he held it in front of the baby (3,8,24). During the next visit Simon decided on his own to show a rattle to 11-week-old Charles. After I told him not to hold it too close to Charles's face, Simon did manage to catch Charles's attention. Later Simon wanted to change Charles, so I showed Simon how to wipe him with a wet tissue and how to fasten the diaper tabs (3,10,13).

Simon learned about breast feeding, something he would eventually observe hundreds of times. Simon first saw a baby suckle when Fran nursed 11-day-old Charles. Simon was both flabbergasted and amused (3,8,5). When Fran and Charles visited us about two weeks later, Simon was quite impatient to see him nurse. He stood right next to her and watched intently but this time without surprise or amusement. Simon soon asked Fran when she was going to give him "the other one," and she explained after ten or fifteen minutes. When Fran did switch Charles, Simon asked about the breast pad that she removed; she explained that she needed it because the milk sometimes drips (3,8,24).

When Charles cried, Simon generally became upset and wanted to do something to soothe him. My suggestion that Simon softly call Charles's name did not work at 4 weeks any more than it had at 11 days, but this time, Simon did not give up his attempt to calm Charles; he spontaneously kissed him and gently patted his head

(3,8,24). Similarly, seven weeks later, Simon tried to soothe Charles by tenderly patting his cheek. Fran had said Charles might be hungry, so Bev tried to give him a bottle, but Charles was not used to it and he wailed more and more forcefully. Simon wanted to try, oblivious that Bev was not in the mood for help. Then Simon loudly and accurately observed, "No, no, he doesn't want it!" Simon became increasingly upset and put his hands over his ears. Finally he held up a toy, which distracted Charles for a while (3,10,13).

Although Simon was generally pleased about having Charles visit and was enthusiastic about helping, he may have found these visits mildly stressful, particularly when we babysat at 11 weeks. Simon, upset that I was holding the baby at the dinner table without letting Simon have a turn, told me to put Charles down. I explained that Charles would start crying and reminded Simon that he did not like to hear it. Simon retorted that he changed his mind—that he did not care if Charles cried. Later, when Bev was amusing Charles, Simon sadly approached me to cuddle in my lap for a moment. Afterward Simon started to play on the floor, and I sat next to him with Charles in my lap. But Simon soon asked me for help in the bathroom and for his bath, even though Bev had been bathing him lately. Before going to bed, Simon said that babysitting Charles was like having our own baby and added that Charles was a "tough baby." But he would not answer whether he had fun with Charles around (3,10,13).

In fact, babysitting Charles did reveal some of the joys and problems we would experience when Asher was born, such as Simon's enthusiasm, his desire to help, and the need to juggle family routines. Although Simon was not yet particularly adept, he was already learning useful skills for interacting with a baby: gently touching, talking, and expressing affection; holding a baby and showing toys; soothing cries in a number of ways. And Simon was keen about learning more.

Separation from Parents
Naturally Simon sometimes resisted separation from Bev and me, but he was quite used to them. He was cared for by a babysitter for at least 12 hours a week from the time he was 6 weeks old until he started full-time daycare at 14 months. As a baby he virtually never fussed when Bev and I left him during the day, and he was easily engaged by an activity, so we rarely saw tears as we left, even during his first week at daycare. By the time we returned from sabbatical, Simon was a daycare veteran. When I dropped him off before work, he typically started to play right away. When Bev or I picked him up

in the afternoon, he usually wanted us to watch him finish "one more game" or "one more picture."

Simon was also used to our going out about one evening a week, although he typically cried when we told him about it. If we had a new babysitter, Simon cried as we left the house, but not for long, since he was so easily engaged in an activity. And he was reasonably cooperative after establishing that the babysitter knew the rules. Once Simon knew the babysitter, he looked forward to her arrival and rarely fussed as we left. If Bev or I went out alone, Simon might protest about a disruption to his routine play and stories but usually just checked that the other parent was staying behind.

Simon experienced some long-term separations from Bev and me when we took a break. Four months before Asher was born, Simon stayed at his grandparents for a weekend (3,7,24–26). After our year in Jerusalem, they were enthusiastic about having him overnight, and we looked forward to the time alone. Simon was understandably upset. He cried when we told him we were leaving for the weekend and wanted to know all the details about where we were going.

Although Simon was well behaved while we were gone—a "gem" according to his grandparents—he did occasionally ask where we were. And he seemed somewhat upset when we came to pick him up three days later. He wanted to be alone with us and was quite reserved as he told us about his weekend. Then, holding back his tears, he asked us where we had gone. That evening he was very clingy and ate uncharacteristically little for supper. He seemed particularly angry with Bev and resisted her offer to read him a bedtime story. When it was time to say good-night, he had trouble settling down; he objected that we were not going to bed too, something he had frequently done lately. Later that night Simon wet his bed, for only the second time in about a year (the other shortly after our return to Montreal).

Four days later Bev's work took her out of town overnight (3,8,0–1). The evening before she left, she told Simon that she would be leaving early the next morning. Simon asked if I was staying with him and seemed reassured that I was. The morning she left, Simon forgot that Bev was going away and looked for her when he wanted breakfast, but he calmly accepted my explanation that she was already on her way. He was quite himself while she was gone; he slept well that night and, although he woke up early the next morning, willingly went back to bed when I told him he needed more sleep. Simon warmly welcomed Bev upon her return, without the anger he had shown earlier that week. At the time I thought Simon's response to Bev's absence boded well for Bev's confinement.

Bev's Confinement

First Visits to the Hospital

Simon was eager to see the baby, so we went to the hospital as soon as Bev had a chance to rest (4,0,3). On the way Simon asked why Bev and I had left the night before without telling him. I explained that we had to go to the hospital since it was an emergency, that we could leave him at home since Roz was there, and that we did not want to disturb him since he was sleeping.

Simon was clearly happy to see Bev and greeted her warmly. She was on her way to feed Asher, so we all went to the nursery. Asher, only a few hours old, was asleep in an incubator. We watched him, saying very little at first. We then exchanged a few comments about his appearance. When I asked Simon what he thought about Asher's size, he said that Asher was smaller than he expected. Simon asked about Asher's clamped umbilical cord; I explained that the nurse would soon remove the clamp and that the cord would fall off and leave a belly button. Simon was obviously interested in his new brother and, once started, continued asking many questions, about the "dirt" (blood) on Asher's face, about his long hair, and so on.

Simon and I gowned up to watch Asher nurse. Asher needed a little coaxing, but he took to the breast soon enough, and Bev drew one of many comparisons between the two boys by telling Simon how enthusiastic he had been the first time he nursed. Simon was absolutely unperturbed by Bev's nursing Asher; he was neither flabbergasted nor amused, just interested. He matter-of-factly asked Bev several questions, such as why she held her nipple back, away from Asher's nose, and he offered to help. He gently stroked Asher's hair and ears and talked to him sweetly, with a high-pitched, modulated tone in a rudimentary form of baby talk. Afterward he helped burp Asher and happily held him in his lap.

Simon was in generally good spirits throughout the visit, but he was upset to learn that Bev and Asher would probably stay in the hospital for two or three days, until Saturday or Sunday. He was particularly concerned that she would not be home for Friday-night dinner, our traditional Sabbath meal. Eventually Asher's disruption of our mealtime routine would become a problem for Simon.

On the way home, Simon and I talked mainly about Asher. We reviewed Simon's first impressions: "He was nice!" "I think he prefers milk than water . . . because he drank the milk and he didn't drink the water." "He was bigger than I expected!" (Yet earlier Simon said that Asher was smaller than he expected.) "I assumed he would have less hair than that." (Perhaps Simon remembered how little hair 11-day-old Charles had.) I also pointed out that Simon had learned how to do some things with Asher, like burp him and hold him. Simon apparently learned well.

Simon: If the baby's really little you have to . . . ah . . . like a
          big boy has to hold him sitting down.
Father: That's right. Absolutely! And when the baby's really
          little you have to make sure that you hold his head
          steady, because little babies—very little babies—don't
          even know how to hold up their heads yet.
Simon: I know. You know what? . . . Like a 15-year-old can
          hold him standing up.
Father: That's right. But not a 4-year-old.
Simon: No (taped 4,0,3).

I then asked Simon what he thought older brothers do. He immediately interpreted my general question personally and responded with something that could hardly have been more appropriate for Asher's birthday.

Father: What do you think older brothers do? What kinds of
          things do you think they do?
Simon: Well, I'll have to help him blow out his birthday
          candles.
Father: . . . Until he knows how to do it himself. Right?
Simon: Yeah, when he's 2, I'll have to help him.
Father: Yes, you will.
Simon: When he's 3, he'll probably know how.
Father: Maybe . . . maybe when he's 3, and certainly when
          he's 4, he'll know how.
Simon: Yeah, certainly (taped 4,0,3).

That evening Simon and I returned to the hospital. There were many other visitors as well—Simon's grandparents, aunts, uncles, and cousins—who not only admired the baby but also showered Simon with affection. At the end of the visiting hour, Simon was upset about leaving Bev. On the way home he suggested that we phone her before going to bed. He also verified that big brothers can visit the hospital as many times as they want. And he finally asked about what was bothering him directly: "Why is Mommy going to miss Shabbat supper?" I explained that she had to stay in the hospital with Asher until Saturday or Sunday. Simon naturally preferred Saturday, but I said the doctor had to decide (4,0,3).

A Hectic Four Days

Simon talked to Bev on the phone at least twice a day. They had pleasant conversations, briefly about Asher but mostly about Simon and what he was doing. And Simon was very busy. He spent most of his time with my parents, my sister Esta, and her family. As special treats they went out to eat and saw a movie. Simon played with his older cousins for hours, something he thoroughly enjoyed and would not interrupt even to visit the hospital with me.

Although I saw Bev and Asher two or three times a day, Simon was barely interested in coming each morning. I had to entice him on the fourth day by bringing something for him to do with Bev. During his visits, we naturally talked about babies: they drink only milk, sleep a lot, do very little, cannot touch things, squeeze fingers, turn their head early on (as Asher already did), and eventually flip over (as he did not). Bev and I compared Asher with what Simon was like as a baby, both in terms of looks (same button nose, blue eyes, and sculpted lips but different hair and complexion) and in terms of behavior (the two boys nursed well, slept well, and were easy to soothe). The information possibly encouraged Simon to identify with his brother and to differentiate himself from him, and Simon learned something about himself while becoming familiar with Asher.

Because of all the excitement, Simon missed his nap every afternoon and stayed up unusually late every night. He was cantankerous by Monday, the day Bev and Asher came home (4,0,7). Simon and I had several altercations about what we would do that piercingly cold day; finally he cajoled me into taking him skating before we went to the hospital. It was his first time on ice skates, and he was quite proud about mastering such a big-boy activity. When we arrived at the hospital afterward, Bev was ready to leave. Simon was bubbling; he wanted to help with everything and, given his mood before skating, was surprisingly cooperative. Simon moved the plants that Bev had received, wheeled Asher's bassinette, and helped dress Asher for the subzero weather. By choice Simon went with Bev and Asher in my father's car, while I took all the paraphernalia in ours. When we got home, Simon enthusiastically helped carry everything he could manage. The waiting was over. But so much else had just begun.

Initial Adjustments

Just in the Door

Simon claimed his new "toy" as soon as Bev undressed Asher. Despite Simon's comment the day Asher was born that a 4-year-old cannot stand up while holding a baby (4,0,3), he wanted to do just that. Bev and I tried to supervise, but Simon wanted his own way. We tried simultaneously to set limits and to show him what he might do with his baby brother.

Simon: I want to hold him.
Father: OK, here you go. Sit back, OK? Do you want to sit back a little bit? OK . . . That's fine. Can you hold him?
Simon: I can stand up with him.
Father: No, you can't stand up.
Simon: I want to . . .
Father: Look, you can't hold him standing up.
Simon: (irritated) Lemme show you!
Father: OK, good, very nice.
Mother: No, no, no! I don't want him walking around!
Father: OK, now you can't walk around with him though.
Simon: (annoyed) I'm just staying here!
Father: OK, because it's the most important . . . OK, now I'd like you to sit down, please. Why don't you sit down and hold him? And you could . . . you say something to him.
Simon: It's easier standing up.
Father: No, it's easier this way. So then he can sit in your lap like this. See. Or you could put him on your knees like that. OK? There you go. There!
Mother: (laughs) (taped 4,0,7).

Despite the strain between Simon and us, Simon interacted sweetly with Asher. But it was time for Asher to nurse, and he eventually started to cry, so Bev took him. Simon made room for himself right next to her and watched with interest. He tried to pat Asher but used his fingernails. Perhaps he was simply inept; perhaps his positive overture turned ambivalent (Dunn and Kendrick 1982a). Regardless, he prompted a confrontation.

Mother: No, no, no! Leave . . . No, don't scratch him, Simon. No, just leave his hair.
Simon: I was just patting him.
Mother: No, you're using your nails; that's not patting. Patting is with the fingers, Simon.
Father: Not with the nails.
Simon: (getting upset) I know, I don't even . . .
Father: Yeah, OK. But you have to use your fingers like this. No! I'm not going to let you do it.

Simon: But I'll do it very . . .
Mother: No! I want you to use your fingers. If you can't use
          your fingers, then I don't want you to do it.
Simon: (annoyed) I know what to do!
Mother: OK. Then you use your fingers like this. That's how
          . . .
Simon: I know what to . . . to do. I want to use my fingers.
Mother: (annoyed) Simon! I'm not going to tell you again. If
          you don't pat him with your fingers, I'm going to ask
          you to leave. I want you to use your fingers, not your
          nails.
Simon: I'm not using my nails!
Mother: I don't want you to use it like this. You're to pat like
          this.
Father: Gently.
Simon: (to Mother) Your nails are even longer!
Mother: I know, but I want you to use your . . .
Simon: I don't even have my nails out (taped 4,0,7).

I tried to distract Simon by getting him to attend to Asher's "cute little ear," but Simon would have none of it. I then invited him to help with lunch. After all, each parent should be able to handle one child. Although my tactic prompted a short discussion about Asher's drinking just milk, Simon wanted to stay with Bev and Asher. Then Bev tried:

Mother: Come here. You want to see how he sucks? Come
          here.
Simon: How does he suck?
Mother: Doesn't he remind you of Charles, Fran's Charles,
          when he sucks?
Simon: (petulantly) No (taped 4,0,7).

Simon was not having fun, so Bev offered to read him a story, a classic standby for nursing mothers. But before Simon got a book, he noticed Asher's sounds and sat down to watch. Understandably, a new baby brother was more interesting than anything Bev or I might suggest.

After a while Bev resorted to the helping myth: "If you get a diaper from his room, then Daddy or you can help change him. OK?" I offered to show Simon which diapers to bring, but he insisted that he already knew and could find them himself. In the end, I had to get them for him anyway, and I then volunteered to show him how to put on the diaper. Again he insisted that he already knew because he had seen it done. Simon proceeded to put the baby blanket on the floor, and I admonished him that we did not want it there. Simon also started touching Asher with a hand Simon had just put in his own mouth, and I admonished him again.

Then Bev said that we had to burp Asher before changing him, so we showed Simon how, but our desire to encourage Simon was clearly tempered by our concern for the baby. And Simon was a bit impatient with our instructions, perhaps because he had already burped both Charles (3,8,24) and Asher (4,0,3).

Mother:	. . . Do you want me to show you what to do?
Simon:	Yeah, I know.
Father:	OK, go like this. Put the . . . hand in front, like this. OK, now you burp him. Come on. There! Hey, you're a terrific burper!
Simon:	Don't hold him.
Father:	OK. You're terrific!
Simon:	Don't be, I'll . . .
Father:	No, I have to make sure his face doesn't fall forward.
Simon:	I will make . . .
Father:	He's already burped already. Because you're such a good burper, he burped right away . . . OK.
Mother:	He's sleeping now.
Father:	OK. That's fantastic (taped 4,0,7).

Asher resumed nursing, and we distracted Simon by talking about his skating lesson. When Asher was almost finished, Simon was confronted with the first disruption to our general routine: Bev was not going to eat with us.

Simon:	I think he's almost finished . . . Look. He's almost finished.
Father:	And then are you going to help me make lunch for you and me?
Simon:	Why isn't Mommy eating lunch?
Father:	Mommy ate at the hospital. Mommy's eaten. And Asher's eaten.
Mother:	You can have . . . something to eat.
Simon:	I don't even want something!
Mother:	OK, fine.
Father:	I'll make something up. . . .
Mother:	(to Simon) Do you want something to drink?
Simon:	No (taped 4,0,7).

Simon liked to eat with both of us. In the ensuing weeks, we would have many confrontations because either Bev or I had to tend to Asher during mealtime.

While I was preparing lunch, Bev reminded me to get some groceries. Simon wanted to come; he pleaded to accompany me though he would miss his nap, and we succumbed to his pleas. Then he asked that we bring Asher—something he would often suggest—but that was impossible. Finally, when I started talking to Bev, Simon was not about to be excluded. "Daddy, let's go make lunch," he suggested, using my own tactic. "OK," I agreed, "let's go and make lunch" (taped 4,0,7).

A Snowy Day at Home

On New Year's Day, a raging blizzard confined us to our apartment—not an ideal situation for a family with a 5-day-old baby and an active 4-year-old boy. Under the best of circumstances, Simon never enjoyed staying in all day, and he became less and less cooperative about things that did not concern Asher. We argued about nap, dressing, eating properly, bath, and so on. Simon also tested long-standing limits. We had an absolute rule about electrical outlets and plugs, and Simon had learned to avoid them at a very young age. Yet the day Asher came home, Simon played with a plug, something he had not done for years. Although Bev and I severely scolded him, he tested us again the next day, and we had to stop him from playing with a plug for a second time.

Later Simon graphically demonstrated what was really bothering him. Bev had just put Asher down to sleep. Simon started patting him and, despite her repeated admonitions, refused to stop, so she eventually shooed him out of the room. When Simon cried and talked back to Bev, I tried to lead him away, but he stood spread-eagled in the doorway, defiantly barring us from going to Asher.

Simon found Asher's first full day at home quite troublesome. Longing for calmer times, he expressed his concern that evening while we were playing.

> Simon: Everyone's angry.
> Father: Who's angry?
> Simon: You, me, and Mommy.
> Father: Why do you think so?
> Simon: . . . Because everyone is upset.
> Father: Who do you think is upset?
> Simon: You and Mommy and me and . . . I assume, Asher.
> Father: Why do you think everyone is upset?
> Simon: I don't know.

Father: I think it's because there's a new baby in the house,
         and it's hard to get used to a new baby.
Simon: I think it's because things aren't as calm in the house
         as before.

Simon got up to close the door, saying that he likes it calm and quiet
in his room. When he sat down again, I tried to pursue the topic, but
he had had enough.

Simon: I don't want to build anymore. I want stories for bed.
Father: (hugging Simon) I love you.
Simon: (warmly returns Father's hug) (4,0,8).

Continuing Downhill
The next day was the last one of winter break. Because Simon had to
get out of the house, I took him skating despite the cold. On the way,
we talked about two relevant topics. First, I tried to explain what was
happening in the house.

Father: (even though Simon was the only one who had slept
         well the night before) It was good that we all had a
         good night's sleep last night, because maybe tonight
         we won't be so cranky. Just the way you get cranky
         when you don't have enough sleep, Mommy and I
         also get cranky. And when people get cranky, they get
         angry.
Simon: (revealing his perspective on how family members af-
         fect each other) And when you and Mommy get
         cranky, I get cranky. And when I get cranky, Asher
         gets cranky.
Father: That's why everyone needs to get enough sleep.

Second, Simon raised a crucial issue that was bothering him.
Throughout the conversation, he was clearly sad and talked in a subdued voice.

Simon: It's hard to raise two childs, isn't it?
Father: (amused) Yes, it's hard to raise two children. There are
         a lot of things to do with two children.
Simon: And a mommy and a daddy don't have time to play.
Father: Why? You don't think we play with you as much?
Simon: No.
Father: But here we're going skating.
Simon: That's not play.
Father: It's not the same as playing in the house?

Simon: No.
Father: Mommy and Daddy will make sure to play with you
          more as the days go on (4,0,9).

Later that day Bev and I discussed the importance of maintaining Simon's playtime routine at home.

As the day wore on, Simon became less and less controllable, perhaps because of the baby but for other reasons as well. He had been away from his regular schedule for two weeks and was about to return to daycare the next day; he had missed most of his naps for a week and had stayed up late, so he was very tired; he was recovering from a cold; and Bev and I were tired and irritable. That evening Simon uncharacteristically exploded with two temper tantrums. Classically they resulted from a clash of wills—the first over an extra box of raisins just before supper, the second when Bev dismantled one of his Duplo creations at bedtime clean-up. So ended Simon's winter break.

Asher's Circumcision
Brit Milah, the covenant of circumcision, is an essential part of Judaism. The ancient ritual is performed on the eighth day of a Jewish boy's life and symbolizes a personal covenant between him and God. Simon was cooperative the day of Asher's circumcision, and we got ready without incident (4,0,10). Although I had told Simon a little about the *Brit Milah* four days earlier, I wanted to explain it in more detail so he would not be alarmed by Asher's bandage. I invited Simon to help me dress Asher. While changing Asher's diaper, I showed Simon that Asher's penis was different from his and said that one of the things that would happen at the *Brit Milah* was that Asher's penis would be made the same. Empathizing with his baby brother, Simon asked if Asher would cry. I said that Asher would cry a little, but it would not hurt very much. I also showed Simon some pictures of the celebration at his *Brit Milah*, explaining that Asher's would be similar.

Many friends and relatives attended the ceremony and they greeted Simon warmly. Simon even received a few big-brother presents but was surprisingly unenthusiastic about them. He was clearly withdrawn and asked to be held. Simon did not watch the ceremony; he ate cake with a daycare friend who had come with her parents. On the way home Simon was still sad and complained about having to go to daycare. Bev and I matter-of-factly said that it was a daycare day and assured him that all his friends would be there. When I said that I had to go to work, Simon asked about Bev. We told him that she was going to stay home to take care of Asher and that they had to rest. Crying a little, Simon said he also had to rest. Nonetheless I dropped him off at daycare. As usual he asked me to stay a few minutes, and, although he did not fuss about my leaving, he was still visibly sad.

Bev picked up Simon that afternoon. He enthusiastically greeted her with an especially big hug. He was quite chipper, very different from the boy I had dropped off. At home Simon was notably cooperative while playing, during supper, and getting ready for bed. He was back to his daycare friends and teachers and, probably more important, back to his routine.

A Passing Whirlwind

The transition to sibling status is a multifaceted process that occurs over an extended period. True, a firstborn definitionally becomes a sibling upon the birth of a brother or sister, but the psychological changes associated with the new role may begin considerably before. Adjustment to the general situation and acceptance of the baby may occur only gradually, and the relationship between the siblings will certainly evolve over their lifetime.

But several psychological and social issues become salient when a new baby is born. The time takes on an unreal aura, probably because of the general level of excitement, because of the emotional impact of the baby, and because normal routines are suspended. This was certainly true in Simon's case. His first week as a brother was marked by Bev's absence, by meeting Asher, and by our groping to adjust to a baby in the house. There were a number of out-of-town visitors, a series of special events, and gifts for both turning 4 and becoming a brother. The result was obviously out of the ordinary, but even more than one might expect since Simon was away from his usual daycare schedule. Still, Simon was somewhat prepared for the events that week.

As Simon's parents, we were primarily concerned with two issues—his general adjustment to the new situation and his acceptance of Asher, the same two issues that concern most other parents upon the arrival of a second child (Walz and Rich 1983). The first week of Asher's life was certainly stressful for us all, so it is not surprising that Simon reacted emotionally, but he was still consistently cooperative when he was involved with his brother. He amply demonstrated a positive attitude toward his new brother when he visited the hospital and when Asher first came home, and he treated Asher as gently as he had always treated other babies.

The whirlwind surrounding Asher's birth passed quickly; we soon established a reasonable routine at home, and Simon returned to day-care. Thus, it is probably a mistake to attribute much importance to any specific event, such as a tantrum or an argument, however salient it may have been. In fact, Simon adjusted to the situation, accepted his brother, and interacted with him better and better in the ensuing months.

Chapter 5
Adjustment to the Baby

The life change associated with the birth of a brother or sister is probably understood best as a role transition—not melodramatically as trauma or even simply as a stressor that possibly elicits coping. There are, of course, potential stresses associated with a new sibling, but a role transition perspective can help explain the sources of stress and the coping strategies that may be observed at this time in a preschooler's life.

The birth of a brother or sister is stressful in part because of the constellation of events that often accompany the baby's arrival, events such as separation from mother during childbirth, moving to a new residence, and modifications in sleeping or daycare arrangements (Field and Reite 1984, Legg et al. 1974, Stubblefield 1955). But changes in existing social relationships are probably the most commonly assumed source of stress. With the arrival of a second child, mothers do spend less time directly interacting with their firstborn, and their interactions become more negative in tone (Dunn and Kendrick 1980, Feiring et al. 1983, Kendrick and Dunn 1980, Taylor and Kogan 1973). Although father-firstborn interactions may not change as much shortly after the birth of a second child, they seem to decline over the baby's first year (R. B. Stewart et al. 1987).

The new baby's disruption of daily life has been identified as another important source of stress for both parents and children (Dunn and Kendrick 1980, LaRossa 1983, LaRossa and LaRossa 1981). New parents find that time management is a particularly pressing concern, and those who effectively deal with time and energy demands tend to adjust to parenthood (Myers-Walls 1979, cited by B. C. Miller and Myers-Walls 1983). Bev and I were struck by this problem when we babysat for Charles before Asher was born (3,10,13; 3,11,18). We discovered how hectic it was to care for Charles and attend to Simon at the same time. We would later learn that adjusting to a baby requires very careful scheduling indeed.

For parents of a second child, one way to cope with time demands is to include the baby in activities with the firstborn (Mendelson and

Gottlieb 1987). Immediately after the baby's birth, mothers may spend somewhat less time alone with their older child and fathers reciprocally somewhat more time, but from shortly before to about 11 months after the baby's birth, the total amount of time that parents spend with their firstborn in caregiving, play, and social activities is surprisingly stable. What does change dramatically is the social context of parents' involvement. Roughly half the time that each parent spends alone with the firstborn before the baby's birth is replaced afterward by time with both children, and virtually all the time spent as a family threesome is replaced by time spent as a foursome. Such changes may effectively solve time and energy constraints, but they also modify the firstborn's overall social experience, since the baby's presence undoubtedly affects both the content and quality of parent–firstborn interactions (Belsky 1979, 1981, Clarke-Stewart 1978, Dunn and Kendrick 1980).

Most parents, assuming that their preschool child will be somewhat upset by the birth of a brother or sister, worry about how the preschooler will adapt to the baby (Walz and Rich 1983). But contrary to popular beliefs, not all children are distressed by a new sibling (Dunn and Kendrick 1982a, Gottlieb and Mendelson 1990, Kramer 1989, Legg et al. 1974, Nadelman and Begun 1982). Indeed some may respond positively by becoming more mature. And even if children are distressed, there is wide variation in the extent and the intensity of their reactions. Thus adjustment or maladjustment to a sibling's birth can take several forms. Children may regress by, for example, being naughty, demanding attention, or needing more help than usual with certain activities; alternatively they may become more mature by, for example, achieving toilet training or needing less help than usual with other activities; or they may show distress in some areas and independence in others.

Researchers have identified some of the factors that predict the amount of distress a preschooler will experience upon the birth of a new brother or sister (Dunn et al. 1981, Gottlieb and Mendelson 1990, Kramer 1989, Nadelman and Begun 1982, R. B. Stewart et al. 1987, Thomas et al. 1961). At the top of the list, firstborns who are distressed before the birth tend to be distressed afterward, yet behavioral difficulties may be mitigated by continuity in parental care, support from parents, and a close reciprocal friendship with a peer. Firstborns younger than 3 years old seem to be more adversely affected by the birth of a sibling than are older firstborns, yet older children may still react, not only after the baby is born but even before. Children show their distress in apparently sex-stereotyped ways; young boys tend to withdraw, and young girls to demand more attention. Finally, the level of the firstborn's distress may change over the baby's first year—higher at 1 month and 8 months than at 4 months and 12 months.

Despite these generalizations we do not know enough to predict adjustment or maladjustment in any particular child. To do so would presumably require more detailed understanding about the child and the situation than traditional methods provide. One of the strengths of case research is that it affords just such detailed understanding.

Daily Life before and after Asher

To fully understand a child's psychological adjustments to the birth of a sibling, it is useful to consider how the baby influences the child's daily life. I kept detailed records of Simon's activities for seven consecutive days during the three months before Asher's arrival—October (3,9), November (3,10), and December (3,11)—and during four of the five months afterward—January (4,0), February (4,1), April (4,3), and May (4,4). (The daily diaries are described in detail in appendix B.) They yielded information not only about what Simon did, where he did it, for how long, and with whom but also about the degree to which other people were involved in his activities. These constitute the settings of daily life, which play an important role in the development of interpersonal behavior (Whiting and Edwards 1988). Because I was a participant-observer, I could collect far more data about Simon and be more specific than has been the case in traditional studies (Douglas et al. 1968, Gottlieb 1985, Mendelson and Gottlieb 1987, Lawson and Ingleby 1974).

What Simon Did

I analyzed Simon's activities in terms of broad codes—care (receive), conflict, daycare, hang around, help (provide), mealtime, play, stories/songs (listen to stories or songs), religious services, sleep (quiet in bed or asleep), talk, travel, and television—to determine which of these activities changed and whether the changes were attributable to Asher's arrival or simply to Simon's development. The amount of time Simon spent sleeping at home was constant across the observation period (73.1 hours per week before Asher's birth versus 73.4 after), but there were some changes in the pattern of Simon's sleep. After Asher's arrival, Simon napped an hour less a week at home on weekends, and probably somewhat less at daycare during the week. In compensation, he slept 1.4 hours a week more at night, but he interrupted his sleep over twice as many times (3.3 times per week before versus 6.8 after). Simon's sleeping pattern may also have changed in unobserved ways: He may have spent more or less time falling asleep and lying quietly in bed upon waking; his sleep may have changed at daycare; and he may have suffered transient sleep disturbances during Bev's confinement (Field and Reite 1984).

Not surprisingly, Simon was involved in daycare activities for the same amount of time after Asher's birth as before (38.0 hours per week before versus 37.8 after). His daycare attendance generally reflected my day at the university; I typically dropped him off and picked him up, although Bev sometimes fetched him early. Daycare took up a substantial part of Simon's waking time and was potentially a source of stability, a counterpoint to the changes at home.

Figure 5.1 shows the amount of time that Simon spent on each of the other activities before and after Asher's birth. First consider the activities for which there were minimal changes: play, care, travel, stories/songs, and religious services. How much time Simon spent in these activities was largely determined by his needs and by daily or weekly routines. Thus Asher's arrival minimally affected how much time Simon spent bathing, grooming, dressing, and the like. It also did not affect daily routines such as traveling to and from daycare, after-dinner play, and bedtime stories and songs, nor did it alter our weekly attendance at religious services. To some extent, activities like

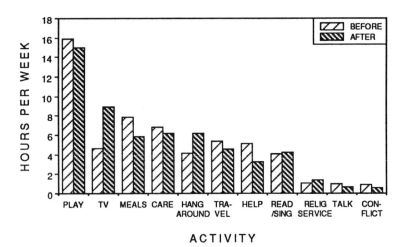

Figure 5.1
Amount of time per week that Simon spent in various activities before and after Asher's birth.

caregiving and even bedtime stories operate on a relatively fixed quota (Lawson and Ingleby 1974, Mendelson and Gottlieb 1987), but we also consciously tried to maintain our household routines after Asher was born to ensure that Simon's life was as stable as possible.

The amount of time that Simon spent in four activities—watching television, mealtime, hanging around, and helping—did change from before to after Asher's birth. A month afterward Simon began spending less time at meals and helping out, contexts in which conversations and social interaction take place around a directed activity (figure 5.2). In contrast there was a large and sustained increase immediately after Asher's birth in Simon's television watching and hanging around, passive, nondirected activities in which any conversation and social interaction were somewhat limited (figure 5.3).

After Asher was born, Simon spent about 25 percent less time at meals—besides those at daycare—a change that was true of breakfast, lunch, and dinner. Although the drop did not actually occur until Asher was about a month old, it was still clearly attributable to his presence. His effect on our family routine—the increased hecticness—is graphically illustrated by a comparison of the diary entries that cover the time from leaving daycare until seven o'clock for October 16 (3,9,22) and April 9 (4,3,16) (table 5.1). On October 16, Bev broke Simon's routine somewhat by picking him up early and taking

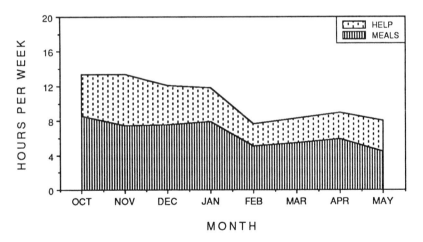

Figure 5.2
Amount of time per week that Simon spent helping out and at meals before Asher's birth—October (3,9,22), November (3,10,18), and December (3,11,23)—and afterward—January (4,0,24), February (4,1,20), April (4,3,19), and May (4,5,1). The data points for March are interpolated values.

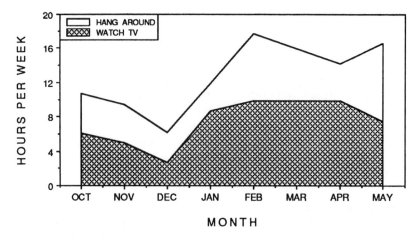

Figure 5.3
Amount of time per week that Simon spent hanging around and watching television before Asher's birth—October (3,9,22), November (3,10,18), and December (3,11,23)—and afterward—January (4,0,24), February (4,1,20), April (4,3,19), and May (4,5,1). The data points for March are interpolated values.

him to the park, yet the rest of the evening unfolded as usual before Asher's birth: Simon helped Bev prepare supper; dinner started relatively late and lasted fairly long; and Simon briefly helped me clean up.

On April 9 Simon watched television instead of helping with supper. As usual after Asher's birth, we began eating slightly earlier than on October 16. We typically ate as early as possible so that we could fit in all of Simon's routine activities before his bedtime. And since Asher also had to be fed, Simon and I sometimes started our meal without Bev; depending on how calm dinnertime was, she would nurse Asher either at the table or in another room. On April 9 Bev had already fed Asher by the time Simon and I arrived home, so Asher sat at the table in his infant seat. When this happened, the meal was often interrupted because Asher might fret or have to be changed. After dinner Simon watched television, I cleaned up, and Bev tended to Asher. Then, as usual at the time, Bev played with Simon while I tried to settle Asher down to sleep.

The comparison between October 16 and April 9 also illustrates that Simon helped out less after Asher was born than before. Overall he spent less time folding clothes, assisting with the dishwasher, vacuuming, and shopping, partly because we had less time to include him in these chores. He also participated less in his favorite adult activity—helping prepare food—which dropped from approximately

Table 5.1
Diary Entries

Time	Activity	Duration (minutes)
Tuesday, October 16 (3,9,22)		
16:00	S and M leave daycare to go to the park.	15
16:15	S and M at park; S rides bike, digs, climbs tree.	60
17:15	S and M drive home.	15
17:30	S helps M prepare supper.	15
17:45	S, M, and F eat supper.	45
18:00	S helps F with dishwasher.	5
18:05	M gives S a bath.	10
18:15	S and F play with Duplo.	45
Tuesday, April 9 (4,3,16)		
17:00	S and F drive home from daycare.	10
17:10	F changes S into pyjamas.	5
17:15	S watches TV next to F, who burps A and talks to A.	18
17:33	S still watches TV while M combs his hair.	2
17:35	S, M, and F eat dinner while A sits in infant seat.	20
17:55	S and A sit on F's lap.	5
18:00	S watches TV while M, F, and A in kitchen.	5
18:05	S still watches TV; F in and out of room; M with A.	10
18:15	M joins S watching TV.	15
18:30	M and S play; F with A.	30

Note: S = Simon, M = mother, F = father, A = Asher.

2.7 hours per week (53 percent of total helping time) to 1.3 hours per week (39 percent of total helping time). There were two primary reasons for the change in food preparation: instead of helping with breakfast, Simon spent time with the parent caring for Asher, and instead of helping with supper, he watched television. The helping myth is also relevant. Although Simon had assumed he would help take care of the baby, he actually spent only a negligible amount of time (0.1 hours per week) arranging diapers, changing or bathing Asher, and so on. Simon never really had a chance to help with the baby, so there was nothing to compensate for the drop in his help around the house. In a sense Simon's role in the family changed: he was a less active participant in the adult world after Asher's birth than before.

Bev and I carefully controlled the television shows Simon watched. Yet his television viewing almost doubled after Asher was born (4.6 hours per week before versus 9.0 after). The increase was due to more time spent watching "Sesame Street" (3.6 hours per week before versus 5.0 after), to an additional program after supper, an extra cartoon show Saturday morning, and an occasional video film. Probably part of the change in Simon's television viewing represented an expected trend; preschoolers spend more and more time watching television from 2½ to 5 years of age as their understanding of television content improves (Anderson et al. 1979). But part of the increase was due to Asher's presence in the family. Bev was often nursing Asher when Simon returned from daycare, so Simon watched television instead of helping prepare dinner. After supper Bev and I wanted to clean up the dishes and get Asher ready for bed with the least possible fuss, so we encouraged Simon to watch "Polka-dot Door." We also used television as a babysitter on the occasional weekend afternoon when we wanted to rest (Steiner 1963).

Hanging around is a more broadly defined activity than mealtime, helping, or watching television. It includes, for example, waiting to play with someone, socializing when people visit, wandering around the house, and talking to someone involved in preparing a meal, cleaning up, or a similar activity. Such seemingly undirected activities have been identified as signs of stress (Dunn and Kendrick 1982a, Nadelman and Begun 1982), yet they should not be interpreted too hastily. Although Simon hung around more after Asher's birth than before, the increase reflected age-related changes in Simon's sleep, not Asher's presence in the family. The greatest increase in hanging around occurred weekend afternoons, when Simon would have otherwise been napping. Yet Asher's presence did affect when Simon hung around—slightly more from 7:00 to 8:00 A.M. because of a shorter breakfast but slightly less from 8:00 to 9:00 A.M. because of "Sesame Street." Asher also affected what activities Simon hung around. Although we had implied that a big brother helps bathe, feed, or change the baby, Simon actually just hung around while Bev or I took care of Asher.

Where Simon Spent His Time
To determine whether Asher affected the location of Simon's activities, I examined the time that Simon spent in the following locations: car, daycare, home, outdoors, public building, synagogue, and visiting another home. Although Simon's time at home dropped slightly after Asher's arrival, the 1.4-hour-per-week change was only 2 percent of nondaycare waking time (40.5 hours per week before versus 39.1 after). The amount of time that Simon spent at friends' and relatives' homes tripled after Asher was born (2.3 hours per week before versus 7.6 after). The increase, a shift of 9 percent of Simon's nondaycare waking time, replaced time outdoors—mostly walking or swimming—and time in public buildings—mostly shopping.

The change in Simon's social context after Asher was born potentially fostered Simon's developmental progress. Simon was beginning to play at his friends' houses and occasionally visited with his grandparents, so the shift to other people's houses was obviously accompanied by a shift in the amount of interaction with other children outside daycare (2.0 hours per week before versus 6.0 after) and with other adults (6.4 hours per week before versus 7.3 after). The change was partly age related—one of the achievements of preschool is forming friendships outside the home—but it was also partly due to Asher. People invited Simon over because we had a new baby, or we arranged visits for him on weekend afternoons so that we could rest.

Just as babies stimulate social interaction between their parents and others (Belsky and Rovine 1984), they can also affect a sibling's social contacts outside the home. Asher's presence prompted Simon to develop new roles by widening his social circle and to elaborate his existing roles by engendering even closer relationships between Simon and his grandparents. If Simon had not been developmentally ready, visits away from home could have been added sources of stress, but, like parental support, contacts outside the immediate family may actually mitigate the stress associated with a new baby (Gottlieb and Mendelson 1990, Kramer 1989).

Attention from Parents
Although Asher indirectly affected Simon's social life outside the home, his main influence was on interactions within the family. One

obvious consequence of a new baby is that parents have less time to spend alone with their other children. How did Asher affect the attention that Simon received from Bev and me? For each diary entry, the level of attention that Simon received was rated on a five-point scale, from 0 for not present to 4 for intensely involved (table 5.2).

Figures 5.4 and 5.5 show the amount of time (excluding daycare and sleeping) during which Simon received each level of attention from Bev or from me before and after Asher's birth. The two graphs are surprisingly similar in the overall pattern and in the changes that apparently accompanied Asher's birth: each of us was either not present or present but not involved more after the birth than before. And each of us spent more time somewhat involved and less time moderately involved, mainly because some of our time shifted from a family of three to a family of four (for example, Simon would necessarily receive less attention with Asher at the table than without). But Bev and I both spent virtually the same amount of time intensely involved with Simon after Asher's arrival as we had before. We purposefully engaged in one-on-one activities with Simon, and it was quite easy to find a relatively small amount of time each day to do so.

To explore these changes in our attention to Simon, I partitioned his activities depending on who between us was involved (attention levels 2, 3, or 4) and considered only activities in which no one else besides Asher might be present. Figure 5.6 shows how much time Simon spent on six activities—play, watching television, receiving care, meals, helping, and hanging around—before and after Asher was born, and it indicates the amount of time that Simon spent on

Table 5.2
Definitions for Levels of Attention That Simon Received from Others

Level	Definition	Examples
0	Simon engaged in an activity alone	playing by himself in his bedroom, watching TV alone
1	one or more people present but minimally involved	watching TV while parents read, playing while mother nursing Asher
2	continuous involvement but at least three others present (TV counts as one individual)	meal at grandparents, watching TV with mother and father
3	continuously involved with one or two others	mealtime, dressing, playing
4	intensely involved with one other person	reading, bathroom care, singing, discipline

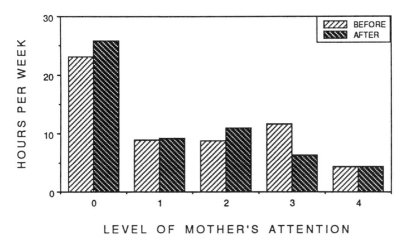

Figure 5.4
Amount of time per week that Simon received each level of attention from his
mother before and after Asher's birth.

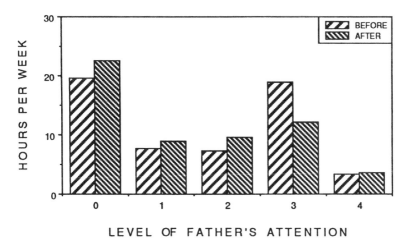

Figure 5.5
Amount of time per week that Simon received each level of attention from his father
before and after Asher's birth.

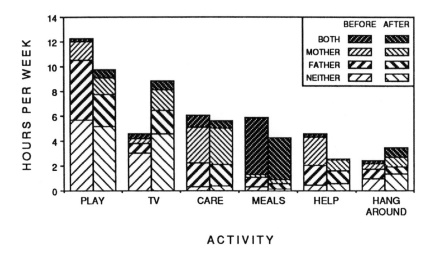

Figure 5.6
Amount of time per week that Simon spent in various activities with both mother and father, with only mother, with only father, and with neither mother nor father before and after Asher's birth.

each activity alone, with only me, with only Bev, or with both of us. Our involvement did not change uniformly for the six activities. Simon spent the same time receiving care from Bev and me after Asher's birth. In contrast, he spent less time playing with me, helping Bev, and at meals with the two of us, but he partly made up for these changes by increasing the time he spent watching television with us and hanging around us.

Implications
Asher's arrival did not herald a major reorganization in Simon's daily activities. Most obviously Simon still spent a large part of his week at daycare, where he and his pals followed predictable routines unaffected by changes in our family. He also experienced reasonable stability away from daycare. Simon spent a fairly constant amount of time on a variety of activities—play, care, travel, stories/songs, and religious services—that we purposefully tried to maintain to mitigate the disruptions associated with a new baby. Moreover Bev and I each spent the same amount of time interacting with Simon one on one after Asher's arrival as before.

Simon presumably benefited from the stability that he experienced during this period of change (Dunn and Kendrick 1982a, Thomas et al. 1961). Indeed predictable family routines are generally important for preschoolers' social and emotional well-being (Keltner 1988); they enable a child not only to construct scripts, or event-schemas, but also to follow them (Nelson 1981). For example, a child who has a predictable bedtime routine will learn everyone's role and the sequence of events—perhaps, Daddy gives me a bath, I brush my teeth, and Mommy reads me a story—and will be able to enact his or her own role, at least more smoothly than without the routine.

Obviously Simon's daily life changed after Asher was born. For instance, he spent more time with friends and extended family, which—like the decrease in how much he helped around the house—meant that his world was differentiating from ours. Yet his outside visits often replaced his nap, so they did not appreciably reduce the amount of time he spent with us. Simon was both developmentally ready and temperamentally inclined to visit other people by himself—two requirements for any successful solution to a situational demand. Therefore his excursions provided valuable entertainment and possibly an important source of support (Kramer 1989).

The amount of time that Simon spent on four activities did change after Asher was born: less time at meals and helping and more time watching television and hanging around. Asher's arrival did not influence the four activities in the same way, however. Mealtime was shortened partly because Asher's needs as an infant were often incompatible with order at the family table. Simon helped less partly because of Asher's schedule—directly because Bev prepared dinner before Simon returned home so that she could nurse Asher at five o'clock and indirectly because I preferred to clean up after dinner by myself so that I could finish as quickly as possible. Simon watched more television since he sat with Bev while she nursed Asher before dinner, since I encouraged Simon to watch after dinner, and since Simon relinquished his weekend nap. Finally, although Simon hung around more mainly because he no longer napped at home, he now hung around when Bev and I looked after Asher.

Superficially such changes can be interpreted as signs of stress. Simon apparently withdrew—spending less time on social or directed activities and more time on asocial or passive ones—which may be typical for boys with a new brother or sister (Dunn et al. 1981, Nadelman and Begun 1982). But these particular changes in Simon's behavior actually reflected changes in our family's schedule, not emotional changes in him. And one of the behaviors may have served positive functions: by hanging around Bev or me when we tended to Asher, Simon was accommodating to the changes in our family. More important, he had a chance not only to talk to us about Asher but also to observe, and possibly learn from, our interactions with the baby. Of course, Simon also had a chance to disrupt and distract, both potential sources of conflict.

According to one study, mothers attend to their firstborn less after the birth of a second child than before, but only when they are *not* occupied with the baby (Kendrick and Dunn 1980). However, the study did not sample the full range of baby-care activities—such as putting the baby to sleep for the night—and did not include family activities—such as mealtime. Indeed I played with Simon less after Asher was born than before because I typically put Asher to bed in the evening. Asher also disrupted dinnertime and considerably reduced the time we spent as a family. Finally, Simon interacted with us less when he watched television, either because Bev was nursing or I was trying to clean up, than he would have if he helped prepare a salad or rinse the dishes.

Signs of Stress and Coping

How children react to the events immediately surrounding the birth of a brother or sister is less important than how they cope in the long run. Furthermore children's adjustment weeks and months after the birth is best predicted by adjustment weeks or months before (Gottlieb and Mendelson 1990, Kramer 1989). Thus, Simon's initial response to his new brother must be placed within a broader context—one that extends from long before Asher's birth to long after.

A Major Transition: Jerusalem to Montreal

I started my case study shortly after we returned to Montreal from a sabbatical year in Jerusalem (2,5,26–3,5,21). For a number of reasons, Simon spent far more time with Bev and me there than he had in Montreal. When we moved to Jerusalem, we had no friends or relatives who could spend some time with Simon, and since he did not start daycare until the fall, he spent virtually every moment of the summer with at least one of us. When he finally did start, he attended only half days, so we had ample time to enjoy his company, especially since Bev was working part time and I distributed what I had to do over the six-day Israeli work week. Even at 2½ years Simon was a well-behaved boy who was equally comfortable going to one of the many parks in our neighborhood, having dinner in an adult restaurant, exploring ancient ruins, or splashing in the Mediterranean. Besides, Israel is a child-centered society, so we had no misgivings about taking Simon on our many excursions around Jerusalem and around the country.

Within two weeks of returning to Montreal, Simon went back to the daycare that he had attended before we left. We thought he might be reluctant to begin daycare, but he was so enthusiastic about returning that we started him a few days earlier than planned. He remembered some of his pals, perhaps because we had periodically looked at his class picture when we were away, and he quickly became part of the group again. Two months later his daycare class moved to another room with two new teachers, a change that did not appear to bother him (3,8,12).

Playing Alone
Parents obviously cannot spend as much time alone with their first-born after a second child is born as before (Gottlieb 1985, Mendelson and Gottlieb 1987), but presumably the change has different implications for different children. Children who generally enjoy solitary play should be less affected than those who depend on others for entertainment.

Bev and I rarely encouraged Simon to play by himself when he was a baby. As working parents we had precious little time at home, so we were enthusiastic about interacting with him when we had a chance. We probably made a mistake, because it became apparent quite early that Simon did not like playing alone. By the time we went to Jerusalem, Simon was reluctant to play by himself and generally relied on us for entertainment. And we did not even have a television there to function as a babysitter.

As a 4-year-old back in Montreal, Simon spent less than half his playtime at home by himself (figure 5.6), and he typically played with friends at daycare. He was either unable or, more likely, reluctant to entertain himself. Instead of playing alone, he preferred to be with Bev or me, even if we were not doing anything. When we were involved with him in an activity and had to leave for a moment, perhaps to answer the telephone, he became quite wild and might jump up and down on the couch. He tried to wake us in the morning so that we could be with him and usually requested company while he watched television, ate, or moved his bowels. Moreover, he was often quite impatient when Bev and I talked to each other, especially if he wanted something but even occasionally when he heard us after he was in bed.

Although we realized our previous mistakes, we had trouble correcting them. About four months before Asher was due, we decided to encourage Simon to play by himself, at least in the morning when he got up early. Like other parents expecting a second child, we were anticipating the baby's demands on our time, so we hoped to encourage Simon's independence (Walz and Rich 1983). When Simon was ready for action at six o'clock one morning, I told him to stay in bed. At about six-thirty, he brought his stuffed toys into our room, which would probably have been acceptable if he lay quietly in our bed, but he did not (3,7,21). Two days later Simon awoke early and got a bagel on his own. But after only two bites he insisted that Bev make him breakfast. We were frustrated by being awakened, so we announced a rule that, until seven o'clock, he was not allowed to enter our room but had to play in his own room. He objected that he could not play by himself and that, besides, he did not want to play before seven (3,7,23).

A week later Simon got up very early and came into our bed. Contrary to what we had told him, we did not send him out; instead, we gave him the option of staying quietly with us. Predictably he accepted but, just as predictably, was not calm for long; however, he eventually left to play with Duplo building blocks (3,7,29). We were making progress. Within a week Simon established a new pattern. He got up early and with only a little prompting played with Duplo in his own room. We praised his building effort, praised the fact that he did it by himself, and pointed out how pleasant the morning had been because we did not have to get out of bed before we were ready. And we told him that he was becoming such a big boy (3,8,3). On subsequent days Simon played by himself early in the morning and, when we finally got up, often proudly showed us his Duplo creations.

Despite his new morning routine, Simon was still reluctant to play alone when Bev or I was available to participate. If we were busy, he would follow us around, interrupt us, and generally try to get our attention. Although the problem was more pronounced for me than for Bev, it eventually declined for the two of us. Simon entertained himself more and more during the fall but often only if he was near Bev or me. Two of his favorite activities were pitching a "tent"—draping several blankets on overturned chairs—and building a "boat"—spreading a blanket on the living room floor. After working hard to set up his scene as precisely as possible, he, like Christopher Robin, would include his stuffed animals in his activity. But he continued playing only if Bev or I was in the room, and he inevitably invited us to cozy up in the tent or go for a boat ride.

Another of Simon's favorites was joining our activity. He helped variously prepare food, serve a meal, water plants, load and unload the dishwasher, load the washing machine, fold laundry, make beds, vacuum, take out the garbage, put away groceries, and virtually anything else that we allowed him to do around the house (see appendix B). Although his help was occasionally intrusive—as when he wanted to pour the juice even though there was a good cloth on the table— we could not dampen his enthusiasm. As a result, his assistance could be frustrating, and we often had to warn that if he wanted to help he had to do what he was actually able to (3,11,0).

Ratings of Distress and Independence
Traditionally, psychologists interested in children's adjustment have used behavioral checklists to assess distress reactions (Nadelman and Begun 1982, Gottlieb and Mendelson 1990, Kramer 1989, Vernon et al. 1966). I therefore examined summary judgments of Simon's behavior made by Bev and me and—since stressful life events may affect children's functioning at preschool (K. H. Rubin and Gordon 1987)—by Simon's two daycare teachers (appendix C). The judgments were made at regular intervals, with three parallel rating scales that each consisted of six subscales (Table C.1, Appendix C): (a) Reaction to Separation, (b) Withdrawal, (c) Anger/Hostility, (d) Insecurity, (e) Dependence, and (f) Independence. Bev and I judged the frequency of the behaviors (Home Behavioral Rating Scale, HBRS), and Simon's teachers judged both the frequency of similar behaviors (Daycare Behavioral Rating Scale, DBRS) and Simon's relative standing in his class on each (Daycare Behavioral Comparison Scale, DBCS).

The ratings provide an overview of Simon's behavior and his reaction to his new sibling. Simon was a generally well-adjusted child, with few problem areas. Both at home and at daycare, he rarely exhibited most of the distress behaviors (subscales a–e) and usually exhibited most of the independence behaviors (subscale f) (appendix C). Yet short-term changes might be obscured by averages across many weeks. Figures 5.7 and 5.8 present, respectively, the overall distress scores (average of subscales a–e) and independence scores for each rater for each scale. Simon's behavior at daycare apparently did not change because of Asher (DBRS and DBCS). Like the transition from Jerusalem to Montreal, the transition to the role of big brother did not disrupt how he functioned at daycare, perhaps because he went there regularly and was familiar with the routine. Thus, daycare was a source of stability for him.

Simon's distress ratings for home were relatively high in July (3,7,5) and generally declined until April (4,3,14) (HBRS). The drop may have reflected Simon's increasing maturity over the forty weeks of

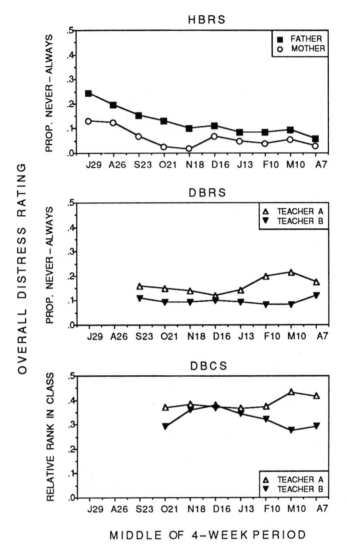

Figure 5.7
Ratings of Overall Distress (scales a–e) by parents on the Home Behavioral Rating
Scale (HBRS) and by teachers on both the Daycare Behavioral Rating Scale (DBRS)
and the Daycare Comparison Rating Scale (DCRS) computed within four-week periods: July 29 (3,7,5), August 26 (3,8,2), September 23 (3,8,30), October 21 (3,9,27),
November 18 (3,10,25), December 16 (3,11,22), January 13 (4,0,20), February 10
(4,1,17), March 10 (4,2,14), April 7 (4,3,14).

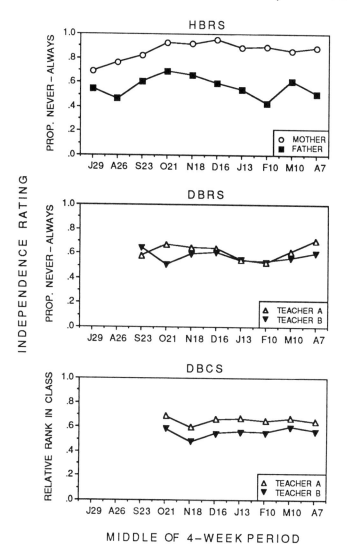

Figure 5.8
Ratings of Independence (scale f) by parents on the Home Behavioral Rating Scale
(HBRS) and by teachers on both the Daycare Behavioral Rating Scale (DBRS) and
the Daycare Comparison Rating Scale (DCRS) computed within four-week periods:
July 29 (3,7,5), August 26 (3,8,2), September 23 (3,8,30), October 21 (3,9,27), November
18 (3,10,25), December 16 (3,11,22), January 13 (4,0,20), February 10 (4,1,17),
March 10 (4,2,14), April 7 (4,3,14).

our ratings, but I suspect that the relatively high ratings early on were partly due to what was happening in our life. Simon was presumably still adjusting to our move from Jerusalem, a dramatic dislocation that entailed extensive changes in our work schedules—we returned to our teaching in September—and in Simon's daily routines. Not surprisingly, Simon's high overall distress scores early on were largely due to high ratings on the Response to Separation subscale, ratings that subsequently dropped. The general decline in our distress ratings was interrupted, albeit very slightly, in December (3,11,22), the month before Asher was born, and less so in March (4,2,14), when Asher was 2 to 3 months old. I suspect that the apparent increases were due to Simon's anticipation of Asher's arrival and to Asher's presence in the family.

The summary ratings yielded a good portrait of Simon's behavior. They were apparently sensitive to his gradual adaptation after our move from Jerusalem and somewhat sensitive to changes associated with Asher's birth. But summary ratings do not capture the richness of a child's responses, and they obscure both the significance and function of particular reactions, however fleeting they may be (Dunn and Kendrick 1982a).

A Skunk Named Blossom
Simon anticipated Asher's arrival in many ways and in some cases was upset by the prospect (for example, he was particularly disturbed about not being allowed to accompany Bev and me to the hospital). That he reacted emotionally to a specific issue, however, does not necessarily mean he was generally upset by what was happening in our family. Yet there were other signs, one of which involved his favorite plush toy, a skunk named Blossom. About two months before Asher was born, Simon insisted on taking Blossom to daycare for his nap. We could not convince him to take something else, though we warned him that we might forget to bring Blossom home. Sure enough, when Bev and Simon returned from daycare one afternoon, he realized that they had forgotten Blossom. He was visibly upset and said that he could not sleep without it, so they walked back to retrieve it (3,11,4).

Despite potential inconveniences, Simon would not accept any of several possible substitutes for naptime that could stay at daycare. He routinely took his toy skunk back and forth. And we did forget Blossom on other occasions, which led to more tears. Once, on the way to daycare, Simon realized that we had left Blossom at home, but it was too late to go back. At daycare he was so upset that we finally called Bev, who agreed to bring Blossom over before naptime (4,0,16).

About a week later, I forgot to take Blossom home. That night Simon came out of his room several times after lights out, and Bev tried to settle him down by helping him arrange his animals. He then noticed that Blossom was missing and cried inconsolably for quite a while (4,0,22).

After Asher was born, Simon still occasionally took Blossom to day-care, but he stopped doing so regularly by the time Asher was about a month old. Simon was also no longer upset when we forgot to bring Blossom home (4,1,19) and once willingly left it there overnight, though we could have easily retrieved it (4,1,26). Simon no longer needed the security that Blossom afforded as much as before.

I'm Only Pretending to Be Little

Although Simon objected to being called little, he consistently iden-tified himself as a baby in pretend play. When we lived in Jerusalem, Simon often played baby animal (2,5,26–3,5,21). He usually initiated the game by climbing into my lap or crawling into our bed in the morning. "I'll be the baby worm, and you be the daddy worm," he might say. Alternatively he might be a baby cat, a baby mouse, or a variety of other baby animals. But the game would often stop with his cuddling up to me. Still, Simon's behavior was genuinely sym-bolic, and he announced the onset of play by allocating parts (Bateson 1956). He did not simply enact his role by showing us how a baby behaves; he role played in the context of a script, however short it might be (Huttenlocher and Higgins 1978).

When we returned to Montreal, Simon did not suggest the game for almost three months. The first time ironically was the same day that a waitress referred to him as a baby, and he insisted he was not. Later he was playing the rocket-ship version of boat. After storing his pretend supplies—milk, vegetables, a tractor, and so on—he decided to bring along a baby, so he added some toys and designated a small plastic container as the crib. In the midst of his preparations, he dis-tinguished himself from the baby by saying, for example, that only he and I could drive the tractor. Yet twenty minutes into the game, he put his feet into the container and announced, "I can't fit into my crib." I mentioned that it was not his crib but the baby's. But Simon replied that he was the baby, and he started to babble, squeak, and wail—his imitation of an infant. "You're not a baby," I corrected. "You're a big boy." "I'm pretending to be a baby," he explained (3,8,8). Here, without the assignment of parts, Simon enacted the baby role in isolation, and as in many subsequent conversations, he maintained he was a baby even when I said he was a big boy.

About two weeks later, Simon resurrected the baby animal game. "I'm a baby duckling, hatching from my egg," he called. I went to his room and found him snuggling in bed. "Hi, Daddy Duckling," he greeted (3,8,22). He frequently repeated the game but varied the animal—to baby camel, baby monkey, and baby bear (3,9,14; 3,9,19; 3,10,29)—but his favorite was a baby cat. One morning I was reading the newspaper when Simon climbed into my lap. "Hello, Daddy Cat," he greeted me in his high-pitched pussycat voice. "Hello, Big Boy Cat," I responded. "No," he explained, "I'm pretending I'm a baby cat" (3,9,28). As happened here, Simon often used the game to attract our attention when we were busy; he also tried the game when he was reprimanded, presumably as appeasement (3,10,5).

About a month before Asher was born, Simon apparently abandoned his baby animal pretense although not the game completely. Thus, he initiated a game in which we were both daddies (3,10,28). At other times I was the mommy turtle, he was the daddy turtle, and a toy was the baby turtle (3,11,17). As Asher's due date approached, however, Simon gradually transformed the game back to its original form. After we talked about the baby's crib one day, Simon suggested that we were both baby bears, "so young that we don't talk" (3,11,21). On the next two days he was the only baby turtle (3,11,22–23).

Shortly before Simon returned to the original baby animal game, he raised a topic central to the distinction between big boys and babies. Simon started the following conversation when he was sitting in Bev's lap.

Simon: (patting Mother's breasts and giggling) I'm patting your polkes. I want to drink from your tsitses.
Mother: You can't drink from my tsitses.
Father: Who drinks from tsitses?
Simon: (pretending to nurse) I do.
Father: Babies drink from breasts. Not big boys.
Simon: (to Mother) I'm going to drink from your tsitses.
Mother: There's not even milk in them now.
Father: Big boys don't drink from a mommy's breast.
Mother: You don't even know how to drink milk from a breast.
Simon: (smacking his lips) Yes I do.
Mother: When you were a baby, you did (3,11,5).

Although Simon did not ask to nurse again in the ensuing weeks, he often touched Bev's breasts, and she found him more affectionate than usual; he hugged her and held her more, and he often wanted to be cuddled.

During this time, Simon did pretend to drink from a baby bottle. He was in synagogue with a prayer book in his lap when suddenly he started to suck his thumb, something he had never done before, even as an infant. Bev asked him what he was doing. "I'm drinking from a bottle," he replied. "That's silly," said Bev. "Everyone will think you're a baby." "But a baby doesn't read a book," Simon countered, although he stopped sucking his thumb anyway (3,11,14). A few days before Asher was born, Simon pretended to nurse from one of his birthday balloons by sucking the "nipple" at its end. But this time when Bev asked him what he was doing, he replied, "Nothing" (4,0,1). Similarly the day after Asher was born, he walked around the house sucking the end of a balloon and refused to talk about what he was doing (4,0,4).

Simon occasionally pretended to be a baby after Asher arrived. When Asher was 1 week old, Simon did not simply adopt the baby role but specifically switched roles with his brother. Simon started the game at the beginning of his bath and extended the theme without support and despite several interruptions. "Let's pretend you're a daddy lobster, and I'm a baby lobster," he first suggested. "And you give me a baby lobster bath." A bit later he said that we have a lobster family, with a mommy lobster, a daddy lobster, a baby lobster, and a big brother lobster. I asked who he was: the baby lobster or the big brother lobster. "I'm the baby lobster," he responded. "My name is Asher, and my big brother is Simon." Toward the end of the bath I asked Bev to get me Simon's pyjamas; Simon indicated that Asher's sleeper, which was hanging in the bathroom, was his. Still later Bev said she was going to feed the baby, and Simon claimed that he was Asher (4,0,10).

At other times, Simon did not necessarily switch roles with Asher but rather pretended that he and Asher were both babies. Once, he was cuddling under the quilt next to Bev, who was nursing Asher in bed. Simon said that Bev was the mommy cat and he and Asher were the baby cats. I asked if they were both the same age. "Yes," he answered, "one year old. No. Zero. We're very little" (4,3,1,).

For months after Asher was born, Simon did not pretend to nurse, yet he was still attracted by Bev's breasts. One morning he and I were leaving for daycare while Bev was nursing Asher. After I kissed Bev and Asher good-bye, I prompted Simon to kiss Bev. Simon kissed Asher and Bev, and then he kissed Bev's breast. "Guess what?" he asked, obviously pleased. "I kissed Mommy's breast" (4,1,28). But the idea of nursing was not totally out of Simon's mind, an idea that he could express, at least in fun. Bev was nursing Asher in bed, and Simon was keeping them company. Simon said he was "a kitty cat" and tried to lie on Bev. But she objected, explaining that there was no room. Simon insisted on lying as close to her as possible and he put his head on her chest. "It's time for the kitty cat to drink milk," he announced, pointing at her breast. "From you." "Not this kitty cat," responded Bev (4,4,28).

Thus, before Asher was born, Simon both strove to differentiate himself from the baby and repeatedly pretended to be a baby, an inconsistency that was certainly not resolved by Asher's arrival. Although Simon was graduated to the status of big brother in the eyes of everyone around him and although he clearly considered himself to be a big boy, he still pretended to be little. Pretend play apparently enabled him to be a baby without the conflict that he faced when he even simply called himself one. Perhaps play was a refuge when, despite his primary concern about being a big boy, growing up seemed too onerous (Paley 1988). Pretend play also may have provided a context for him to explore family roles and thereby establish his own identity.

From Teething Rings to Infant Seats
Simon was not particularly jealous that all his old supplies would be used for Asher, yet at one time or another Simon tried out virtually all our baby equipment, often seemingly for the sake of play or experimentation. Several weeks before Asher was born, Simon picked up a teething ring that happened to be among his bath toys. "Something hurt in my mouth," he said. "A new tooth. I need to chew this." But implicitly reminding him that he was a big boy, I said that he had all his teeth, and he stopped gnawing the teething ring to talk about how many teeth he had (3,11,6).

Simon had many chances to get into baby supplies while we were preparing for Asher's arrival from the hospital. He crawled into Asher's cradle after I had just wrapped up the mattress. When I pointed out that the cradle was for babies, he claimed to be a baby cat, and later I had to prevent him from climbing into Asher's crib (4,0,4).

Simon was still getting into baby equipment—for example, the cradle, the infant seat, and the crib—when Asher was about 2 months old (4,2). Each time Simon was told that the object was not his, that he might break it, and that he should get out, but he was not deterred from immediately using any equipment he saw for the first time. One day he came home to find Asher's stroller in the apartment. Even before greeting Bev, he asked where it came from and started to climb into it (4,2,15). Similarly, he immediately sat in Asher's new infant seat the first time he noticed it (4,2,22).

Pretending to Have a Baby

On two occasions, Simon shifted from playing baby to playing mother (Harris 1969). A week after Asher came home, Simon constructed one of his blanket tents, brought his stuffed animals inside, and announced that he was having a baby (Kramer 1989, 112). When Bev and I ignored the comment, he continued the game as usual, without carrying the pretense of birth any further (4,0,13).

Simon returned to the topic the next day. He asked for Bev's baby books—her reference books on prenatal development, birth, breast-feeding, and such. Bev and I objected, since we wanted to keep them intact and since they were not suitable for a 4-year-old. When we asked him why he wanted them, he explained that he was having a baby. I reminded him that he had had a baby the day before, but logic was hardly relevant. Bev suggested that Simon use his own baby book, *101 Things to Do with a Baby* (Ormerod 1987), but Simon said that he needed her books. "They tell lots of things," he explained, "for instance, how to breast-feed." Bev then pointed out that Simon was a boy and that boys do not have babies, but he said he was pretending that he was born a girl. Nonetheless, we did not give Simon the books, and, in the end, he watched television instead of giving birth (4,0,14).

Coping with a New Sibling

Despite our increasing knowledge about children's reactions to a new brother or sister, it is still difficult to predict how a particular child will respond. It is, of course, easier to construct a coherent explanation afterward. Yet my account of Simon highlights the diversity of topics that are potentially relevant. Three of them—sources of stress, reactions to stress, and coping with stress—are particularly important.

The birth of a sibling may threaten children's security by precipitating changes in day-to-day family life, existing relationships, and daycare arrangements (Dunn and Kendrick 1980, Feiring et al. 1983, Kendrick and Dunn 1980, Legg et al. 1974; R. B. Stewart et al. 1987). Changing routines and relationships may be disruptive because they invalidate scripts acquired through experience that are presumably necessary to support children's behavior. Any transition demands that old scripts be revised for interacting with role partners whose behavior has changed and that novel scripts be established for interacting with new role partners.

The arrival of a new sibling does not occur in a social vacuum and does not necessarily turn a child's world upside down, so it is not a

crisis in the usual sense of the term. Asher's arrival minimally affected the structure of Simon's day-to-day life. For example, Simon
was enrolled in daycare. Changes in our family obviously had no
influence on the daycare's schedule, and Simon was not upset
enough to affect his interactions with his teachers and friends. At
home Asher's arrival sometimes adversely affected the way Bev and
I interacted with Simon, but during this study most of our time with
him remained unchanged. At least one of the changes in Simon's routine that was attributable to Asher—spending more time with relatives and friends—probably had a positive affect on Simon by helping
him adjust to a potentially stressful situation (Kramer 1989).

For some children, the birth of a brother or sister may precipitate
major changes. Alternatively it may affect only a few elements in a
child's life that, because of the child's age, temperament, or personality, are critical for the child's well-being. Maturity demands, which
are really requirements for a child to adopt a new role, may upset
some children but not others. In Simon's case, playing alone was particularly problematic, so our encouragement for him to do so may
have been stressful, and even minor reductions in how much we
played with him may have been upsetting. Moreover, some activities
may seem interchangeable for an adult but not for a child. When I
took Simon skating a few days after Asher came home, I assumed it
was more than a reasonable alternative to playing a board game or
building with Lego blocks, but Simon complained that skating was
not play (4,0,9).

Simon's case substantiates the claim that some firstborns react emotionally to a new brother or sister even before the baby is born (Freud
1909/1955, Gottlieb 1985, Nadelman and Begun 1982, Volterra 1984).
Thus, ratings of Simon's distress increased slightly during the month
before Asher's arrival, but there were more convincing demonstra-
tions of Simon's concern; he became upset about not accompanying
us to the hospital, worried about the baby's safety, began taking his
favorite security object to daycare, and, despite his usual insistence
that he was a big boy, pretended to be a baby and occasionally even
to nurse.

Many people assume that young children generally react negatively to a new brother or sister, but the available evidence belies this
view (Dunn and Kendrick 1982a, Gottlieb and Mendelson 1990,
Kramer 1989, Legg et al. 1974, Nadelman and Begun 1982). Four-year-
old children are typically not very upset after the birth of a sibling,
and any distress they may experience usually subsides quite quickly.
The ratings of Simon's behavior revealed little disturbance during the

early months of Asher's life. Yet Simon—just like Bev and me—did react somewhat to Asher's arrival. He still occasionally took his skunk, Blossom, to daycare, pretended to be a baby, tried out Asher's baby supplies, and claimed, although only twice, that he was going to have a baby.

Even if behavioral indicators of stress are extremely salient to parents, they should not be overinterpreted. Young children reacting to a new brother or sister may be momentarily aggressive, may throw one or two tantrums, or may occasionally have a toileting accident, yet such transient evidence of distress should not obscure that older siblings usually behave age appropriately. And I must emphasize that Simon's distress never spiraled out of control; indeed it diminished with time (Kramer 1989, R. B. Stewart et al. 1987). Thus, what emerges from my account is a portrait of a preschooler who coped remarkably well—just like most other children in the same situation and just as he had coped six months earlier with a major dislocation from Jerusalem to Montreal.

It may be difficult to specify how individual children cope with a particular stressor, but behavioral signs of stress are often also signs of coping. In Simon's case, it is possible to discern at least three coping strategies: reliance on an attachment object, information seeking, and pretend play. Although Simon certainly did not use them consciously to manage stress, they likely served that function. The most basic strategy was taking Blossom to daycare for naptime, the one time of day that he was forced to be alone. Blossom was a source of security when he was by himself and it helped him meet the clearly understood rule to sleep or at least rest quietly (Mahalksi 1983). But Simon's reliance on Blossom was merely a stop-gap measure, since a security object can only contain stress to a manageable level. In contrast, his two other coping strategies may have actually engendered personal resources to deal with the transition.

Information about an upcoming stressful event facilitates coping in both adults and children (Garmezy and Rutter 1983, Lazarus and Folkman 1984). Seeking information is seen as a coping mechanism for pregnant women and new mothers and for children and adults experiencing other life changes (Deutsch et al. 1988, A. J. Stewart 1982, A. J. Stewart et al. 1986). Prospective parents often attend prenatal classes and otherwise seek advice from experts, relatives, and friends. As their pregnancy progresses, women seek information about different topics. Their primary focus shifts from pregnancy early on, to labor and delivery before birth, to motherhood immediately afterward. Information seeking may simply reflect the work of

worrying about a stressful event, but it may also involve more positive motives, such as a desire for mastery, that are elicited by the
challenges of the situation, and it may facilitate the definition of new
roles associated with the transition. Women who visualize themselves as a mother during pregnancy adjust better postpartum than
women who do not, perhaps because imagining themselves in the
new role makes it easier for them to adopt it (Leifer 1980, Oakley
1980, Shereshefsky and Yarrow 1973).

Before Asher was born, Simon sought information, which potentially allayed his concerns about the events surrounding the baby's
birth and about how to keep the baby safe. While he may have asked
various questions because he was upset, the ensuing discussions possibly helped him cope with his stress. Thus, worrying about what
would happen when Bev and I went to the hospital, he asked us
about it. Our descriptions and assurances may have relieved his anxiety, for he was quite unperturbed when he awoke to find us gone.
His strategy probably also helped him construct a definition of his
own role as big brother, as, for example, when he asked how to protect the baby and imagined himself participating. Anything that fostered the transition to his new role, even before Asher was born,
would likely mitigate the stress associated with becoming a brother.

Pretend play was not only one of the most obvious signs of Simon's
stress but also an adaptive way to cope with feelings and conflicts.
According to theorists with quite different orientations, pretend play
is a mechanism for alleviating anxieties and fears or for fulfilling
wishes (Freud 1908/1959, Piaget 1951/1962, Peller 1954, K. H. Rubin
et al. 1983, Vygotsky 1967). Children may consolidate their understanding of life events through fantasy, so play might serve some of
the same functions as information seeking. Besides, pretend play presumably allows children to adopt "demeaning" roles and to regress
within a safely framed episode. Although Simon vehemently denied
that he was a baby, he could pretend to be one without suffering
internal role strain or exposing himself to external sanctions. He may
have done so because he was ambivalent about being big or about the
prospect of becoming a big brother. If so, fantasy simply provided a
safe haven for acting little, an interpretation supported more by solitary role enactment than by social role play. When Simon tried out
Asher's baby supplies, he may have simply been incorporating real
objects into a solitary pretense.

But most of the time Simon's pretense occurred as social role play,
both at home and certainly at daycare where he played, unobserved
by me, with his pals (Paley 1988). When he assigned the role of baby

animal to himself and the role of daddy animal to me, he may have been communicating ambivalence about his own role or status, yet several other explanations also come to mind. First, consider Robert Trivers's (1974) analysis of parent–offspring conflict. He suggested that by using mimicry or deception, an offspring might adopt infantile behavior to avoid parental rejection or weaning. In other words, the offspring tries to maintain parental attention and caregiving through behavior that has previously elicited these benefits. The analysis has been extended to account for firstborns' apparently regressive behavior after the birth of a brother or sister (Dunn and Kendrick 1982a, R. B. Stewart et al. 1987). However, applying the analysis in this context raises additional issues. Unlike other offspring, children may be aware of the significance of their behavior. If they understand the implications of adopting infantile behaviors, they may censor themselves and opt for behaviors that probably will not be sanctioned. Thus, older children are more likely to mimic baby talk than abandon acceptable toileting or feeding habits, and pretend play may be the most socially acceptable way for a preschooler to act like an infant. Also unlike other offspring, children may anticipate the birth of a brother or sister, so they may exhibit infantile behavior even before the baby arrives. It is possible, though not probable, that they preemptively avoid a predicted loss of parental attention by imitating babies or resurrecting previously abandoned behavior.

Pretending to be a baby may have served a second coping function for Simon. The acquisition of any new role is necessarily achieved at the expense of other roles, so role transitions may be accompanied by a sense of loss or grief (R. Rubin 1967, Walz and Rich 1983). For example, women may long for the role of bride after their first child or for the role of mother of one after their second. One way of coping with the loss is to imagine or review past events, perhaps by reminiscing or looking at old photographs. A preschooler who has become a sibling (or one who is about to) may similarly sense losing the role of baby or only child. In either case, pretend play may be a concrete way of imagining the lost role.

A third possible explanation of Simon's role playing relates to the development of his self-concept. According to many, the self-concept develops from social interaction and social comparison (Bannister and Agnew 1977, Harter 1983). Social interaction may provide the content for self-concept development by establishing the distinction between self and not-self or between self and other. Simon was confronted with a dilemma: he considered himself to be a big boy yet understood that he was still little in many respects. Presumably he was motivated to resolve the contradiction, and one solution may have been to exile his baby persona to pretend play, which affords the opportunity to adopt various roles, thereby enabling children to view themselves as both different from and related to others (Mead 1934). Thus, by pretending to be a baby, Simon explored not only how he was different from a baby but also how my normal interactions with him were different from my interactions with him as a baby. His inevitable explanation that he was pretending to be a baby was actually an assertion of his real status, and his declaration that he was pretending to be a girl giving birth constituted an assertion that he was a boy and different from Bev.

I cannot confidently say which hypothesis best accounts for Simon's pretend play, yet the explanation in terms of role definition probably accounts for most of the data: pretend play considerably before Asher was born, pretend play in the absence of any other signs of distress, pretend play away from Bev and me, and the wide variety of scenarios including baby-daddy, mommy-baby, baby-baby, and daddy-daddy. It is also consistent with the explanation that information seeking is useful because it fosters role definition. But none of the explanations of pretend play may be appropriate; alternatively, all may be valid, each accounting for different bouts of play or similar bouts on different occasions. Simon may have pretended to give birth to allay the anxiety he felt about an imagined threat to Bev, or perhaps he was symbolically claiming the baby as his own, in which case it was a positive sign of acceptance. He may have enacted the baby's role because of general distress about having a new brother, or perhaps he was trying to identify with Asher. He may have suggested pretenses about complementary social roles to solicit attention, or perhaps he was exploring the social world and defining his own role.

Regardless, parents and researchers should appreciate that pretend play does not necessarily reflect profound jealousy or disturbance. Since it is so easy to attribute a wide variety of children's behaviors to presumably inevitable emotions, we may disregard the real significance of what we observe. Even if pretend play is motivated by mild distress, it may reflect conflicts about self-definition as much as distress about shifts in parents' attention. We should also realize that, whatever the motivation, pretend play may be an adaptive strategy for coping with stress, for learning about the self, and for exploring the social world.

Adaptation to a new brother or sister involves not only the type of behavioral adjustment I have discussed here but also responsiveness to the baby. The distinction is particularly important, since adjustment and responsiveness are apparently unrelated (Gottlieb and

Mendelson 1990, Kramer 1989). Some children who seem upset by a new sibling because they throw tantrums or refuse to comply with their parents may still accept and pleasantly entertain the baby; others may appear adjusted when alone with their parents yet reject the baby. A full account of a preschooler's adaptation to a new brother or sister must include a description of how the child responds to the baby.

Chapter 6
Rivalry and Conflict?

Suspicion of rivalry—competition for resources, equality, or dominance—breeds jealousy. And throughout the ages people have assumed that rivalry and jealousy unavoidably mark sibling relationships. A source as old as the Bible provides classic examples: Cain's jealousy of Abel over God's acceptance of a sacrifice; Jacob's rivalry with Esau over a birthright and over Isaac's blessing; and Joseph's brothers' anger with him over his own self-importance and over Jacob's favor. These legends are as understandable today as they have been for thousands of years, perhaps because they reflect a universal truth about sibling relationships. But as a part of Western mythology, they also bias our expectations and attributions.

Many people accept assertions, however unfounded, that "all children suffer great jealousy of younger sisters and brothers" (M. Klein 1927/1975,173). When a young child becomes a sibling, virtually every negative emotion and seemingly aggressive behavior can be interpreted as evidence of jealousy, but the interpretation begs the question. In fact, intense jealousy and hostility are not necessarily part of becoming a brother or sister, and occasional ambivalence can be embedded in generally positive feelings (Dunn and Kendrick 1982a, Gottlieb and Mendelson 1990, Kramer 1989).

Before Asher was born, Simon virtually never hit us and was always gentle when he felt the baby. Then one day he swatted Bev's tummy without apparent provocation. Bev angrily asked for an explanation, and Simon responded that he was patting her. Bev said that it was a little too hard, which upset Simon. He insisted that he was only patting, not hitting (his term), and he denied that he wanted to hurt her or the baby (her hypothesis). When I entered the scene, Simon initially tried to avoid the topic but eventually reiterated that he had not meant to hurt Bev or the baby and that he had patted her because he wanted to feel the baby. I suggested that he should ask Bev first and then gently feel her belly, a term that made him laugh. Bev then invited him to feel the baby move, and Simon's face lit up when he did (3,11,10). Bev and I did entertain the possibility that Simon harbored hostile feelings toward her or the baby, but even if he had intentionally struck her tummy, feeling the baby transformed his mood, and his obvious pleasure transformed ours.

After Asher was born, Simon's attitude and behavior toward him were generally positive, and their emerging relationship appeared friendly. Important relationships, however, inevitably foster some conflict and may occasionally be highly charged. Brothers and sisters—like husbands and wives or parents and children—sometimes disagree and do not always resolve their conflicts smoothly. But warmth and hostility are not polar opposites in a sibling relationship, which may include responsiveness one moment and indifference the next, expressions of love and feelings of jealousy, or positive interaction punctuated by occasional conflict.

Competition for Things

Although Simon tried out most of Asher's baby equipment, he never seemed jealous that much of what Asher now had was once his. But Simon did react to Asher's new toys, particularly a large teddy bear, and to Asher's pacifier.

A Teddy Bear Named Asher

The day after Asher came home from the hospital, Simon complained that he had not gotten any presents while Asher had so many, and he was not assuaged when we reminded him of all the gifts he had received for his birthday, for Chanukah, and for becoming a big brother (4,0,8). He especially envied a large blue teddy bear, which he named Asher Bear. He immediately wanted to pick it up when he first saw it at the hospital. I tried to intercede—with one of his first lessons in Asher's proprietary rights—and told Simon that the bear was Asher's. When Simon picked it up anyway, I suggested that Asher would surely not mind sharing it (4,0,5).

Two days later Simon eagerly carried Asher Bear when Bev came home (4,0,7), and he played with it quite often over the next few days. At one point he wanted to sleep with it, but, forestalling an expropriation, we pointed out that there was no room in his bed. Simon was quite upset and negotiated that Asher was now too little to play with the bear and would not even be able to play with it when he was 2 years old. We replied that Asher did not mind if Simon played with the bear during the day but that he had to leave it on the couch at night (4,0,8). About nine weeks later, Simon tried to claim

Asher Bear again. He said that he wanted it on the wall of his room. Reminding him that the teddy bear was not his, we explained that he was just borrowing it, but Simon said he wanted it for himself (4,2,18).

Simon's behavior in these few incidents may look like classic examples of sibling rivalry, but it is not surprising that Simon continually attempted to claim Asher Bear: it was an extremely attractive toy, and Asher could not use it, whereas Simon could. Moreover, Simon did not seem to envy any of Asher's other possessions, even those that had formerly belonged to him. Simon's reaction to Asher Bear reveals more about his feelings for a big furry toy than about his feelings for a little brother.

He Doesn't Want His Pacifier!

Simon often tried to soothe Asher's distress, but was not always responsive to Asher's cries and even occasionally interfered when Bev or I tried to calm him. Simon once seemed more concerned about where Asher sat than about Asher's distress. It was dinnertime, and as usual, Simon wanted Asher right next to him. But Asher was fretting, so I reached for him. "He wants to look at me," objected Simon. "Just leave him. Let's see what he does" (4,1,14). Simon also sometimes suggested that we just let Asher cry if our soothing Asher would interrupt Simon's play (4,3,9). And Simon was even once so absorbed by the television that he ignored Asher, who was crying right next to him (4,4,25). But such incidents were in fact extremely rare.

Yet there was a recurring problem related to Asher's pacifier, perhaps because Simon had previously had one himself. Simon had started using a pacifier when he was a newborn but only while sleeping or occasionally while resting in bed. We did not wean him from the pacifier early in infancy, and several subsequent plans to take it away failed. About two months before going to Israel we pretended that the pacifier was lost and matter-of-factly told Simon that he had to sleep without it. He threw a tantrum that grew louder and louder when we did not respond. Eventually we gave in after pretending to look for the pacifier and rationalized to ourselves that it was probably a bad time to force Simon to give it up since we were just about to move (about 2,4,0).

In Jerusalem it was not unusual for children even older than Simon to use a pacifier even when playing outdoors. Regardless, we talked to him about giving up the pacifier by his third birthday. As the day approached, Simon became more and more agitated and finally announced that he would not give it up until we got back to Montreal (about 2,11,15). When we returned home, he was reluctant to follow through with his plan. But unlike many of his Jerusalem friends, none of his Montreal pals used a pacifier. Simon conformed by relinquishing his pacifier at daycare, though he still used it in bed at home. According to his latest plan, he would wait until he could give his pacifier to the baby—a concrete example of a preschooler's passing the torch (about 3,6,0).

The issue was finally resolved when the dentist confirmed that Simon's teeth were being displaced by the pacifier. The dentist successfully goaded Simon to give it up with an offer of two surprises if he did. Since Simon was worried about his teeth and excited about the prizes, he complied within a week. He put his pacifier on a shelf, where we could save it for the baby, and insisted on visiting the dentist to claim his reward: two plastic trinkets (3,6,29).

When Asher was born, we bought a pacifier for him identical to the one Simon had used. We had thrown out Simon's old pacifier and had never said anything about its absence; neither had Simon. But he may have still remembered it. And although he seemed to ignore Asher's pacifier at first, he started objecting to it by the time Asher was 2 months old. Asher was once sucking calmly on his pacifier; Simon took it from him and was surprised when Asher started to cry (4,2,21). Another time Asher was fretting in the back seat of the car. Bev tried to give him his pacifier, but she could not reach, so she asked Simon to help. He refused, asserting as usual that Asher did not need it, so Bev explained that Asher would be more comfortable with it. Simon continued to defy her, fabricating that he could not reach, so she eventually stretched to give it to Asher. We admonished Simon both about not listening and about not wanting to help his brother. A bit later when Asher dropped the pacifier, I asked Simon to give it back to him, and this time he at least tried (4,3,0).

During the same period, Simon occasionally gave the pacifier to Asher but not consistently or necessarily when it was appropriate. Once after briefly watching Asher, who was craning his neck and chest off the mattress of his crib, Simon tried to push Asher's head down and put the pacifier in his mouth (4,2,3). Sometimes when Simon objected to the pacifier, he at least suggested an alternative soothing technique, such as giving Asher a toy (4,3,14). Yet he typically gave Asher his pacifier if we insisted and even occasionally suggested it on his own (4,4,25). But before Simon ever resolved his ambivalence about Asher's pacifier, Asher stopped using it.

Simon did not object to the pacifier because he enjoyed Asher's crying; indeed he was actually upset by Asher's distress. Rather he seemed jealous of the pacifier itself, though I never saw him suck on it. If he had wanted to, he may have restrained himself because it was one infantile object—unlike Asher's other supplies that he had tried or the balloon that he had sucked on just around Asher's birthday (4,0,1; 4,0,4)—from which he had not fully dissociated himself. Alternatively Simon may have been somewhat reluctant to pass the torch because he wanted to keep one part of his previous role for himself. Or Asher's use of the pacifier may have undermined Simon's attempt to define himself as a big boy. After all, pacifiers were clearly babyish if Asher used one, and Simon probably remembered that he had given up a similar pacifier not long before. He may have wanted to reduce the similarity between his baby brother and himself to assert his own status as a big boy (Melson and Fogel 1982).

Competition for Attention

Although Simon apparently envied Asher's teddy bear and pacifier, sibling rivalry is classically related to dethronement, or a loss of attention, in the family (Adler 1927/1959, Levy 1937). This is not simply a childish worry. Mothers who give birth to a second child are also concerned that the relationship with the first will change (Walz and Rich 1983). At a global level, they are involved with their firstborn somewhat less shortly after the birth of a sibling than before; perhaps more important, much of the time they spend alone with the firstborn is eventually replaced by time with both children (Mendelson and Gottlieb 1987). At a more detailed level, there are negative changes in the mother–firstborn relationship, at least as assessed through behavioral observations of necessarily limited interactions (Baldwin 1947, Dunn and Kendrick 1980, Feiring et al. 1983, Field and Reite 1984, Kendrick and Dunn 1980, Kreppner et al. 1982, R. B. Stewart et al. 1987, Taylor and Kogan 1973). After the arrival of a second child, mothers directly interact with their firstborn less, firstborns assume more of the responsibility for initiating interactions, and the interactions become more negative in tone.

Are such changes due to the care and attention that mothers devote to the new baby? No and yes (Kendrick and Dunn 1980). When mothers are busy with their second born, mother-firstborn interactions actually increase, but negatively as well as positively. Confrontations arise because firstborns tend to make demands or be naughty when their mother is involved with the baby. But, interestingly, the confrontations are less pronounced when the mothers breast-feed rather than bottle-feed, perhaps because mothers who breast-feed provide better distractions for the firstborn or are more willing to interrupt the feeding to attend to the older child. Thus, mothers can avoid difficulties with their first child while they feed the second.

Before Asher was born, Simon had trouble amusing himself and was typically upset when we were busy and unwilling to include him in our activity. The problem diminished as he learned to be more resourceful and as we encouraged him to play alone, yet we were still concerned about how he would react when we had to tend to the baby. Simon himself realized there might be a problem if he and the baby needed attention at the same time, as when he wondered what would happen if he and Asher had a bath at the same time (3,10,6).

After Asher was born, Simon did receive somewhat less attention from Bev and me, and the issue of jealousy over our attention did arise. Here I examine Simon's reactions to two specific situations. The first, when Bev nursed Asher, is the classic case of exclusion from mother. The second, when I carried Asher in the Snugli (a cloth pouch, worn on the chest, to hold the baby) provides an interesting parallel that involves exclusion from father.

Mommy's Feeding Asher Now

Before Asher was born, Simon knew that mothers breast-feed their babies. Although he was quite taken aback the first time he saw Charles suckle, he was equally inquisitive (3,8,5). Two weeks later, during a conversation about why Bev and the baby had to stay in the hospital, we talked about the baby's nursing.

Father:	. . . Also, a baby has to be in the hospital for a few days after it's born to make sure it's all right. And Mommy has to stay there to help take care of the baby.
Simon:	Why can't the nurses take care of the baby?
Father:	Mommy has to nurse the baby—the way Fran nursed Charles.
Simon:	How do you nurse a baby?
Father:	You feed it, so it gets milk from its mother. Just like Charles, or like you used to when you were a baby.
Simon:	(smiled)
Mother:	Where does the baby nurse from?
Simon:	Where?
Mother:	(pointing) From its mommy's tsitses.
Simon:	(jokingly) From her head (3,8,19).

Although Simon was apparently amused, he was still curious, and he wanted to watch Fran breast-feed Charles again when they visited us several days later (3,8,24).

Simon was also interested in Asher's nursing. From the outset, he sat right next to Bev and watched intently, gently stroking Asher, talking to him softly, and playing with his hands or feet; when given the chance, he was happy to help with the burping (4,0,3; 4,0,7). Simon's questions and comments, which continued over the months, prompted many conversations about nursing: why Asher did not eat any food besides breast milk (taped 4,0,7), if Asher bit her (4,0,7), when Asher would stop (4,0,7), if breast milk is warm or cold (4,1,5), for how long wine could affect breast milk (4,1,7), how Bev knew when a breast was done (4,1,14), if Asher hurt her breast (4,2,6), and if Bev's breasts got smaller when Asher drank (4,2,23).

The only problem initially was Simon's enthusiasm about participating coupled with his relative ineptness, as when he burped Asher too hard (4,0,22). But Simon seemed unperturbed by Bev's nursing. Bev's first evening home from the hospital, Simon went to wish her good-night and found her feeding Asher. Simon kissed her as usual and, with only minimal encouragement, also said good-night to Asher by gently patting him and kissing him. Then he went to bed without a fuss (4,0,7).

Two problems eventually did arise, however; Simon invariably asked Bev to feed Asher near him, and he occasionally acted out. One day Simon and I were playing when Asher awoke for his feeding. Simon asked Bev to bring Asher into the room, but he started to jump around when Bev began nursing. I persuaded him to settle down and eventually read him a bedtime story, next to Bev, who was still feeding Asher. When she was done, she put Asher in Simon's lap, and with my help Simon elicited a loud burp from Asher, for which we praised Simon (4,0,14).

By the time Asher was 2 weeks old, Simon occasionally reacted when he was excluded during nursing. One morning Bev awoke first and ate alone so she would be ready before Asher cried to be fed. Simon got up and waited for me, and he was very hungry by the time I was ready to eat. As we sat down to breakfast, he realized that Bev was not going to eat with us because she was nursing Asher. Simon was very upset even though she was close by. He argued that the three of us always ate together and he gradually lost control. Finally Bev brought Asher to the table, but Simon was still crying because she was not eating with us, and I had to calm him down in his room (4,0,18). Eventually Simon accepted that Bev sometimes had to feed Asher while he and I ate. Six weeks later he matter-of-factly asked her to join us at breakfast, although he still objected when she said she would come only after Asher was finished nursing (4,2,1).

Simon usually ignored Bev's nursing if he was busy watching television, for example, or playing with my computer. Otherwise he wanted her right next to him, even if she had to move Asher, and he often acted out while she nursed, generally by jumping on furniture or roughhousing or by sitting too close and distracting Asher. I then had to lead him away so Asher could finish nursing. Simon might ask Bev for something even if I was available to help, but she usually just said she was busy nursing. Although he often accepted the situation, he occasionally voiced his concern. "Why does he eat so many times in the day?" he once asked. ". . . He should eat only one time in the day" (4,2,13).

Yet despite any difficulties Simon may have had with the situation, he never directed his negative reaction toward Asher but consistently treated him gently, often with warm affection. Simon might kiss Asher while he nursed (4,0,27), observe what he was looking at (4,1,4), or notice his responses to what was going on (4,1,9).

A Snugli Is Not Funny

Simon was not at all surprised when he first saw Bev nurse Asher, but he was astounded—and quite unpleasantly so—the first time he saw me carry Asher in a Snugli. Simon responded unlike he had responded to anything else about his baby brother. Asher, who was 4 weeks old, was crying shortly after a feeding, so I put him in the Snugli to soothe him. "Isn't it funny?" I asked Simon. He did not laugh. He approached sheepishly, touched the Snugli, and backed away, saying nothing. He was jealous and upset. I tried softening the blow by suggesting that we look at a picture of him as a baby in the Snugli. "No!" he refused. "And it isn't funny." When I then invited him to sit down next to me, he refused again and said that "the Snugli won't help Asher. Asher will cry and cry louder and louder." Yet Simon sat down anyway. He said that Asher wanted to be held, offered to hold him, and unzipped the Snugli. Asher, quiet until then, started to cry. Instead of pressing the point, I put Asher into bed. I then joined Simon watching television, and he climbed into my lap (4,0,29).

What was to become a common situation arose again two days later. Asher was fretful, so I carried him in the Snugli before putting him to sleep. As with every other caretaking task, Simon wanted to help. He asked if he could hold Asher in the Snugli but did not pursue the topic when I did not respond. Then, unable to play my role, he opted for Asher's; he asked if I could hold him and Asher at the same time. I replied that I could if I held him on my back, which made Simon giggle. Then he gratuitously untied the waist strap of the Snugli and walked away (4,1,0).

Simon adopted different approaches to the Snugli. He told me I should take Asher out of the Snugli because it did not help, the same rational persuasion he had used for the pacifier, but I explained that the Snugli really did calm Asher. When I then suggested that Simon sit with me, he walked away. "I'll never sit with you," he said, "if Asher's in the Snugli." He just might have said, "This town ain't big enough for the two of us" (4,1,2). Another day I was sitting with Asher in the Snugli. Simon sat in my lap, leaning his chest on Asher's back and kissing Asher's cheek. Perhaps he decided, "If you can't lick 'em, join 'em " (4,1,4). A month later Simon came out of his room after bedtime, and I picked him up facing my chest to carry him back. "Daddy, you have to carry me around until I fall asleep, and then slip me into bed," Simon instructed, describing my routine with Asher. I laughed as if he were telling a joke, and he laughed too—but perhaps he thought, "What's good enough for the gosling is good enough for the gander" (4,2,1).

Typically I was the one who carried Asher in the Snugli, but not always. Although Simon finally accepted it, he sometimes objected if it disrupted his agenda, regardless of who had the Snugli. At times his protests were mild; he simply asked that the other parent take Asher. Once Simon and Bev were playing doctor and patient. "Could you please take off the baby," Simon requested in a professional tone, "so I can examine you?" Bev then explained that Asher would cry if she put him down, so Simon suggested that she give him to me (4,2,4). On one occasion, however, Simon strongly reacted to the Snugli. He was in the bathroom and wanted me to stay with him, but I had Asher in the Snugli and did not want to carry him there, especially since I was quite tired. After considerable arguing, Simon had a full-blown tantrum (4,1,17). Although he rarely had such outbursts, it is worth noting that he reacted similarly when Bev did not join us for breakfast because she was feeding Asher. In each case Simon was upset that Asher disrupted one of his well-established routines—eating with us or having company in the bathroom—and his reaction highlighted the importance of such routines.

Nevertheless, Simon usually accepted the intrusion of the Snugli quite well; he even kissed Asher one time after I told him that I could not play because I was carrying Asher (4,1,8). Simon also did not object when I hugged and kissed him good-night with Asher in the Snugli. Afterward he usually kissed his baby brother, who might be sleeping peacefully. One night he gently stroked Asher's face, gave him a little hug, and straightened out the Snugli because Asher's ear was twisted under the collar (4,2,22). Again, we see Simon's affection for Asher, which was just as difficult to curb when Asher was in the Snugli as it was when he was nursing.

Yet we were carrying Asher to calm him down or to get him to sleep, so Simon's interest in him, no matter how sweet, was usually unwelcome at that moment. When Asher was in the Snugli, Simon tried variously to open his eyes, play with his hands, squeeze close to him, cover him with a blanket, stroke his cheek, give him back his pacifier, or talk to him. And whatever else he did, Simon almost always kissed him. Except when we said good-night, we typically tried to restrain Simon from disturbing Asher in the Snugli, but we could not abate Simon's enthusiasm; he enjoyed such interactions with his brother and tried to prolong them. One evening Simon climbed into my lap while I was carrying Asher in the Snugli. I offered to put Asher to bed since he was already asleep, but Simon wanted him there. He kissed Asher several times, patted his head, and talked to him sweetly. I asked Simon to stop kissing Asher, but he would not, so I got up and put Asher into his crib (4,2,16). Unlike six or seven weeks earlier, Simon not only willingly sat in my lap with Asher in the Snugli but even resisted my taking Asher away.

Awareness of Jealousy

Children's books about baby brothers and sisters inevitably address the firstborn's jealousy. One of Simon's books, *Billy and Our New Baby* (Arnstein 1974), exclusively concerned the older brother's feelings. Simon discovered the book in his cousins' room, and we took it home with us (3,6,26). Although he listened to it a few times, he lost interest quickly. But he still occasionally listened to other books on the topic, such as *The New Baby* (Althea 1973) and two books about conflict between older siblings (Hoban 1973, Roche 1979). He also watched at least one relevant sequence of "Sesame Street" (number 1927) in which Telly was upset that the grown-ups could not play with him because they were too busy with the new baby (3,9,2).

Thus Simon was certainly exposed to the idea of becoming angry with a baby brother or sister, but he was reluctant to admit any such feelings. I once asked Simon if he thought his friend Jeff would sometimes become angry with his new baby sister. "Everyone gets mad, of course, with the baby," replied Simon. Yet Simon could not, or would not, say why. He was also slightly irritated when I asked if he thought he would become angry with our baby. He responded that he did not want to talk about babies because it was "too annoying" (taped 3,9,29).

After Asher was born, I tried to find out if Simon was aware of his own feelings about Asher Bear. I was reading him the story of Joseph's multicolored coat. "How would you feel," I asked, "if Mommy and Daddy gave Asher a special present but didn't give you one?" "It wouldn't matter to me," Simon answered. (4,1,2). Either he was oblivious that his feelings about the teddy bear were relevant or he was unwilling to talk about them. Another time he was more obviously reluctant to discuss what was bothering him. He announced that he wanted a crib of his own. He initially explained that he wanted one just for pretend but then said that he wanted one for real. I suggested that he was too big for a crib. He said he wanted a big one so that he would fit, but he changed his mind again and said that one like Asher's would be cosy. Eventually he said that he wanted a crib so he could sleep in Asher's room. "Asher's room?" I questioned. "You mean Mommy and Daddy's room." Simon agreed and then pointedly changed the subject (4,2,2).

Simon eventually admitted that he occasionally had negative emotions about Asher. I was reading Simon a section of *Billy and Our New Baby* (Arnstein 1974) in which Billy was particularly upset with his brother. I asked Simon if he ever became angry because of Asher. "Yes," he answered, "when Asher gives me a headache." He was complaining about the crying, like most other preschoolers with a baby brother or sister (R. B. Stewart et al. 1987). But although he admitted that he was sometimes upset with Asher, Simon was struck by how angry Billy was in the story, and he denied feeling so angry with Asher (4,3,22).

I read Simon the same book a few weeks later. Simon laughed when Billy wanted to act like a baby and when he wanted a bottle. Simon also denied feeling jealous about Bev's love for Asher.

Father: (reading Billy's part) "Maybe Mommy loves the baby more than she loves me."
Simon: No way!
Father: (reading) "Other little boys and girls who have a new baby in the family feel the way you feel sometimes."
Simon: Not me, because I'm already a big brother and I'm not so little. (He meant that he already was a big boy.)
Father: (reading Billy's mother's comment) "Remember that I love you in a very special way."
Simon: And the baby (taped 4,4,8).

Simon may have been actively repressing his real feelings about Asher. Young children have trouble acknowledging common feelings such as anger and sadness, perhaps because admissions of bad feelings challenge their essentially undifferentiated self-esteem (Glasberg and Aboud 1981). Thus, even if Simon could have appropriately labeled jealousy, he might not have acknowledged the feeling because that would have been tantamount to saying he was bad. Yet Simon's denial of jealousy may simply have been true. In fact, he was genuinely struck by the intensity of Billy's response and was incredulous about the suggestion that Billy's mother loved the baby more than she loved Billy. Simon, apparently quite secure about our feelings for him, was rarely jealous over our attention to Asher.

Don't Do unto Brother

Before Asher was born, we had a chance to stress how wrong it is to hit a baby. Simon's friend Jeff said he sometimes hit his baby sister in the face when she cried. Later Bev mentioned Jeff's comment. I immediately told Simon how horrible that was. Simon agreed. Bev explained that babies sometimes cry, but hitting never helps, and we stressed that hitting a baby is wrong (3,11,17).

Simon indirectly expressed negative feelings toward me and Asher during Asher's first few days at home. Simon had Asher Bear tell me I would have "garbage on my head." When I objected that he should not say such things, he explained it was the bear. Later Simon pretended the bear was warning to pounce on Asher. Although we might have taken the opportunity to talk about his feelings about the baby, we simply told him it was "not right to say things like that" (4,0,8). Pretense may provide an acceptable way to express the negative feelings presumably elicited by a new brother or sister (Field and Reite 1984, Freud 1909/1955, Volterra 1984). Yet Simon's resentment was quite limited, and I found no evidence that he harbored such sentiments for long. Although he repeatedly pretended to be a baby animal, I never saw him pretend to be hostile to Asher again. And possibly with the exception of withholding Asher's pacifier, Simon was virtually never intentionally hostile to Asher during this study.

Physical Play and Exploration

Yet as a 4-year-old, Simon lacked both experience and foresight, so his behavior occasionally appeared negative, and, whatever his intentions, lapses in his gentleness were certainly salient to us. Even if a young child knows how to be kind to a baby, the child's enthusiasm, curiosity, egocentrism, and lack of restraint conspire against the infant. Parents must be just as careful perhaps about misinterpreting the child's intentions as they are about protecting the baby.

During Asher's first month, Simon was sometimes a bit rough with him, perhaps burping him too forcefully, holding up a toy right in his face, or swinging his arm too vigorously (4,0,22–4,0,24). Simon merely seemed enthusiastic but inexperienced—not purposefully hostile. When we interceded on Asher's behalf, Simon usually complied immediately with our directions to treat Asher more gently.

By the time Asher was 6 weeks old, Simon repeatedly tried to get Asher to smile by stroking his face but was not always successful. He would then stroke Asher's face more vigorously, and stroking sometimes became poking. He was not intentionally aggressive; on the contrary, he enjoyed making Asher smile. Yet we assumed Simon's behavior would disturb Asher and tried to curb it, though Asher did not complain. We should have consistently told Simon that he might disturb his brother, suggesting a positive alternative, but practice sometimes departed from theory, and we could be quite impatient, especially when Simon did something we repeatedly warned him about.

Once Simon pushed a teether into Asher's face, perhaps ineptly showing it but perhaps intentionally. Although the behavior was actually quite mild, it was likely the most negative thing Simon had done to Asher until then. I explained that it was not fair. Bev said Asher loved him and poking his brother was not nice. So far, so good. Then we should have shown Simon how to present a toy to Asher, but I impatiently took the teether, shoved it in Simon's face, and asked him if he liked it. Understandably, Simon became sullen. We then reiterated that he had to be nice to his brother (4,1,29).

We communicated Asher's point of view more reasonably on other occasions. Simon once put his foot in Asher's face. Bev explained that although Asher was little, he would soon grow bigger and tell Simon he did not like something like that. She added, perhaps unrealistically, that she wanted Simon to be nice to Asher all the time. Finally, she asked if Simon would like someone to put a foot in his face, and he said no. "Well," she reasoned, "that should be an indication that *Asher* doesn't like it" (4,2,10).

Putting a foot in Asher's face and other forms of boisterousness may have simply been Simon's invitations to physical play, invitations to roughhouse that Asher would enthusiastically accept more and more in the ensuing years. When Asher was still a baby, Simon's physical play often involved rocking Asher's chair, pushing him along in his infant seat, shaking his arms and legs, covering his face, or blowing on him (4,2,2–17). Although all of these seemed playful, they were sometimes potentially dangerous or disturbing. We always told Simon to stop rocking or moving Asher's seat because Asher might topple over. We were similarly consistent about Simon's not covering Asher's face, and we usually told him to stop shaking Asher's arm or blowing on him, particularly if Simon was too vigorous or if Asher became upset.

Simon often ran through several options, apparently searching for an acceptable game. One day, finding Asher in his infant seat on a large swivel rocker, Simon started to spin the rocker around. Given the obvious and immediate danger, I forcefully told him that he was "absolutely not to do that." Startling at my intensity, Simon claimed he was only moving the chair a little. I then explained that if he spins the rocker, Asher could fall and hurt himself. Simon tried a substitute and shook the rocker, finally stopping only after several instructions to do so. Then Simon blew in Asher's face, which elicited a cry from Asher and another admonition from me. I demanded that he leave Asher alone, and Simon withdrew sullenly from me (4,2,7).

Simon sometimes shook Asher's limb or blew on him with acceptable restraint but did not always control himself. Bev and I were therefore not consistent about limiting these games. Simon was once playfully blowing on me through a cardboard tube and then on Asher. I told Simon not to, but he showed me how softly he was doing it. He was indeed gentle, and I praised him. Later, when he was about to blow on Asher again, Bev told him not to. Simon argued that I had said it was all right, but Bev insisted no. Simon then hit Asher's rattle with the tube and tossed the tube into Asher's lap. He was understandably upset by the inconsistency and showed reasonable self-control in venting his frustration on Asher's rattle (4,2,11). Simon's intentionally negative behavior was most likely momentary defiance or anger toward us, not hostility toward Asher, and Simon always restrained himself from hurting his brother.

Bev and I assumed that Asher would be disturbed by Simon's shaking, blowing, and such, yet Asher seldom objected. Neither did he react when Simon touched his eyes, ears, nose, and mouth. A baby, perfectly oblivious to a caregiver's feelings, innocently explores her face by yanking her nose and poking her eyes. The baby does not mean to hurt her and does not even know that yanks and pokes are painful. Some of Simon's apparently negative behavior was also simply exploratory. He occasionally tried to touch Asher's eyes or poke his finger in Asher's ear. Simon seemed unaware that he might hurt Asher; he simply wanted to find out what Asher's eyes and ears felt like. Yet even if Asher did not respond, we told Simon to stop (4,2,2).

Most of all, Simon was interested in Asher's mouth. He continually tried to feel it inside, frequently during play or while attempting to elicit a smile (4,1,22; 4,2,3). Whatever the situation, Bev or I told him to stop, usually explaining that he had germs on his fingers and we did not want Asher to get them. But we never did stop Simon from putting his hands in Asher's mouth. Bev eventually gave up trying and once simply told Simon to wash his hands if he was going to do it (4,4,26). There are at least two possible reasons that Simon's behavior was so persistent. First, he may have been responding naturally to Asher's baby features; indeed parents commonly stroke the area around a baby's mouth with their fingertips (H. Papousek and Papousek 1987). Alternatively, Simon may have been curious about Asher's mouth because he wondered what breast-feeding felt like. He once asked Bev if Asher's sucking hurt her (4,2,6), and he even put his nose in Asher's mouth, apparently to find out for himself (4,1,9; 4,3,3).

Regardless, Simon had friendly intentions, and his exploration of Asher's face was very similar to Asher's exploration of his. One day Simon leaned over Asher, who was lying on his back. Asher played with Simon's face by pulling and poking, which amused Simon very much. But at one point, Asher hurt Simon by poking his eye. When I said that Asher did not mean to do it, Simon agreed, adding that Asher also did not mean to hurt when he pulled hair. Simon then leaned over Asher again and laughed when Asher reached for his face. He also tried to put his hand in Asher's mouth and to let Asher's hands get into his (4,4,6). Both boys clearly enjoyed such physical play and exploration.

Ssshhh, Asher's Sleeping
Simon liked Asher nearby and typically enjoyed interacting with him, so much so that he often tried to kiss or touch Asher when the baby was asleep. The day after Asher came home from the hospital, I had to prevent Simon from touching him through the bars of his crib (4,0,8). A few weeks later, I still had to explain that Asher had to sleep, even if Simon wanted him at the breakfast table (4,0,24).

In the ensuing weeks Simon's noise often woke Asher, so we tried to inhibit Simon's exuberance while Asher was sleeping, but we only made awakening Asher a point of contention. Simon once disturbed Asher by building a construction set near his crib. When Bev asked me why Asher was up, I mentioned the clicking of the parts. Simon was upset by the implied blame, fully aware that he was not supposed to wake the baby (4,1,29).

Sometimes Simon tried not to disturb Asher's sleep, but he was not always successful. I was lying down with Asher in the Snugli one evening after supper. Simon very quietly whispered for me to come and play, but his restraint quickly evaporated when I quietly put Asher into the crib. Simon boisterously bounced on the bed, and I scolded him for making noise. As it happened, Asher had trouble settling down, so when Simon wanted to play blast-off, we told him to count down softly. Simon insisted that a countdown had to be loud. I tried to explain to Simon that he did not like noise when he wanted to sleep, and it was not fair to make noise while Asher was falling asleep. In the end, Simon did not count down, but he was persuaded more by my insistence than by reason (4,1,29).

Thus, we tried to encourage Simon to consider Asher's needs and understand what was fair. I do not think that Simon was too young to take Asher's perspective. He always restrained himself around the babies' sleeping room at daycare and often reminded me to be quiet when we walked by. He occasionally considered Asher when he was out of sight, as when he did not want to flush the toilet because he thought Asher was sleeping in his crib (4,2,2). We always praised Simon for such restraint and usually admonished him for making noise but never succeeded in changing this behavior. Simon continued to disturb Asher's sleep, most often unintentionally because Simon could not, or would not, curb his exuberance. Yet disturbing Asher's sleep was more of an offense against us than against Asher, since we had to deal with his mood if he woke up too early.

Learning about the Baby's Rights

Contrary to popularly held preconceptions, young children with a new brother or sister are not necessarily consumed by sibling rivalry (Dunn and Kendrick 1982a). Simon was a good case in point. What appeared to be negative feelings or antagonistic behavior was usually not related to jealousy of Asher. A baby brother or sister will necessarily detract from a young child's attention some of the time. And since Simon enjoyed adult company, the issue of sharing our attention with Asher was potentially quite serious. Yet the problem was mitigated for reasons already noted: Simon's daycare routine, our attempts to maintain certain family routines, the time Simon spent with friends and relatives outside our home, and the time we spent alone with Simon.

But obviously it was sometimes impossible for Bev or me to be involved exclusively with Simon, especially when Bev breast-fed Asher and when I carried him in the Snugli. The situations were surprisingly parallel, since each excluded Simon, who could therefore have responded jealously. And just as when we were busy with any other task, Simon did occasionally try to get our attention; he might ask Bev for help while she was breast-feeding or suggest that I take off the Snugli and play with him. Yet Simon virtually never reacted negatively toward Asher. Simon was interested in his baby brother and tried to make him respond, occasionally distracting him from nursing or preventing him from falling asleep. Although it would have been easy to misconstrue Simon's motivation, Simon appeared jealous more of Asher's attention to us than of our attention to Asher.

Young North American children are typically not adept at interacting with babies (Berman and Goodman 1984, Bryant 1982). Therefore, apparently aggressive or negative behaviors may actually be well intentioned. But however important the intentions, the baby must be protected. Although we tried to encourage Simon's interaction with his baby brother, we intervened when we had a sense that Simon might hurt or disturb Asher, even if Asher did not complain. We also tried to teach Simon that Asher had proprietary rights and a right to be comfortable, needed to eat and sleep, might get hurt, and so on. And we often called upon Simon to yield his own needs, enthusiasm, curiosity, and desires to Asher's rights. At 4 years of age, Simon was not always prepared to do so, but by highlighting Asher's point of view, we may have helped Simon understand Asher as a person, thereby fostering a positive attitude toward him (Dunn and Kendrick 1982a, Howe and Ross 1990).

Chapter 7
Brotherly Feelings and Attitudes

Various behavioral methods have been used to study the early relationship between brothers and sisters. Researchers have observed interactions to measure how much time the children are involved with each other or have globally categorized the type of interaction—for example, as positive, negative, or imitative—or have coded specific behaviors—such as kissing, watching, smiling, and hitting (Abramovitch et al. 1979, 1980, Baskett and Johnson 1982, Dunn and Kendrick 1982a, Lamb 1978a, 1978b). Investigators also have examined the functions served by sibling interactions—for example, caregiving, teaching, and companionship—and have characterized the role each partner plays within different functional contexts (Cicirelli 1975, Howe and Ross 1990, R. B. Stewart 1983; R. B. Stewart et al. 1983). And they have focused on the qualities of the relationship, such as warmth, closeness, and rivalry (Dunn and Kendrick 1982a, Furman and Buhrmester 1985, Mendelson et al. 1988, Mendelson and Gottlieb 1988).

The three behavioral approaches are certainly useful, but a strictly behavioral focus obscures many important features of the early sibling relationship, especially since young children have limited social skills for effectively interacting with a baby. Indeed, children's motives and intentions are not always apparent from their behavior; for example, seemingly aggressive acts may really be unskilled play, and intrusiveness may actually be exploration of the baby. Therefore a complete account of a young child's relationship with a baby brother or sister must include information about qualities like friendliness, getting along, and such (table 1.1). And the information must be drawn from a variety of sources, even from situations in which the children do not interact, because at the outset, feelings and attitudes are probably more relevant than behaviors. Simon did have a wide range of positive feelings and attitudes about Asher, and here I examine five of them: acceptance, identification, affection, help, and protection.

Acceptance

New mothers generally want their baby to be accepted by the family (Mercer 1981, R. Rubin 1967), and, after a second child, they are particularly interested in the firstborn's attitude (Walz and Rich 1983). Acceptance of the baby brother or sister is one aspect of the firstborn's adjustment to the transition (Kramer 1989). More important, it is a necessary precursor to a relationship that goes beyond rejection or indifference.

Like other psychological changes associated with a new sibling, acceptance may begin even before the baby arrives. Many preschoolers are enthusiastic enough about the prospect of a baby brother or sister to request one from their parents, and Simon was no exception. Before Asher was born, Simon occasionally suggested that we have a new baby, perhaps because he saw so many infants in Jerusalem or more probably because several of his friends already had, or were expecting, a sibling. He was pleased when he learned his suggestion would became a reality (3,4,21).

Simon's enthusiasm for a new baby did not diminish in the ensuing months; like most other children in his situation, he felt positively about the prospect of becoming a brother (R. B. Stewart et al. 1987). We were once talking about a picture of a big boy dog who expected a baby brother (figure 3.1). Simon wholeheartedly replied yes to my question if the big dog was happy about being a brother (taped 3,9,5). And just before Asher was born, Simon told my student Judy that the same dog felt good. Judy then asked what the big brother dog would wish for if he could wish for anything in the whole wide world. "A baby dog," replied Simon (taped 3,11,23).

Shortly after Asher was born, Simon was enthusiastic about the prospect of even more babies, which surely meant that he accepted the one we had.

> Simon: You know, some people have more than just two children.
> Father: You're right.
> Simon: Yeah, some people have nine children.
> Father: (amused) That's a lot of children.
> Simon: Maybe Mommy will have more babies.
> Father: Would you like that?
> Simon: Yeah!
> Father: Would you like Mommy to have nine children.
> Simon: Yeah, I really would.

Father: Well, I don't think Mommy is going to have nine
           children.
Simon: Maybe (4,0,17).

Now We Are Four

A clearer indication that Simon accepted the baby was how readily he changed his concept of our family. He thought about the baby as a family member almost from the outset. For one thing, he considered himself a brother prior to becoming one, but there were also other indications that he accepted the baby as ours.

Before Asher was born, we usually referred to the baby simply as "the baby"—not "Mommy's baby" or "our baby." Still Simon had ample reason to assume that the baby was Bev's, although I heard him say so only once, and he seemed to be joking. He patted Bev's tummy and said, "Mommy's fat baby" (3,11,0). Yet Simon often did refer to the baby possessively.

Simon: When is *our* baby coming out?
Mother: In December.
Simon: Why did *Fran's* (not Fran and Charles's) baby come
           out before *my* baby?
Mother: (echoing the possessives) Because *Fran's* baby was
           ready to come out now and *our* baby will be ready in
           December (3,8,5).

Simon was incredulous about an implicit suggestion that a new baby might not belong to the whole family. We were looking at the picture of the dog family. "And the second baby," I asked about the dog shown inside the mother. "Is it going to be his *mommy's* baby or his *daddy's* baby or *his* baby or what?" "Well," Simon replied immediately, "all of them!" (taped 3,9,29).

At the very least, Simon's language indicated proprietary feelings for his unborn brother. Perhaps he was also claiming the baby as his (Mercer 1981, R. Rubin 1967). Alternatively he may have simply included the unborn baby as part of the family. Like other children his age, he thought about the nuclear family in terms of common residence and love (Pederson and Gilby 1986). "It's for the whole family," he once said about a pumpkin that Fran had sent us, "not everyone we love—only the people that live in this building" (3,9,23). And based on residence, the baby surely was also a member of the family. Thus, in a conversation about moving, Bev and I assured Simon that the three of us would stay together. "And the baby," Simon immediately added, "the baby's in your uterus" (3,10,9).

At least two months before Asher was born, Simon thought about a family in terms of four members. I proposed that we draw a picture of a family and asked who was going to be in it. "A daddy, a mommy, a big boy, and a baby," replied Simon. Simon's family consisted of charming tadpole figures, just like the ones all young children draw (figure 7.1) (Gardner 1980). He first sketched the baby, with a nose, the eyes, and "a smiling mouth." He then drew the mommy and the daddy, also with smiling mouths. But he wanted the baby holding the daddy's hand and the daddy holding the mommy's hand, which was beyond his artistic ability, so he asked me for guidance. "And the big boy is going to have to go in the middle of the mommy and the daddy," he said after completing the other figures (taped 3,10,10). Simon's drawing of a family—four happy people holding hands— was a very pleasant image indeed.

A child who accepts the idea of a new baby will not necessarily

Figure 7.1
Simon's drawing of a family that includes (from left) Baby, Mommy, Big Boy, and Daddy (3,10,10).

accept the reality, and Simon was not pleased the first time we talked about Asher as a member of our family. We were watching Asher and discussing names during our first visit to the hospital. Simon proudly remembered how to pronounce Asher's two Hebrew names. I then said that Asher had another name and asked Simon what he thought it was. When he guessed Mendelson, I asked why. "Because our name is Mendelson," Simon reasoned. "That's right," I said. "Asher's name is Mendelson because he's now a part of our family." My elaboration stopped Simon cold; he grew quite solemn and immediately changed the topic (4,0,3).

Yet Simon did accept the baby as part of the family. Thus, he included Asher when he distributed goodies. Several months before Asher was born, Bev's mother gave Simon four roses from her garden, suggesting that each was for one of us. He completely accepted the idea and later showed me the roses: "One of these is for you, one for Mommy, one for me, and one for the baby" (3,8,11). In the ensuing months, Simon spontaneously shared other objects with the unborn baby, qua member of the family. He once told me that four Duplo cars he had constructed were "the daddy car, the mommy car, the boy car, and and the baby car" (3,9,19). Another time he asked, "Do you want to come and see what I cut for you and Mommy and me and my baby brother or baby sister and me?" (3,10,17). Simon continued after Asher was born. One morning he awoke just before seven o'clock and played in his room for about forty-five minutes. He diligently cut out pictures of watches from magazines and then proudly distributed his assortment—some for Bev, some for Asher, and some for me (4,0,9).

Occasionally Simon may have actually served his own interests by offering a goody to Asher. Simon once asked for a pet—either a rat or a gerbil. We suggested a fish and then negotiated how many. I proposed two. Simon countered, "Four—a baby fish, a big brother fish, a mommy fish, and a daddy fish" (4,1,27). He included a baby either to justify four fish or to complete the parallel between the fish family and his own. Another time Simon included Asher obviously to bolster his own request. He was inspecting a rack of postcards and asked if we could get a picture for the four of us—not four pictures but one picture for the four members of his family (4,2,15).

Yet Simon often included Asher without an ulterior motive. Within a week of the postcard request, Simon found some tinsel and said that each of the four pieces was a present for one of us (4,2,18). Later the same day he mentioned that he mailed a picture home for Bev, Asher, and me. (His daycare class was learning about the post office.)

When I asked whose idea it was to send it to Asher, Simon replied with a distinctly what-do-you-think tone that it was his (4,2,18).

Why was Asher on Simon's family gift list? Perhaps Simon was following the lead set by his grandmother in early September. Perhaps he sought our approval, for we usually praised him for sharing with the baby. Perhaps he was simply showing brotherly affection. But even if all of these played a role, I suspect the real reason was quite simple: as far as Simon was concerned, Asher was part of our family and therefore deserved certain privileges.

Simon quickly included four family members in pretend play. He frequently announced that he was a baby creature and that someone else was the mommy or daddy creature. Ten days before Asher was born, he defined his three-member family, including a daddy turtle without anyone present to play the role. "Let's pretend we're the turtles," he suggested to Judy. "I'm the baby turtle, and you're the mommy turtle, and our daddy has gone out to work" (taped 3,11,23). When Asher was a month old, Simon already specified a four-member family, this time without anyone present to play two of the roles. "Let's say you're the daddy lobster," he suggested during his bath, "and Mommy's the mommy lobster, and I'm the big brother lobster, and Asher's the baby lobster" (4,1,0).

Juggling Family Constellations

Although Simon thought the unborn baby was part of our family foursome, he also thought it was apart from our family threesome. Simon understood that the baby had to be cared for, and he knew that both Bev and I worked outside the home. One day he spontaneously asked, "Who's going to stay with the baby at home?" "Either Mommy or Daddy," replied Bev. But Simon said he meant when we both had to go out, so she explained that we would get a babysitter then (3,7,27). Simon again raised the topic a few weeks later but this time with a twist that clearly reflected his notion of a family of three plus one. It was a mild evening, and we all walked downtown for a light supper. Afterward Simon asked Bev, "Who's going to stay with the baby when you and I and Daddy go out?" Bev responded by naming some of his babysitters (3,8,22).

But Simon also envisioned that the baby's arrival would create a new family subsystem, the division between children and parents, which he would eventually accept quite willingly. The following conversation was about a sheep family:

> Father: I have a suggestion that the mommy sheep, the daddy
>   sheep, and the baby lamb all go away and do some-

	thing, and the big brother lamb will stay home and play by himself.
Simon:	No.
Father:	You don't think that's a good idea? No. How about if the mommy . . .
Simon:	(excited and obviously identifying with the sheep) Sometimes you guys go out and I stay with the brother.
Father:	You stay with the brother? Oh! You're going to take care of the brother?
Simon:	Yeah . . . sometimes . . . and not always (taped 3,9,16).

Asher had a regular babysitter by the time he was 2 months old. Anne stayed with him under three circumstances, and each defined a distinct family constellation. She occasionally took care of him when Simon was at daycare and Bev and I both had to be out of the house; she babysat regularly on Saturday mornings so Bev, Simon, and I could go to synagogue together; and she she stayed with Asher and Simon when Bev and I went out for the evening.

We first fulfilled Simon's prediction about the family threesome by leaving 2-week-old Asher with Anne so we could all go to synagogue. Simon was quite pleased. Indeed, he had tried to preserve the family threesome earlier that morning when he insisted that we eat together; he strenuously objected that Bev could not sit with us at breakfast because she was nursing Asher (4,0,18).

When Asher was 1 month old, Simon talked about the four of us going away but with more understanding than before Asher was born. Although he first seemed to reject Asher, he subsequently considered Asher's wants and needs. Simon suggested that Anne stay with Asher while the three of us go away on a trip, but Bev reminded him that she had to stay home to feed Asher. Simon then suggested that only he and I go away, yet he added that Bev should come with us or stay at home, depending on what Asher wanted to do. Simon finally said that it depended on how far away we were going and how cold it would be—presumably because Asher could not yet go out in the winter weather (4,1,7).

One month later I overheard a conversation that clearly demonstrated Simon's unwillingness to reject Asher. A stranger jokingly asked Simon if she could have his baby brother. Taking the stranger quite seriously, Simon insisted no. But the stranger continued the joke by telling Simon to ask his mommy and daddy if it would be all right. Simon still vehemently insisted no (4,2,0). What we thought did not matter; he was not about to let the stranger have his baby brother. And Simon often even suggested that we include Asher in our activities.

Simon: One day the four of us should go out to dinner.
Mother: What do you mean?
Simon: Daddy, me, you, and Asher should go to a restaurant for dinner. You know why I suggested that Asher go?
Mother: Why?
Simon: So you can feed him if he's hungry. Except we'll have to go to a restaurant that allows babies (4,2,9).

Yet Simon did not abandon the possibility that he might accompany Bev and me while Asher stayed at home. Thus Simon juggled family foursome and family threesome, at times even in the same conversation. Once Bev and I were talking about the possibility of moving. Simon seemed worried, so I assured him that no matter where we went, he would also go. "And Asher," Simon added, "except if you, me, and Mommy go some place like a restaurant" (4,4,0).

Simon also included Asher when he partitioned the family foursome in yet another way by considering "the boys" separate from Bev. He and I were making plans for an outing, and he suggested that Bev and Asher join us. I explained that Bev would be napping, so we would go by ourselves. "So then just the boys will go," Simon proposed, trying to involve at least Asher (4,1,3). Another time he suggested that we have two more girls so that there would be three boys and three girls, an ideally symmetrical family (4,4,29).

The Two of Us

Simon was generally comfortable about our going out for an evening, perhaps because he always had a regular babysitter of his own. The babysitter would usually play with him before bedtime, so an important criterion for keeping a babysitter was that Simon enjoyed her company. But Anne was busy with Asher, so she had little time for Simon, who clearly understood the problem and even proposed a solution. One evening I told Simon that Bev and I would be going out and that Anne would stay with him and Asher. Simon tearfully asked why we did not "invite" someone else to stay with him. Bev said that Anne came to stay with Asher but that Simon was a big boy and could play by himself (4,2,6).

The next day Simon complained that Anne only took care of Asher and did not do anything with him. Bev then effectively accepted Simon's first proposal: she said that her parents would come next time, so one could play with him while the other took care of Asher. Simon nevertheless was not placated until he complained to me and I also said that Bev's parents would come next time (4,2,7). When they finally did stay with him and Asher, Simon did not object to our going out, and he took brotherly charge, claiming that he knew what Asher wanted better than his grandmother (4,2,20).

Simon eventually accepted the family division between parents and children. Of course, he and Asher were very different at the time—a big boy versus a baby—so there were not many realistic chances to group himself with his brother. Yet he often did when he was not allowed to have something he wanted; he would then ally himself with Asher against me. The strategy actually worked, mainly because I was amused as well as pleased that he would recruit Asher to his side. He once asked me to read a story when we were lounging around with Asher. I was reluctant, but he persuaded me with phrases like "Here's *our* story" and "Please read *us* a story" (4,2,16). Another time Simon constructed a "little cabin" out of pillows in our bed, but I wanted to lie on my pillow. Simon became angry and took Bev's pillow to complete the enclosure. He then announced that it was only for "little people" and, in case I did not understand, he explained that it was just for Asher and him. Amused, I put Asher next to him. "Hi, Asher," Simon greeted. "Isn't it fun to be in our own little cabin?" (4,2,24).

Thus, Simon included Asher as part of his in-group. In effect, he classified Asher as "one of us"—one of four Mendelsons, one of three boys, or one of two children. He could have done it dispassionately, based purely on objective criteria. After all, Asher was in fact a boy child in our family. But Simon's acceptance of his brother was more than just a simple cognitive process. It may have been based on his desire for Asher to be similar to him, and it certainly was accompanied by positive emotions.

Identification

Simon often pretended to be a baby and frequently tried out most of Asher's supplies. Imitation of a baby brother or sister can be interpreted as regressive or as a bid for parental attention, negative signs of mild stress (Dunn and Kendrick 1982a, R. B. Stewart et al. 1987, Trivers 1974). But the same behavior can be interpreted as an attempt to find or promote similarities with the baby, a positive sign of identification within a close relationship. Certainly a young child's imitation of a parent is interpreted positively, where it may be both a cause and a consequence of identification (Kohlberg 1966, Maccoby and Martin 1983).

Young children may be more responsive to individuals they consider like themselves than unlike themselves, at least along the dimensions of gender, age, and familiarity (M. Lewis and Brooks-Gunn 1979). This might help explain both why same-sex siblings apparently interact more positively than different-sex siblings (Abramovitch et al. 1979, Dunn and Kendrick 1982a, but see Lamb 1978a, 1978b) and why 2- to 3-year-olds interact more positively with a same-sex baby than with a different-sex baby, but not why 4- to 5-year-olds, regardless of sex, prefer baby girls (Melson and Fogel 1982). I suggested that Simon may have wanted a brother so that the baby would be like him, a hypothesis supported by one of Simon's proposals for the baby's name. Simon overheard many discussions about names, but he once spontaneously raised the topic with an intriguing proposal—that we name the baby Simon. Bev and I offered reasons for not doing so: it would be confusing if they had the same name, and, just as he was named in honor of someone special, the baby should have a special name of his own. Yet we could not dissuade Simon, who reiterated his suggestion (3,7,25).

After our first visit to the hospital, Simon and I talked about the name we finally did choose. I wanted him to like the name and to accept his brother, so I tried to show him that their names were connected. Simon started the conversation by saying that Asher's name was funny. "No, it's a very nice name," I disagreed. ". . . In the Torah [Bible] Simon and Asher were brothers! . . . And in our family, Simon and Asher are brothers." Simon was amused. Later I mentioned that I had greeted Asher by his name when he was just born. Simon asked how I knew it. I responded with a question of my own, "Who gets to choose a boy's name?" "A mommy and a daddy," Simon replied knowingly. "That's right. Mommy and Daddy chose your name, and Mommy and Daddy chose Asher's name," I said, drawing a parallel between the brothers. And I added that we thought it would be nice if our two boys had the same names as two brothers in the Torah (taped 4,0,3).

Bev and I also tried to encourage Simon to see that Asher was like him in other ways (Walz and Rich 1983). When Asher was still in the hospital, we often compared him and Simon as a baby. We noted a few differences. Unlike Simon, Asher had lots of dark hair and ruddy skin. But we were primarily struck by the many similarities. We repeatedly told Simon how much Asher resembled him, since they had the same mouth, nose, and blue eyes, for a few of many possible examples. We also told him how similar they were in other ways, since Asher, like Simon, nursed well, slept well, was easy to soothe, and needed phototherapy for jaundice (4,0,3–4,0,7).

In the ensuing months, Simon often overheard such comparisons, especially when people saw Asher for the first time. The resemblance between the boys was striking, so the conversation invariably turned to their similarities. And when anyone said that Asher was cute in front of Simon, we typically added, "Just like his big brother" (4,1,11). Simon also joined our many conversations about family resemblances, often indicating his desire to be similar to his brother.

Simon: (to Mother, who was holding Asher) Asher smells like you.

Mother: Actually he smells like Daddy.

Simon: No, he smells like me (4,1,19).

Simon: (to Father, referring to what Asher was wearing) I was asking [Mommy], maybe I could get socks and a nightgown like that.

Father: But that's a baby's nightgown.

Simon: Except, I mean in a bigger size (4,1,28).

Mother: Bubby Pessy said that when Daddy walks down the street, people are going to wonder why his sons have blue eyes.

Simon: I know. We should get Asher the same jacket and pants and boots and hat [as mine], so we'll look the same (4,2,5).

Father: (to Asher) You look so much like [Auntie] Roz.

Simon: Asher looks like me.

Father: Asher looks like you too.

Simon: Asher looks more like me than like Roz (4,3,15)

Thus, unlike their comparisons with unfamiliar babies, preschoolers may compare themselves with a baby brother or sister on a variety of dimensions. Regardless of sex, the children may be quite similar or quite different in terms of general appearance, specific features, body build, temperament, abilities, preferences, and so on. These dimensions, which are often not as obvious to an outside observer as sex, may actually be more important, to both children and their parents. And parents may choose to highlight similarities—as we did— or to emphasize differences. Whether or not because of our comparisons, Simon did strive to find similarities between him and Asher, which was consistent with his other positive feelings for his baby brother.

Affection

Simon rarely harbored negative feelings for Asher. Did that mean he felt positively about his brother or simply neutral? Before Asher was born, he certainly expected to love the baby. When his friend became a new brother, he agreed that Jeff was going to love his sister, and to the same question about himself, he replied, "Yeah! . . . Everybody does" (taped 3,9,29). Of course, emotions cannot be willed, so we tried to foster Simon's affection for Asher as do other parents with a second child (Walz and Rich 1983). We used two conscious strategies: telling Simon that Asher loved him and encouraging Simon to show his own tender feelings physically. Simon also experienced our affection to him and witnessed our demonstrativeness to Asher.

Asher Loves You

Even before Asher was a week old, we interpreted his behavior to Simon as affectionate. The following conversation occurred just as we arrived home from the hospital:

Simon:	(high soft voice) Open your hand. Open your hand. (excited) He opened his hand!
Mother:	He did?
Simon:	Yeah. He's grabbing my finger.
Father:	That's right. *He likes you. He likes to grab your finger.*
Simon:	(softly brushes his face against Asher's cheek)
Asher:	(turns to Simon, rooting)
Father:	*He tried to kiss you there.*
Simon:	(laughs and brushes Asher's face again)
Asher:	(roots to Simon again)
Simon:	(pleased) There. *He kissed me!*
Mother:	*He kissed you* (taped 4,0,7)

More often, however, the topic of Asher's affection was raised in the abstract. I even made a game of telling Simon that Asher loved him. I adapted it from my standard good-bye at daycare in which I would kiss Simon and rhetorically ask, "Who loves you the most?" "Mommy and Daddy love you the most," I would then answer. But Simon often answered first, confidently saying, "Mommy and Daddy." After Asher was born, I added a twist, and Simon smiled the first time I replied, "Mommy and Daddy . . . and Asher" (4,0,8). Yet Simon did not change his own response to the question, though I repeated the amended answer several times over the next few days. Thus, the morning Simon returned to daycare after winter break:

Father: Who loves you the most?
Simon: You and Mommy.
Father: And Asher.
Simon: Actually, you and Mommy love me and Asher.
Father: And Asher loves you too.
Simon: (kisses Asher) (4,0,10).

Although Simon did not acknowledge that Asher loved him, he kissed Asher when I told him so, which encouraged me that my strategy might be useful.

In the ensuing weeks, the subject of love came up in various ways besides my daycare farewell. I once talked about loving more than one person, and Simon attributed love to Asher.

Father: (to Asher while Simon was in the room) Hello, little
         fellow. We love you very much.
Simon: Actually you and Mommy love me and Asher.
Father: (agreeing) . . . We love you very much. . . . (Then Fa-
         ther observes that it is possible to love more than one
         person at the same time) For instance, you love
         Mommy and Daddy and the bubbies [grandmothers]
         and the zaides [grandfathers].
Simon: Yeah. And Asher loves the bubbies and the zaides too
         (4,0,17).

Later the same day I told Simon, "Mommy and Daddy love you very much, and we also love Asher." Simon then volunteered that he loved Asher (4,0,17). Several days later, Simon deduced an important lesson about a family, again attributing love to Asher, at least implicitly.

Mother: I love you.
Simon: Actually you and Daddy love me and Asher.
Mother: And what else?
Simon: Everyone loves everyone (4,0,20).

But our daycare farewell did not change. Then one day I asked, "Who loves you the most?" And Simon haltingly replied, "Mommy and Daddy . . . and Asher" (4,2,19). Within a few days, he stopped hesitating and simply rattled off, "You and Mommy and Asher," his usual response for the remainder of his daycare days.

Simon truly understood that family members love each other. Before Asher was born, Simon answered questions about family relationships and said that a parent must love (3,11,2). Afterward he extended the idea.

> Simon: (referring to Asher, who was looking at him) You see, he always watches me—not you or Mommy.
>
> Father: That's because he loves you.
>
> Simon: He loves all of us, and we love all of him. That's what a family is for.
>
> Father: We love all of him, or all of us love him?
>
> Simon: We love all of him, and all of him loves us (4,4,0).

But did Simon really believe that his brother loved him? Although he had ample evidence of Asher's limited abilities, he was still willing to say that Asher loved people. And he never questioned us when we said that Asher loved someone, which was particularly telling since Simon did challenge Bev when she said that Asher experienced another emotion. Once when Simon returned home from daycare, Bev told him that Asher had missed him. Simon immediately asked Bev how she knew, to which she responded that she was just kidding (4,2,8). Perhaps Simon would have accepted Bev's statement if we told him that Asher missed him as often as we told him that Asher loved him. Alternatively, Simon may have so fundamentally believed family members love each other that he even believed a baby loves his big brother.

Hugs and Kisses
Words are cheap. Simon may have very well talked about love in the family because he knew how important it was to us. A more convincing indication of his feelings for Asher would have to come from actions, actually the only way to communicate love to a young baby. The day Asher came home, I prompted Simon to say good-night to him. Simon first kissed Bev and then gently patted and kissed his baby brother (4,0,7). Over the weeks Simon kissed and stroked Asher countless times. Simon often spontaneously showed his affection, as when he gently stroked Asher's cheek after watching him for a while in the infant seat (4,0,18). At other times he followed our suggestion, as when Bev told him to give Asher a good-morning kiss (4,0,21). But sometimes he simply followed our lead. The first Friday night home from the hospital, Bev lit the Sabbath candles and, as usual, she, Simon, and I kissed each other in a traditional Sabbath greeting. Bev and I then kissed Asher, and so did Simon (4,0,18).

We often praised Simon for expressing his affection for Asher in word or deed. Simon once asked me to play boat with him, but I explained that I had to hold Asher because he would not settle down.

Simon came over to kiss Asher, and I kissed Simon, telling him that he was nice to kiss his brother and that Asher would kiss him back when he learned how. Simon then kissed Asher many times more (4,1,8).

By the time Asher was 1 month old, Simon constantly kissed him, patted him, and stroked him. Indeed Simon seemed unable to inhibit himself. He even kissed when he had a cold, despite our repeated warnings about getting too close (4,1,4). And Simon circumvented obstacles to kiss Asher. One morning leaving for daycare, Simon could not kiss Asher good-bye because he was already in bed, but Simon was not to be deterred. "I'm giving you a kiss for Asher," he told Bev as he kissed her an extra time. "Afterwards, give it to Asher" (4,2,2). Kissing was simply something Simon did to Asher, even when Asher was asleep and during almost every interaction. Simon expressed his love in a way that Asher could feel, if not understand.

Help by Sharing

Besides accepting Asher as part of the family and generally demon- strating his affection for him, Simon also held two attitudes that were consistent with his role as a big brother: he believed he should help Asher and should protect him. During Asher's first days at home, Simon was enthusiastic about helping to change, burp, bathe, and dress Asher, to put Asher to bed, and so on. Simon was usually will- ing to listen to instructions about how to do something new and then wanted to jump right in. Bev and I tried to include him as much as possible, so we usually asked him if he wanted to help with a variety of tasks. Invariably he said yes in a do-you-have-to-ask tone and seemed genuinely pleased to be involved with his brother. But his eagerness did not always translate into helpfulness. For one thing, he was not skilled, so he could not adeptly hold Asher, and he had trouble dressing him. For another, his assistance was sometimes problematic, as when he quickly lost interest in helping Bev give Asher a bath but not in playing with the water and spilling it on the floor (4,0,8). Thus, despite his prior expectations, Simon spent vir- tually no time helping take care of Asher (.29 hour per week based on daily diaries). Yet he still demonstrated a helpful attitude in other ways.

Where's the Baby Going to Sleep?
A baby takes up very little space, but the baby's paraphernalia—a crib, a changing table, a collection of toys, a library of books, and so

on—pose problems. Indeed collecting the supplies and finding a place for everything are practical challenges all expectant parents face. Simon involved himself in our preparations for the baby, which reflected his general willingness to help, and his reactions showed how willing he was to share.

At the time we lived in a two-bedroom apartment. Simon's room, a den and office before he was born, still had most of the original furnishings, to which were added his bed, toys, and books. Like most other second borns, Asher would eventually have a collection of hand-me-downs—old clothes and baby toys—that we had put aside for a second child. Initially Bev and I avoided telling Simon that the baby would use his things, but we often talked about what the baby would need, so Simon may have overheard conversations about handing down "his" possessions. Regardless, he understood early on that we could use his old clothes for the baby. One day he asked about the clothes in a suitcase we had removed from storage. I said they were old and were too small for him. "Let's save these for our baby," he offered. "OK, Daddy?" (3,7,11).

Simon's offers to share were not indiscriminate; besides baby clothes and baby toys, he also proposed giving the baby a bottle of Johnson and Johnson Baby Lotion and a box of Baby's Own Soap (3,10,5). Yet his suggestions were not only limited to baby items. One day he removed some blankets from a cupboard and explained, "I took out these blankets for when it gets cold for me and the baby" (3,10,6). He had a sense of the baby's needs and was relating them to his own, something he had done even two months earlier when we were in the car.

> Simon: We should get a bigger car . . . so we'll have room for another [carseat] for the baby.
> Father: We don't need another, because soon we're going to get you a big-boy carseat.
> Simon: Then we can give this one to the baby.
> Father: Exactly.
> Simon: If you stop suddenly, he needs these straps. But I don't because I'm a big boy (3,8,10).

Simon intuitively realized that the baby posed a space problem. Early on he asked where the baby was going to sleep (about 3,6,15). I replied that the baby might sleep in his room eventually but in ours at first. Simon tearfully said that he wanted the baby to sleep in his room all the time. Six weeks later he returned to the topic and asked why the baby was going to sleep in our room. Fumbling, I said that we would be there if the baby woke and needed something and that Simon might be disturbed by the baby's cry. "No. I don't get up," countered Simon, with a tremor in his voice, "even if I hear a noise." He was visibly upset and certainly not about to be convinced by reason (3,7,22).

The issue was by no means settled for Simon. Two months later, I elicited virtually the same conversation and the same emotional reaction simply by asking him about his friend's new baby sister.

Father: Where do you think Jeff's baby is going to sleep?
Simon: In [Jeff's] room.
Father: . . . And our baby?
Simon: In my room.
Father: . . . Well, eventually the baby is going to sleep in your room, but I don't know if he or she is going to sleep in your room right away.
Simon: (worried) How come?
Father: Because, when the baby's really little, it's not so convenient for the baby to be sleeping in your room.
Simon: How come?
Father: Because the baby would get up in the middle of the night and . . . um . . . would disturb you when it cried.
Simon: . . . It doesn't disturb me.
Father: No? You don't think so?
Simon: No.
Father: I think it would wake you up.
Simon: (sadly) No, it wouldn't.
Father: Well, I think when the baby is really little, little, just for a little while . . .
Simon: No!
Father: . . . the baby will stay in Mommy's and Daddy's room for a while.
Simon: (almost crying) Nooo. I . . . I don't want it to stay there for a little while. . . . But only in the day it will stay there for a little while. In the night it will always sleep in my room (taped 3,9,29).

By the end of the conversation, Simon sought a time-sharing compromise. Returning to the same topic a couple of weeks later, I tried to ensure that Simon understood what would happen. He was somewhat less emotional but still proposed a compromise. I started the conversation by asking him if he would help me set up the baby's crib. As usual, he agreed enthusiastically. We continued:

Father: When the baby is very, very little, we're going to put [the] crib in Mommy and Daddy's room.

Simon: I have a good idea! We could put it between our rooms. With half in your room and half in my room. You know how I do that?

Father: How would you do that?

Simon: Put it in the hall.

Father: Put it in the hall? Maybe sometime we will put it in the hall.

Simon: Sure.

Father: . . . And then the baby is going to . . . When the baby's really little, the baby will probably sleep in Mommy's and Daddy's room most of the time. But not all of the time. And then . . .

Simon: Sometimes he'll sleep in my room.

Father: And then as the baby gets older, just a little bit older— sleeping through the night—then we'll make room in your room . . . for the crib (taped 3,10,19).

Yet it dawned on Simon that the benefit of having the baby in his room would entail a cost.

Simon: . . . But then we can't set up so many toys.

Father: Where?

Simon: In my room.

Father: Well, you know what we'll do? We'll take the couch away to make room for the baby's crib. . . . So you'll still have room for toys. OK?

Simon: Then we'll have lots and lots of room for toys.

Father: Yeah. Is that all right? Do you think that will be a good plan?

Simon: Yeah. Yup.

Apparently assuaged, Simon tackled the main reason we had offered for not letting the baby sleep in his room.

Simon: I . . . I never wake up when I hear a sound.

Father: You don't?

Simon: Yeah. . . . Only if something shouts or screams or something.

Father: Or cries?

Simon: (immediate) No! Not cries.

Father: You don't think that you would wake up if you heard
           a baby crying at night?
Simon: No! But I'll wake up if you want me to help the baby.
Father: OK.
Simon: You'll call me.
Father: Yeah. OK. Well, we'll have to see if you wake up
           (taped 3,10,19).

We finally settled on a plan that a good time to move the crib into
Simon's room was when the baby starts sleeping through the night
and that we would make more space by taking out the couch and
getting more shelves for all the toys.

Preparations for the baby shifted into high gear a few weeks before
Bev's due date. We began washing Simon's baby clothes and putting
them away in a drawer in Simon's bureau. True, Simon had continually insisted that he wanted the baby in his room, but I did not know
how he would react to an actual invasion of his space, so I cautiously
directed his attention to the clothes. I had him look in the drawers,
first at the baby's clothes in the bottom two drawers and then at his
in the top two. He stared at the baby's clothes, which had all once
been his. I asked if it was all right to put them in the third drawer.
Simon replied yes but added that there was still some room there for
his own clothes too. I told him he had plenty of room for his clothes,
but if he needed more room, he could put his clothes in that drawer
as well (3,11,19). Thus, he was reasonably willing to share his space,
at least if it did not cost him too much.

No matter how explicit we were, Simon continually returned to the
topic. He wanted the baby in his room and was inevitably upset by
our stand that the baby was going to sleep in our room at first so
Simon would not be disturbed but that the baby would eventually
sleep with him. A few days after Asher was born, Simon tried to find
out how long he would have to wait. "When is Asher going to sleep
in my room?" he asked tearfully (4,0,8). Yet though he was usually
upset when he talked about it with us, he matter-of-factly had the
following conversation:

Judy: Does the baby cry a lot or keep you awake at night,
           or . . .
Simon: No! . . . He's not even . . . he's not even sleeping in
           my room.
Judy: I remember when my little girl was a baby at home.
           She used to wake up and cry in the middle of the
           night, and I couldn't sleep.

Simon:	(perhaps referring to an incident that occurred early one morning) . . . Sometimes, a few days in the night, my baby wakes up and cries. And then I come into my Mommy's and Daddy's room and I ask them why Asher is crying.
Judy:	. . . So, the baby's not sleeping in your room? Where does he sleep then?
Simon:	In my Mommy and Daddy's room.
Judy:	Ah, so that means you get some peace and quiet, I guess.
Simon:	Yeah. But sometimes I hear my baby cry.
Judy:	. . . and what do you do then?
Simon:	I just look at some things in my room (taped 4,0,14).

But Simon still wanted to share his room, and we still talked about when he could. One day Bev put Asher down for a nap in Simon's room. Returning from daycare, Simon quietly went into his room to see for himself and came out smiling broadly. Later he asked if Asher was going to sleep in his room that night. Bev explained again that Asher would disturb him, and Simon was again perturbed by the answer (4,1,8).

Notwithstanding our plans, Asher never did sleep in Simon's room in our apartment, and Simon eventually understood why. When Asher was about 2 months old, we did have him sleep in the living room at night because he disturbed Bev and me. After three weeks of doing so, Simon told us not to put the crib next to the wall to his room because Asher's squeaks would keep him up (4,3,0). And to his cousin's question if Asher slept in his room, Simon replied, "Not yet, because when he gets up at night, he still squeaks" (4,3,26). Asher continued to squeak; we continued to stall. And at last we moved to a house where the boys had rooms of their own. But they did eventually share a room—starting when they were about 3 and 7 years old—to make way for their sister, Dana, who was born six months later.

Actually Sharing

Sharing in theory is different from sharing in fact, and Simon's offers might not have been genuine, or he might have tempered his generosity when he realized the costs. During Asher's first week at home, Simon balked at two suggestions to share with his brother, perhaps because the suggestions were ours or because the objects were special. In the first case, I suggested that we wash one of Simon's plush toys so that we could give it to Asher, but Simon proposed a substitute that could not be washed (4,0,9). Simon also did not want Asher to use his blanket, though we needed to bundle Asher up for the cold weather (4,0,10).

Yet early on Simon was willing to share other objects, at least ones that were not particularly special. Until the day before Asher was born, Simon had used a high chair, without its tray, to reach the table. But he gave it up because a 5-year-old friend of his ate supper with us that evening and sat on a dining room chair (4,0,2). The day after Asher came home, I asked Simon if he minded leaving the high chair at Bev's parents' house for his baby cousin. "But we need the high chair for Asher," he objected, and I had to persuade him that Asher would not need it for at least six months (4,0,8). The same day, Bev mentioned that we would engrave a little silver cup for Asher. Simon offered his because it was too small for him. Bev praised him but said we would get one with Asher's name on it.

Gradually Simon became genuinely generous about sharing with Asher. He once offered a costume that he had worn in Jerusalem during Purim, a Jewish holiday marked by dressing up and general merrymaking (4,0,18). Seven weeks later, when we were preparing for a Purim party, Simon wanted Asher to join in the fun and asked what Asher would wear. I suggested a hat because Asher was going to be in the Snugli. Simon immediately got a cloth bag—something special—that he used for storing collectible treasures such as rocks and string. We put the bag on Asher's head, laughed, and agreed that Asher would wear it (4,2,6). The day of the party, Simon was excited and enthusiastically dressed himself in a cat costume. Yet despite his own excitement, he remembered Asher's hat, and after the party Simon suggested, "Why don't we save [my cat costume] for Asher?" We praised the idea. But then Simon asked a pertinent question: "Well, what if Asher doesn't want to be a cat?" We said that we would let Asher decide (4,2,10). Sharing the costume may have entailed no real sacrifice, since Simon knew it would be too small for himself, but it was still special, and he truly thought about what Asher would want.

Simon also willingly shared privileges that he might have considered his own. The traditional ritual of the Sabbath meal includes a blessing for children. The first time Asher joined us for Sabbath dinner, I wondered how Simon would feel about not being the only one to receive the benediction. After I blessed and kissed Simon, he was immediately ready to continue the ritual, yet he was delighted when I told him it was Asher's turn. I blessed and kissed Asher, exactly as I had always done with Simon. But this time I had help: Simon kissed Asher as well (4,1,18).

Simon did eventually share in the true sense of the word and even let Asher use his most prized possessions. Simon and I were once playing with Asher when I gave Asher one of Simon's two stuffed lions to lean on. Simon then offered the other lion, the one he preferred and always used as a pillow. I said that Asher was fine as he was. But even so, Simon switched the lions, explaining that Lisa was softer (4,2,16). When Asher was crying a few days later, Simon spontaneously offered the same blanket he had refused to share on a cold winter's day (4,2,19).

Naturally we wanted to encourage sharing, especially items that were suitable for Asher. I even successfully co-opted a doll for Asher that Simon never played with, although it did take several days. Simon asked me to put the doll away the first time he noticed that I had given it to Asher. "You don't mind if Asher plays with it, do you?" I asked rhetorically. But Simon ignored me, even when I repeated the question (4,2,24). A few days later, before an outing, Simon found the doll in Asher's tote bag. "I don't exactly think we should bring this," he calmly remarked. "It may get lost." I agreed and said that I should have asked him before taking it. Then he changed his mind, saying it might be all right if we kept the doll with Asher. But I thought better of it and replaced the doll (4,3,0). Finally, a week later, Simon noticed that I had taken the doll again, but this time he did not object. "It's all right if Asher uses it," he said, "because I was thinking I have too many stuffed animals" (4,3,7).

Simon gave a very sensible reason why we should not bring his doll: it might get lost. As the weeks passed, there was another legitimate reason for not sharing toys: Asher put everything in his mouth, and Simon did not like his toys to get wet. One day I was about to give Asher one of Simon's Duplo cars. Simon said he did not mind as long as Asher did not put it in his mouth because he did not want saliva on it. But Asher immediately tried to mouth the toy, so I stopped him (4,4,18). Yet we did not always prevent Asher from doing the inevitable. Bev, Simon, and I were at the table, and Asher was on the floor. Bev gave Asher one of Simon's Construx toys, but Simon objected, saying Asher would break it. And just then Asher started to gnaw it. Simon said that was what he did not want, so he exchanged his toy for one of Asher's (4,4,26). Even though he was unwilling to share, he still considered his brother and found something else to amuse him.

Protectiveness

Before Asher was born, Simon assumed that he would help protect Asher from harm. He frequently mentioned that we would have to prevent the baby from touching the stove and also understood that the baby would not be allowed to put small objects in his mouth. Simon's concern for the baby may have occasionally been self-serving, for example, to limit the baby's access to books that Simon was allowed to touch. But more often it was genuine, as was his concern for the baby's safety in utero.

Although Simon was unsure about how to protect the baby from the stove, he reasonably could be confident about preventing the baby from mouthing small objects. One day, before Asher was born, Simon overheard Bev suggest to a friend that she take things out of her 10-month-old's way. Simon, who was playing with Lego building blocks, told me, "I don't want the baby to touch little things—like these [small pieces]" (3,8,17). About two weeks later, Simon expanded on his reason. Bev asked him if he thought he would let his brother or sister play with his toys. "Sometimes I will and sometimes I won't," he replied. ". . . I won't let him play with the Lego. He might eat it" (3,8,29).

Asher's abilities at first were so limited that safety was a moot issue, yet mouthing small objects still remained an important topic. Despite many conversations about the danger of small objects and about babies drinking only breast milk, Simon once offered Asher something little to eat—a piece of breakfast cereal. When I told him not to, he said he was just showing it to Asher. But a bit later he put another piece in Asher's hand. I explained that we could not give him little things since he could put them in his mouth and choke on them; we could only give him big things, like a rattle. Simon then said that we could not give him a plastic bag, even though it was big, and I wholeheartedly agreed (4,1,8). Simon had learned the lesson well. One day while playing with Lego building blocks, he told Asher, "You can't play with this." And to me he said, "Because he'll put it in his mouth. . . . When he's older, he can play with it" (4,2,22). Moreover, Simon virtually never gave Asher anything a baby should not have.

Simon also reiterated his concerns about Asher's safety in the kitchen and revived a proposal he had made five months earlier. During our conversation, Simon said that Asher would soon be reaching and grabbing things, that we would have to make sure he did not go into the kitchen and touch things or he would pinch or otherwise hurt himself, that we could shut the door to the kitchen when we went out, which would be the sign that Asher is not supposed to go in, and, finally, that we would have to put signs all over. The conversation stopped when I asked Simon how signs would help since Asher could not read (4,3,17).

Simon's protectiveness extended beyond Asher's physical safety to his feelings. Simon—in his role as big brother—wanted to censor what Asher saw, perhaps because we—in our role as parents—restricted what Simon watched on television. Simon once said Disney's *Fantasia* was "a bit too scary for Asher," and he described the scary parts. I asked if it was too scary for him. "No," he replied, "only for babies" (4,2,0). Another time, Simon did not think Asher should watch an episode of "The Smurfs"—although maybe when he was 4 or 5 or 6—because it was too scary (4,2,13). And Simon also did not want to show Asher a picture of a fire because Asher might not know that it was not real (4,5,2).

Simon's protective attitude toward Asher was genuine. And although Simon rarely had the chance, he did act on his attitude. Once he carefully picked a crumb from Asher's face, explaining that it was near his eye (4,1,17). Another time, Asher was in his infant seat with a toy safely pinned to his sleeve so he could move it; Simon unfastened the pin, explaining that he did not want Asher to stick himself (4,1,24). Finally, Simon was making the last touches on a diaper-box house for Asher, explaining that he was just cutting off one more jagged edge because he did not want Asher to hurt himself (4,5,4).

Feelings and Attitudes Matter

Simon had a wide range of positive feelings and attitudes about Asher, which I would probably have overlooked if I had held traditional preconceptions about children's responses to a baby brother or sister. And it is noteworthy that I drew much of my evidence from situations in which Simon was not even interacting with Asher, a significant departure from most other studies on early sibling relationships (but see Dunn and Kendrick 1982a, chap. 4, for another exception). Clearly, investigators who limit themselves to strictly observational measures risk overlooking potentially valuable sources of information.

Simon did not necessarily express his positive feelings and attitudes directly to Asher. Surely a boy must translate brotherly emotions into behavior to enact the brotherly role—perhaps so, yet all the behaviors do not have to be directed to the sibling, just as parental behaviors—such as earning a salary, grocery shopping, or meeting with teachers—are not always directed to the child. Besides, expressions of acceptance, identification, affection, help, and protection were important elements of Simon's experience as a brother, and such positive feelings and attitudes about Asher were potentially powerful motives for Simon's behavior.

Simon's acceptance of Asher may have been presaged by his enthusiasm about the prospect of a new baby. More important, Simon readily incorporated the baby into his concept of our family, revising his concept from threesome to foursome even before Asher was born. But a family of four consists of several subsystems, a fact that Simon apparently understood. He assumed that in certain circumstances we would maintain our original constellation as a threesome and grasped that the baby's arrival would create a division, which is easily blurred when there is only one child in the family, between parents and children. After Asher was born, Simon readily accepted the new division and even occasionally aligned himself with his baby brother against us.

Simon's acceptance of Asher must be contrasted with often-reported anecdotes about young children who reject a new brother or sister (Field and Reite 1984, Freud 1909/1955, Volterra 1984). Yet parents and researchers should be careful about interpreting isolated remarks such as, "Mommy, take the baby back to the hospital." It is true that a short, direct statement is often more striking than the types of evidence I have reviewed here, but occasional negative remarks by young children do not mean that they generally reject the baby any more than occasional negative remarks by exasperated parents do. Acceptance that is demonstrated richly in various ways probably reflects truer feelings than one or two comments made at stressful moments.

Acceptance and rejection are not simply opposite emotional responses to the new baby. Acceptance also encompasses restructuring the family concept, a cognitive task that may pose several challenges for young children. They may not understand the family or family roles well enough to be able to incorporate the new baby into their family concept, and the necessary effort to solve the various cognitive problems, as well as incomplete or incorrect solutions, might also elicit emotional responses. Children who, for example, do not grasp the coordination of social roles may not realize that a woman can simultaneously be a mother to two children, which might prove more threatening than imagined loss of attention. Similarly, children who cannot coordinate part-whole relationships might misunderstand what the baby means to the family as a whole; although the baby creates a new family system and new subsystems, it does not destroy the existing ones.

Real acceptance of a baby brother or sister is more than the absence of rejection, but it is also more than a cognitive achievement. Real acceptance implies positive feelings and attitudes. Even children say that positive emotions are one of the functions that families serve, and most kindergarteners consider love to be a defining characteristic of a family (Gilby and Pederson 1982). Simon also believed family members love each other. And even before he become a brother, he expected to love the baby, an expectation that was realized afterward by his genuine affection for Asher.

Naturally we were pleased about Simon's feelings, and we tried to encourage them in a variety of ways. At first we explicitly told Simon to show his affection and, later when no encouragement was necessary, we still praised him for doing so. We also interpreted Asher's behavior as affectionate. Even without behavioral evidence, we told Simon that Asher loved him, an idea that Simon gradually accepted. Our demonstrativeness to Simon and Asher, which reflected our own deep feelings for the boys and was not meant for instructional purposes, nonetheless provided a continually present model.

Most children believe that family members are supposed to do things for each other and help each other (Pederson and Gilby 1986). Simon thus expected to do things for Asher, whom he considered part of our family. The adults Simon knew supported his expectations by telling him that he would help. Simon's willingness to help with the baby was apparent even before Asher was born. To some extent, his enthusiasm reflected a general desire to assist with adult tasks. He often volunteered to help—and his volunteering often grew to insistence—when Bev or I cleaned up, repaired something, went grocery shopping, prepared a meal, or did any other household task. But in the end, he did not directly help with his baby brother as much as he expected to. Still he was helpful in other ways. Before Asher was born, Simon participated in our preparations. He suggested that we keep a variety of items for the baby, offered to share his old clothes and his toys, and talked about how we would protect the baby from harm. After Asher was born, Simon did share, although he was understandably selective, and he did watch out for Asher's safety.

Simon's repeated offers to share his room with Asher reflected helpfulness, acceptance, and, perhaps, an understanding of the division between parents and children. The insistence about his room also demonstrated that he wanted the baby nearby. Simon may have simply wanted to stake a proprietary claim, or he may have wanted the baby to be like him in yet another way. Regardless, such interest was probably the very foundation of Simon's relationship with his baby brother.

Chapter 8

A Brother's Responsiveness

Most relationships can be characterized as either reciprocal or complementary (Dunn 1983). Child-child relationships are reciprocal: the partners are similar in various ways (such as in status, ability, perspective, and understanding) so they contribute equally to the interaction. By contrast, child-adult relationships are complementary: the partners are dissimilar in significant ways, so the behavior of each partner differs from but complements that of the other. Sibling relationships are at once both reciprocal—because of shared history, interests, and emotional intensity—and complementary—because of differences associated with an age gap. Put differently, interactions between brothers and sisters are a "blend of behaviors comprising adult and peer systems" (Pepler et al. 1982).

Reciprocity in a sibling relationship is achieved only gradually since there is a general progression from asymmetry, when the younger child is just born, to relative symmetry, as both children pass early childhood, and presumably to complete symmetry, as they approach adulthood (Abramovitch et al., 1979, 1980, Dunn and Munn 1985, Lamb 1978a, 1978b, Pelletier-Stiefel et al. 1986). Initially the two children behave differently toward each other; for example, a baby may simply watch an older brother or sister, but the older child may start positive interactions like pat-a-cake or negative ones that involve yelling or hitting. Such asymmetry probably results from disparities in competence and from role expectations associated with birth order. True, the relationship changes as the disparities narrow. During the second year of life, the baby gradually directs more social behavior toward the older sibling, becomes increasingly nurturant and protective, and participates more actively in sibling conflict.

Thus, research conducted when the younger child is a toddler cannot necessarily answer questions about the origins of sibling relationships. A child interacting with, say, an 8-month-old brother or sister will display skills that have been honed for many months. Besides, children generally respond differently to infants under a year and to toddlers (Whiting and Edwards 1988). Only a few sibling studies have included babies less than 6 months old, and most of these were restricted to a handful of relatively brief observations during the baby's first year (Dunn and Kendrick 1982a, Gottlieb and Mendelson 1990, Kramer 1989, Kreppner et al. 1982, Murphy 1988, R. B. Stewart et al. 1987). Thus, we know little about the early sibling relationship, about children's initial skills for interacting with a baby brother or sister, and about the development of specific skills.

Besides not providing data, the sibling literature does not even provide a useful framework for addressing these questions. Luckily the parent-child literature does, and it is instructive to examine a preschooler's earliest interactions with a baby brother or sister by comparing and contrasting them with parental responsiveness. Responsiveness, an essential aspect of sensitive parenting, can be defined as contingent, appropriate, and consistent reactions to a baby's needs and signals (Lamb and Easterbrooks 1981). A responsive parent reads the signals—the cries, the coos, the smiles—and meets the baby's needs—for soothing, nourishment, and so on. Responsive parenting is important both practically and theoretically, since it may be a prerequisite for the development of secure attachments. Parents who are sensitive to their baby's needs become effective sources of comfort when the baby is upset and provide a base for exploration at calmer moments (Ainsworth et al. 1978, Bretherton and Waters 1985).

Usually young North American children are not called upon to meet a baby's needs—that is a role reserved for parents or other caregivers—and if they were, they probably could not respond contingently, consistently, or appropriately. Yet infants do form attachments to their older brothers and sisters (Dunn and Kendrick 1982a, Howe and Ross 1990, Samuels 1982, R. B. Stewart 1983). Perhaps such attachments result from day-to-day contact. Alternatively, young children might have suitable skills for interacting with a baby or might easily acquire them. Indeed children in most cultures are nurturant to infants younger than 1 year old (Whiting and Edwards 1988). And my observations provided clues about how Simon's interactional competence developed in tandem with Asher's. Since Simon defined himself as a big brother and had feelings and attitudes consistent with his new role, it is not surprising that he successfully learned how to enact that role.

Crying and Fretting

Defining responsiveness as reactions to a baby's needs and signals raises important questions about how Simon responded to Asher's behavior. Here, I consider Simon's reactions to Asher's cries and Simon's attempts to soothe Asher. Crying is the most obvious and arguably most powerful signal at a baby's disposal (Lester and Boukydis 1985). Simplistically it means "change something." Babies may be hungry, understimulated, overstimulated, tired, wet, hot, cold, or in pain, or they may just need contact comfort. And although the reason for crying is not always clear, crying usually elicits adult attention. Most parents try to discover and alleviate the source of distress, yet some respond less promptly or less successfully than others and some even abusively (S. M. Bell and Ainsworth 1972, Frodi 1985, Grossmann et al. 1985).

Three types of explanations have been proposed as to why parents respond to their baby's cry (A. D. Murray 1979, 1985). According to the first, the cry is an innate releaser of parental behavior. Like other attachment behaviors, crying presumably evolved to elicit nurturance and protection from caregivers (Ainsworth 1969, Bowlby 1969). If so, adults' ability to respond to crying would have had to evolve concurrently and might conceivably be controlled by a neurally based innate releasing mechanism (Eibl-Eibesfeldt 1975). But babies' cries vary in meaning, depending on context and intensity, and they elicit a range of responses—some comforting, some otherwise—so they are more reasonably viewed as "graded signals" that affect caregivers' motivational states (Wilson 1975).

According to the second interpretation, parents respond to cries for the same reason that they respond to any other noxious sound: to reduce aversive stimulation (Ostwald 1963). But this would explain avoidance of the baby better than approach to alleviate distress. According to the last explanation, the cry elicits both empathy, an involuntary emotional response, and altruism, an attempt to reduce the baby's distress. Awareness of the infant's state presumably supports an altruistic goal (comforting the baby) over an egoistic one (reducing one's own empathic reaction) (Hoffman 1975). And an altruistic response will occur if the cry is sufficiently intense to activate the caregiver's distress but not intense enough to elicit avoidance or aggression (Tomkins 1963).

The empathy model of adults' responses to babies' cries has received the most empirical support (A. D. Murray 1985), but aspects of all three models may be valid. Thus, adults are more aroused by infants' cries than by other annoying sounds, which is consistent with both releaser and empathy models, and the relative importance of each model may differ depending on the adults' experience. For unseasoned caregivers, more strident, urgent cries elicit less sympathy, consistent with the aversiveness model. Other factors also probably influence individuals' responses to a baby's cry. Socialization experiences may be crucial, since role demands might motivate parents, especially mothers, to respond to a crying baby under their care. And experience with a particular baby may also be important, since the success or failure of prior interventions might temper current reactions to the baby's cries (Goldberg 1977, Lamb and Easterbrooks 1981).

The majority of firstborns dislike hearing their baby brother or sister cry (Murphy 1988, R. B. Stewart et al. 1987). Yet although the adult literature provides a useful framework, it is still premature to decide which, if any, of the available explanations best accounts for young children's reactions. Preschoolers would presumably respond emotionally to a baby's distress if the cry were an innate releaser or a graded biological signal, but the aversiveness model might be more appropriate to account for their reactions, especially since they probably lack experience with crying babies. The empathy-altruism model may be irrelevant to young children who have limited perspective-taking abilities (R. B. Stewart and Marvin 1984, Howe and Ross 1990). Yet preschoolers might empathize intuitively since they cry quite readily themselves. Role demands—either to help the baby or to leave the baby alone—could conceivably influence young children's responses to their sibling's distress (Berman and Goodman 1984). And preschoolers may acquire effective strategies for coping with a baby brother's or sister's distress through experience. Clearly more information is called for.

Cries Are Upsetting
Before Simon was a brother, he became visibly upset and defensively covered his ears in response to Charles's crying (3,10,13; 3,11,18). Simon typically did not like intense stimulation and frequently put his hands over his ears if someone was vacuuming. Once, he requested that I turn off the car radio, which reminded me of the time he had covered his ears when baby Charles was crying. I asked if he found the crying too loud or if he did not like to hear Charles sad. "Because it's too loud," Simon responded vehemently. "When Charles cries, it's the loudest" (4,0,0).

Shortly after Asher was born, Simon covered his ears while complaining about the crying and, answering the same question, said that he did not like the noise (4,0,27). In the ensuing months, Asher's crying continued to upset Simon, who still occasionally covered his ears if Asher could not be soothed (4,2,23). Simon sometimes complained calmly that the crying bothered him (4,2,7) but at other times became vociferously upset, as when he was unable to escape Asher's crying in the car and shrieked that it was hurting his ears, which obviously exacerbated the problem (4,2,21).

Asher's crying powerfully motivated Simon, and one of Simon's responses—covering his ears, ostensibly to avoid the noise—was as consistent with the aversive model as imaginable. But Asher did not cry very loudly, especially at 3 weeks. Besides, Simon responded far more intensely to Asher's or Charles's cries than to a vacuum cleaner or a radio. Thus, I suspect that Simon did not really understand why he was disturbed by the cry—perhaps only because he had less control over the crying but perhaps because he was responding to a biological signal. Whatever the reason for Simon's reaction to the cry, Simon often tried to soothe Asher.

Soothing the Baby

Before Asher was born, we frequently joked that babies do only four things, and one of them was cry. Simon once replied that he would try to make the baby feel better (3,8,18). But another time he admitted that he did not know what to do and was upset by the prospect of not being able to figure it out (3,10,6). Yet by the time Asher arrived, Simon had observed a number of ways to soothe a crying baby, like holding, carrying, feeding, talking, and distracting. Perhaps more important, he had practiced soothing techniques. He tried to soothe Charles by rocking him and softly repeating his name (3,8,5). Another time he held him, called to him, gently patted his head, and kissed him (3,8,24). And he tried to distract him by showing him a toy, a balloon, and a tape recorder (3,10,13; 3,10,30; 3,11,18). Simon had also soothed his cousin Michael by patting his cheeks and giving him a bottle (3,10,10).

Several times Simon needed instructions about how to calm Charles. I once suggested that Simon try softly calling Charles's name and another time that he try distracting Charles (3,8,5; 3,11,17). Simon was clearly eager to stop the crying and responded to the instructions well. Simon received his first lesson in how to soothe Asher during the drive home from the hospital. Bev tried to calm Asher by rocking his carseat and having him suck her finger, but he cried most of the way. Then she told Simon that I always tried to quiet a baby by singing, "Ooh, ooh" (sustained, modulated, soft, and low pitched). It worked for them. Simon learned an effective soothing technique, and his efforts were immediately rewarded when Asher stopped crying (4,0,7).

Asher was a predictable, easy-to-soothe baby who cried mainly from hunger or fatigue. Early on Bev and I usually attended to Asher as soon as he started to fret, so Simon rarely had a chance to soothe him. Yet Simon often witnessed our responsiveness and concern, which quite possibly bolstered his. He also overheard or participated in problem-solving conversations about why Asher might be upset.

> Father: What happened on the way home?
> Simon: [Asher] was crying.
> Father: . . . Why do you think he was crying?
> Simon: I don't know.
> Father: Do you think maybe he was hungry?
> Simon: Maybe. Maybe he wanted to be patted on the back (taped 4,0,7).

Such conversations, especially those between Bev and me, could well have alerted Simon that it was necessary to interpret Asher's cries and to choose an appropriate soothing strategy.

Simon periodically tried to calm Asher but did not always succeed, which could have deterred his efforts (Goldberg 1977, Lamb and Easterbrooks 1981); yet his failures actually impelled him to try harder, even if doing so was inappropriate. Unsuccessfully attempting to distract Asher from crying, Simon might gradually become more and more boisterous. And apparently insensitive to Asher's negative feedback, Simon would be oblivious to making things worse (4,1,17) (Whiting and Edwards 1988).

Predictably Asher changed at 2 months. He stayed up for longer periods, which meant that Simon had more time to interact with him, and he fretted more insistently, which may have been why Simon attended to him. Whatever the reason, Simon tried to soothe Asher more often than before, yet he had much to learn and he continued to benefit from imitation. The following exchanges all occurred when Asher was crying:

> Simon: It's all right. It's all right. (delayed imitation of Father) (4,2,4).
> Father: Aah, aah, Asher. Aah, aah, Asher. . . .
> Simon: Aah, aah, Basher. Aah, aah, Masher. . . . (direct imitation of soothing and delayed imitation of Father's rhyming Asher's name) (4,2,9).
> Simon: Asher aah. Asher aah. (delayed imitation of Father or response to instructions) (4,2,18).

Simon eventually assumed that he knew how to soothe Asher. Simon once offered to help Bev's mother when Asher started to cry. She rhetorically asked Simon if he thought she knew what to do. He simply explained that he knew better what Asher wanted (4,2,20).

Yet Simon still benefited from his grandmother's experience. Four days later I was unsuccessfully trying to soothe Asher, so Simon suggested that it was time to "stroller" him—ride Asher around the apartment as Bev's mother had done (4,2,24).

Simon also invented soothing techniques or at least adapted them. He once drew on his own experience to devise a strategy for calming Asher. Asher cried when I accidentally caught his foot in his infant seat. Simon got his favorite blanket, explaining that it would make Asher feel better. "Here Asher," Simon said in a modulated voice while gently stroking Asher's face. "This will make you feel better. There. Are you all right?" (4,2,19). Another time Simon extended the distraction strategy that he had learned before he became a brother. He was in the kitchen with Asher, who was in his infant seat. When Asher started to fret, Simon successfully distracted him for a couple of minutes by showing him toys and kitchen implements. Eventually Asher resumed fretting, so Simon pulled Asher's seat into the dining room. He explained afterward that he thought Asher would be happier there, which, as it happened, was true (4,3,2).

Simon benefited from instructions about how to soothe Asher. This was probably truer about how to give a pacifier than about any other soothing technique, perhaps because Simon was so ambivalent about it. Simon was once trying to calm Asher by saying "Aah, aah, Asher . . ." and by rocking Asher's chair, but Asher did not calm down, and Simon began shaking the chair a bit too vigorously. I then suggested that Asher needed the pacifier, and Simon volunteered to give it to him. I first told Simon to wiggle the pacifier in Asher's mouth to get him to suck, but Simon did not succeed. Next I demonstrated and Simon tried again. This time Asher actively spat out the pacifier, which prompted Simon's comment that Asher did not want it (4,2,12). Yet despite counterexamples, Simon successfully gave Asher the pacifier at other times, even when the two of them were alone (4,3,6).

Simon's final strategy for dealing with Asher's distress was a backstop measure, presumably because he understood that attending to Asher was really Bev's and my responsibility—part of our role definitions. He often simply mentioned that the baby was crying, but sometimes specifically asked one of us to take care of the problem, especially when he was busy or if his own attempts failed. Asher once started to cry when Simon was playing with my computer. Simon tried to soothe him, calling for me at the same time, and, the moment I came, Simon returned to the computer—a far more interesting pastime (4,2,10).

In time Bev and I did not always respond promptly to Asher's cries. Depending on their intensity and cause, we might give him time to calm himself. But Simon castigated us for not responding quickly enough—for not fulfilling our responsibility. Asher once began to cry while I was helping Simon dress, and I continued what I was doing. "Don't you hear Asher?" demanded Simon, who was obviously upset. And later that day, Simon admonished Bev, "Why don't you do something [about the crying] right away?" (4,4,4). Another time we were letting Asher cry in bed, since nothing calmed him. "If you don't do something, I will," Simon huffed as he want to give Asher the pacifier (4,4,8). We tried to explain why we did not always respond to Asher right away, but our explanations probably sounded hollow, especially since we often did not heed our own advice.

Simon:	(to parents when Asher was crying in his crib) Who's going to deal with Asher?
Mother:	No one.
Father:	Asher has to deal with himself.
Mother:	When a baby gets a little bit older, he has to learn how ⍳ fall asleep by himself, even if he cries a bit.
Simon:	. . . But isn't someone going to give him the pacifier?
Mother:	No. But it's nice of you to suggest it (4,4,28).

Simon may have learned a reasonable lesson—but not Asher. He continued to cry, and I eventually gave him the pacifier and rocked him to calm him.

Sometimes Simon may have been egoistically motivated to escape the sound of Asher's cry, but there were many reasons to believe that he was genuinely concerned about his baby brother. First, Simon was unselfishly willing to interrupt his own play so Asher could be soothed. Second, instead of trying to avoid the noise, Simon frequently approached to help, even if someone else was available. And if Simon did leave the room, he would likely return with something that might distract or placate Asher (4,2,19). Third, Simon's concern was not obviously related to the level of Asher's distress. Simon responded nurturantly not only to loud crying but also to fretting. He also occasionally insisted that we do something even if Asher's crying was barely audible from another room (4,4,7). Last, Simon was even concerned when he simply imagined Asher's distress. He seemed worried that Asher's circumcision might hurt (4,0,10). And right after a fairly traumatic incident—going to the hospital to have a split eyebrow sutured—Simon thought about Asher and spontaneously said he hoped the same thing did not happen to him (4,5,1).

Taking the Initiative for Social Interaction

For most of the time that parents spend with their new baby, they are probably feeding, diapering, bathing, dressing, soothing, or otherwise attending to the baby's needs. And caregiving, an essential part of the parental role, sets the stage for social interaction. Unlike parents, older brothers and sisters in Western society do not usually have role-related responsibilities that ensure social contact with a baby, especially with a young baby. Simon interacted directly with Asher only minimally during this study—on average, for less than 10 percent of his nondaycare waking time (5.1 hours per week)—and the two boys were together but not involved for only 18 percent (10.3 hours per week).

Table 8.1 shows the amount of time that Simon spent in various activities with Asher from month to month. When Asher was 21 days old (4,0,24), Simon interacted with him overall for 4.18 hours per week; his involvement decreased a month later (4,1,20) to 2.88 hours per week, but in subsequent months increased to 5.67 (4,3,19) and 7.66 (4,5,1) hours per week. If anything, such totals overestimate the time that Simon and Asher spent with each other, since mealtime interactions, which accounted for most of their contact, were not continuous, and the week-to-week fluctuations were due largely to changes in how much time Asher spent at the table during meals. But by the time Asher was 5 months old, Simon also hung around Asher quite a lot. Finally, note that Simon spent virtually no time caregiving, even if he did occasionally respond to Asher's distress. It may be surprising that Simon interacted with Asher so little during this time. But why did Simon interact with him at all, and what prompted their social encounters?

Watching Asher

A brief visit to any hospital nursery provides ample evidence that adults and children enjoy looking at infants, especially a new member of their own family. Simon was similarly attracted to babies even before he became a brother. He might simply watch or greet an unfamiliar baby (Berman et al. 1977, Melson and Fogel 1982), but he did more with babies he knew; he wanted to hold them, talk to them, play with them, and so on.

Simon was interested in most babies he saw, usually at least enough to approach them. Perhaps he was attracted by the novelty of unfamiliar babies or by changes in those he had not seen for a while. But this could not explain why he was attracted to Asher. Simon was also interested in babies with whom Bev or I interacted.

Table 8.1
Total Time Simon Spent on Each Type of Activity Interacting with Asher (Hours Per Week)

Activity	Month, Simon's Age, and Asher's Age				Mean
	January (4,0,24; 0,0,21)	February (4,1,20; 0,1,17)	April (4,3,19; 0,3,16)	May (4,5,1; 0,4,28)	
Meals	2.75	1.19	3.58	3.58	2.78
Hanging around	.17	.94	.93	2.58	1.16
Play	.25	.50	1.08	1.11	.74
Baby care	.67	.08	.08	.31	.29
Television	.17	.17	.00	.08	.11
Care	.17	.00	.00	.00	.04
Total	4.18	2.88	5.67	7.66	5.10

Note: The ages indicated for Simon and Asher are for the middle of the diary week.

Perhaps he wanted to prevent us from interacting with them because he was slightly jealous of our attention. Presumably this could also account for his interest in Asher. Yet there are other possible explanations of Simon's interest in babies: he may have wanted their attention and simply watched them as a first step in getting it, much as he would have watched a group of children before trying to join the fun. Or he may have wanted to be part of our activity, just as he would have wanted to make pasta or vacuum the carpet if that was what we were doing.

Yet Simon delighted in just watching Asher, often without trying to interact with him or help care for him and even when Asher was asleep. Simon also enthusiastically shared his observations, indicating how much Asher pleased him. The day after coming home from the hospital, Asher was sleeping in his crib and Simon wanted to touch him through the bars. I told Simon not to disturb Asher, so Simon simply watched, gleefully commenting when Asher moved (4,0,8). Another time Simon watched with enjoyment when Bev was making Asher laugh and told her to continue when she stopped. Rather than interrupt their play to join in, Simon was satisfied with vicarious pleasure from Asher's amusement (4,4,4).

One reason adults like to watch babies is quite simple: babies are cute. They possess a set of babyness features—a round head that is relatively large for the body, a round face with protruding cheeks, a high protruding forehead, large and widely spaced eyes, a small round nose, a small chin, and short heavy limbs—that according to ethologists elicit an "attraction-to-babies" response (Fullard and Reilling 1976, Lorenz 1935/1970, Maier et al. 1984, Power et al. 1982, Sternglanz et al. 1977). Indeed adults prefer pictures of babies over pictures of adults, and their preferences are predicted by differences in babyness. Although there are no data from preschoolers, 9-month-olds and children from 7 years on also prefer pictures of babies (Berman 1986, M. Lewis and Brooks 1974).

Simon possibly enjoyed watching his baby brother because he found him cute, a characteristic he often attributed to him by 11 weeks. Simon was once helping dress Asher in new clothes, repeatedly telling us how cute the clothes were and telling Asher how cute he was (4,2,20). And when Simon saw Asher in the tub for the first time in several weeks, he smiled broadly, admired Asher, and said how cute he was in the bath (4,3,3). Simon could very well have been imitating us, since Bev and I often told both boys that they were "cute," "delicious," "special," and so on. Yet even so, Simon's appreciation of Asher was heartfelt. Certainly any parent can identify with Simon's response to these common situations.

Can I Hold the Baby?

Before Asher was born, Simon inevitably asked to hold familiar babies every time he encountered them, which is a common response to an infant, even for an adult. Perhaps Simon asked to hold babies for the inherent pleasure. Alternatively, he may have wanted to do something that he thought was grown-up or to control an obviously prized "object." In Asher's case, he may have wanted to claim the baby as his own. Just as we arrived home from the hospital, Simon wanted to hold Asher—immediately controlling or claiming—and stand up holding him, an especially grown-up thing to do (4,0,7). In the ensuing month, Simon rarely asked to hold Asher again, and he did limit himself to appropriate contexts—burping Asher, listening to bedtime songs, or watching television (4,0,14; 4,0,17; 4,0,26).

But Asher eventually outgrew Simon, which eliminated Simon's option of holding him. I once put Asher in Simon's lap for a photo and realized that Simon had not held Asher for several weeks. After the picture, Simon wanted Asher to stay in his lap, but Simon quickly discovered that Asher was too heavy (4,1,21). One of the last times Simon held his baby brother, I was lying on my back, raising and lowering Asher in the air, and Simon wanted a turn with the baby. Although I did not let Simon try, I did put Asher in his lap. And although Simon announced that he was big enough to carry Asher, Simon eventually started to squirm because he was quite uncomfortable just sitting with him. By then Asher began fretting, perhaps because he was uncomfortable from the way Simon was holding him, so Bev distracted Simon with an invitation to help in the kitchen (4,2,13).

I Want Him Right Next to Me

Although Simon was at first so intent on carrying Asher, virtually none of their interactions took place while Asher was in his arms or on his lap; indeed, Simon held Asher for less than ten minutes during Asher's first five months of life. Yet the two boys did interact with each other in other situations, especially when Asher was in his infant seat.

The day after Asher came home from the hospital, we put him in his infant seat at the table while we ate lunch. As would happen repeatedly, Simon wanted Asher right next to him, and we gladly obliged. Throughout the meal, Simon leaned over to admire Asher and to amuse him, with chucks and pats (4,0,8). Since Asher's schedule initially did not mesh with ours, he did not join us again at the table until two weeks later, but by then Simon was no longer satisfied with simply having Asher next to him; Simon also wanted Asher's attention (4,0,22). Several weeks later Simon was demonstratively upset when Asher could not look at him because the infant seat was facing me. Still, it was simple enough to placate Simon; I turned the infant seat around, so Asher faced him (4,1,11).

Usually Simon directly asked that Asher sit right next to him, but Simon sometimes attributed his own wishes to his brother. Simon was once playing with Asher before lunch, patting him and talking to him. "Asher says he's going to sit next to me," Simon announced (4,0,27). A week later Asher was fretting in his seat at the table. "He wants to be next to his big brother," Simon explained (4,1,3).

Simon occasionally asked to have Asher near him for apparently self-serving reasons—as a play object—that ignored Asher's needs. For example, he once wanted us to awaken Asher to bring him to the breakfast table, and we had to explain that we do not wake a sleeping baby (4,0,24). Yet at other times Simon did consider Asher. Once, Simon specifically said that he did not want Asher next to him because Asher might catch the germs from his cough (4,0,30). And Simon remembered the lesson about sleeping babies. He said we should bring Asher's infant seat, which happened to be in the car, up to the apartment; he wanted Asher next to him at dinner but only if Asher was awake (4,2,4).

By 9 weeks Asher had developed a will of his own, and Simon was not pleased about losing control. Simon, as usual, wanted Asher next to him at the breakfast table. Asher was looking at me at one point, so I started to talk to him. Simon then immediately wanted Asher's attention and manually tried to turn Asher's head around, although Asher clearly resisted. I told Simon not to force Asher, but Simon turned Asher's head anyway and began talking to him. Asher watched him briefly and then looked back at me, so Simon tried to repeat the maneuver. Admonishing Simon, I suggested that he simply call Asher, but Simon, upset by then, objected that Asher had turned to me even though I had not called. I said that Asher was old enough to move his own head, and Bev rhetorically asked if Simon always liked to look in the same place. Simon resumed eating, and Asher eventually looked at him on his own. "You see," we said by way of encouragement. "He's looking at you now" (4,2,2).

By the time Asher was 3 months old, Simon expected him at the table during our meals and was upset if Asher did not join us. But Simon spent more time interacting with Asher than eating, so one evening we decided to let Asher play on the floor during dinner. When Simon asked to have Asher next to him, we said that Asher was fine where he was, but Simon argued, "It isn't nice for us to eat with Asher on the floor." Easily persuaded, I moved Asher to his usual place—a member of the family at the dinner table—and left him there, even though, predictably, Simon started talking to him and snuggling him (4,3,2).

Simon really wanted his baby brother nearby, sometimes even during activities that Simon normally did alone with Bev or me. He asked to include Asher not only at the table practically every day but also in other situations: watching television, playing, sitting in the back seat of the car, taking a bath, listening to a story, and cuddling in bed (4,0,21–4,4,24). He also periodically suggested that we take Asher with us to a variety of places: grandparents' apartment to watch a video movie, my office to play with Judy, Israel for a hypothetical trip, the barber shop, synagogue, Albany for a planned visit, daycare to join him for lunch, Florida for an upcoming vacation, and grandparents' house for dinner (4,0,27–4,3,1).

Simon's requests for Asher's company help explain why Simon frequently approached when Bev was breast-feeding Asher, when I carried Asher in the Snugli, or when we were otherwise involved with Asher in caregiving or play. The conventional interpretation would be that Simon was jealous of Asher over our attention, and rivalry may have spurred Simon some of the time. But not always. Simon often wanted Asher nearby even if we were not present or during one of Simon's own activities. Another plausible interpretation is that Simon was jealous of us over Asher's attention. When Asher was nursing or asleep in the Snugli, Simon's social bids—patting, kissing, and calling—were in fact often directed to Asher, not to us, and Simon wanted Asher, not us, to look at him at the table.

Simon was once so interested in Asher's attention that he was willing to let him cry. Simon was watching Asher crying in his crib. I was about to pick up Asher to soothe him. "He wants to look at me," Simon said. "Just leave him. Let's see what he does." I lifted Asher anyway, assuring Simon that even though Asher liked to look at him, he did not want to just then (4,1,4).

Simon was also satisfied with Asher's attention, even if they were not interacting with each other. And Asher had indeed begun to monitor Simon—to watch him intently—whether or not Simon responded to him (Abramovitch et al. 1979, Lamb 1978a). Simon often invited me to watch television next to him, particularly when I was holding Asher. If I watched the program, Simon usually continued watching as well, but if I started to interact with Asher, Simon also attended to the baby—kissing Asher, stroking his face, and talking to him, at least for a while. Yet sometimes Simon simply asked me to turn Asher toward him, and Simon would continue watching television. I once suggested that if he wanted Asher facing him, he should face back. "Why?" Simon asked quite sincerely. "He can face my ear" (4,1,22).

Simon's constant requests for Asher to be next to him and his unflagging effort to attract Asher's attention ensured not only that Simon had contact with Asher but also that he had the chance to learn how to interact effectively with him. Thus, Simon's motivation to have Asher nearby and to receive Asher's attention, which led to their earliest interactions, was actually the foundation of their eventual relationship.

Asher's Smile and Laugh

Babies' cries command attention, rally support, and signal that something needs to be changed. They dramatically and bluntly communicate "come here" or "stop what you're doing." Babies' smiles are also powerful signals that shape caregivers' behavior. They communicate in a distinctly human way "stay here" or "continue what you're doing." And perhaps because smiles so clearly communicate what babies like, most adults go to considerable lengths to make babies smile. The ability to recognize a smile develops early (LaBarbera et al. 1976, Odom and Lemond 1972, Oster 1981). Even infants seem to prefer smiling faces over neutral ones. And undoubtedly every 4-year-old can easily recognize and interpret smiles. But it remains to be seen how babies smiles might affect a young child's behavior.

Two types of smiling are distinguishable in young infants (Emde et al. 1976, Gewirtz 1965). The first, endogenous smiling, is sometimes mistakenly attributed to gas because it occurs spontaneously without an external cause, indeed often when the baby is asleep. The baby's mouth spontaneously turns up at the corners, but the expression appears flat since, unlike a real smile, it does not involve the whole face. Endogenous smiling declines over the first weeks of life as social smiling increases. Initially the baby may smile in response to a variety of visual, auditory, or tactile stimuli. But by 1 or 2 months of age, smiling is confined mainly to social situations, perhaps because social interaction involves coordinated, multimodal stimulation that is contingent upon the baby's own behavior.

When Asher was about 2 weeks old, Simon noticed him smile (4,0,19). I assume the smile was endogenous, but Simon accepted it at face value and was clearly excited. In the ensuing weeks, he looked out for other smiles and either saw or, more probably, imagined them. Simon once kissed Asher just before I entered the room. "Look, Daddy," he told me as he was about to kiss him again. "He smiles when I kiss him." In fact, Asher had not smiled, but Simon was still enthusiastic (4,0,22).

Simon apparently made Asher smile when he was 1 month old, and Simon readily learned what caused the smile. He was kissing Asher's nose and forehead and patting his face. Eventually he stroked the side of Asher's mouth, and Asher smiled, which obviously pleased Simon. A bit later he wanted to show me so he stroked the side of Asher's mouth. Asher's expression changed slightly—barely a smile—but Simon was still pleased. "Did you see, Daddy?" he asked excitedly (4,1,3). Over the next days Simon repeatedly tried his new trick, both for himself and for others. And everyone, including Simon, invariably laughed with pleasure when Asher actually smiled. Anyone who has ever interacted with a young baby can certainly identify with Simon's efforts to make Asher smile and with his joy over success.

I was struck by how effectively Asher's smile shaped Simon's behavior. One day Simon made Asher smile by patting his cheeks. "Look," I said, "he's smiling." Simon was pleased and resumed patting his brother who continued to smile. "Look, Mommy! I found another way to make him laugh [sic]. You bend your fingers like this and pat him here," said Simon, showing Bev exactly how he had patted his brother (4,1,7).

In the ensuing days, it became easier and easier to make Asher smile, much to Simon's delight, and Simon continued to demonstrate or mention Asher's smiles. "I sure am glad I have a brother who smiles so much," he said, acknowledging his own pleasure (4,1,17). More important, Asher's smiles sustained Simon's interactions with him, since Simon repeated any action that initially elicited a smile. "I was twitching his lip," Simon reported one day, "and he was doing great big smiles" (4,1,24).

By the time Asher was 2 months old, Simon's interactions with him were not one-sided. Asher continued to monitor Simon intently, and we often told Simon that Asher was smiling or looking at him, comments that possibly reinforced their relationship. And as is usual for mothers of a second baby, Bev obviously encouraged Simon's interactions with Asher (Walz and Rich 1983). Once, Asher was staring at Simon, who was watching "Sesame Street." "He watches you all the time," Bev remarked. "He's smiling at you. He thinks you're pretty neat. . . . You get the most smiles out of Asher" (4,2,1).

By 10 weeks of age, Asher acquired other skills—laughing and reaching for fingers and faces—that delighted Simon and fostered social interaction. Asher's laugh particularly encouraged boisterous physical play. I was once tending to Asher on our bed. Simon came over and started singing to his baby brother, "Baa, Baa, Black Sheep," and a variation, "Asher, Asher, little Asher." Simon then straddled Asher and, patting him, bounced up and down on the bed. Asher laughed over and over, and so did we (4,2,24). Simon's singing was probably delayed imitation of me, since I had earlier entertained Asher with the alphabet song to the same tune, but straddling and bouncing were clearly Simon's invention, perhaps a precursor to the rough-and-tumble play that would emerge months later and that the two boys still enjoy now.

At other times Simon did imitate how to make Asher laugh. Bev used to blow on Asher's chest with a "horsey" sound. Simon was once intrigued by Bev's game and eagerly took over. Asher giggled each time Simon blew on his chest, which made us all laugh and sustained Simon's behavior. Predictably, Asher's enjoyment peaked; he stopped giggling and eventually began to scowl. Even so, Simon continued, unresponsive to the change in Asher's mood, so we ended the game by telling Simon that Asher had had enough (4,2,26). Here, as on other occasions, Simon's behavior was influenced more by positive, than by negative, feedback from Asher. And Bev or I had to highlight Asher's negative signals.

Simon eventually acquired a useful bag of tricks—sometimes by chance but mainly by imitation—to make Asher smile or laugh. Simon copied the way we exercised Asher's legs (4,3,29), played peek-a-boo (although he had trouble getting it right, even when Asher was approaching 5 months of age [4,4,20]), and Bev's surprising "hiccough," which repeatedly elicited Asher's laughter (4,4,22). Simon's motivation to amuse his brother never waned, and he often took over when someone else was having fun with Asher. Thus, Simon's general desire for his brother's attention progressed from wanting Asher near him, to wanting Asher facing him, to wanting Asher looking at him, to wanting Asher smiling at him, to wanting Asher laughing at his games.

Origins of Sibling Responsiveness

Simon was interested in Asher and concerned for his distress, just as many other children are with a new sibling (Dunn and Kendrick 1982a, Gottlieb and Mendelson 1990, Howe and Ross 1990, Kramer 1989, Legg et al. 1974, Murphy 1988, R. B. Stewart 1983, R. B. Stewart and Marvin 1984, R. B. Stewart et al. 1987, Trause et al. 1981). Such behaviors are noteworthy not only because they violate negative stereotypes of firstborns' reactions to the new baby but also because they may predict a positive relationship between the children later on. Young children who are interested in and entertain a newborn brother or sister interact positively with the baby eight and fourteen months later (Dunn and Kendrick 1979). However, identifying continuity in the sibling relationship is only a first step. We must also explain both the original behaviors and transformations in them over time. And unlike research with necessarily limited observations of many children at widely spaced intervals, a single case study can reveal the complexity of a child's interactions with the new baby.

My account of Simon's interaction with Asher, best described as complementary (Dunn 1983), begins to address questions about the origins and development of sibling responsiveness. Obviously a young child cannot be expected to fulfill the proposed definition of parental responsiveness—contingent, appropriate, and consistent reactions to a baby's needs and signals (Lamb and Easterbrooks 1981)—yet Simon seemed to demonstrate at least some of the components, just as other children do in various cultures (Whiting and Edwards 1988). In particular, Simon often perceived and correctly interpreted Asher's needs and signals, and he often responded contingently and appropriately to them, even if he did not do so consistently. Of course, he had much to learn, but the foundation appeared to be there.

Simon was upset by Asher's crying and responded to it more emotionally than to other loud sounds. At times Simon apparently just wanted to avoid the noise, so he covered his ears. But when he could not avoid loud crying, his reaction escalated—to screams or refusals to give Asher the pacifier—even if it made the problem worse. Thus, Asher's intense crying elicited either egoistic concerns or disorganized behavior (A. D. Murray 1985, Whiting and Edwards 1988).

Yet perhaps partly because of his own definition of the big brother role, Simon often responded nurturantly to Asher's distress. He assumed a big brother helps care for the baby, and responding to Asher may simply have followed logically from that belief. But Simon's nurturance more probably reflected the same genuine concern for Asher that engendered his other positive feelings, his discussions about safety, and his reaction when he simply imagined Asher's injury.

Whatever his motivation, how did Simon actually acquire the skill to soothe Asher? Even before Simon became a brother, he had observed soothing techniques, had tried some himself, and had occasionally been instructed in their use. Afterward Simon may have learned possible explanations for Asher's crying from our problem-solving discussions, and he clearly imitated our attempts to calm Asher. He also extended the soothing strategies that he learned and devised strategies based on his personal experience. But if he were busy or if all else failed, Simon recruited one of us, just as we occasionally recruited each other in similar circumstances. Eventually Simon's soothing techniques probably benefited more and more from practice and from positive feedback associated with successful attempts. Although Simon was somewhat oblivious to negative changes in Asher's mood, he always responded well to positive changes. And even if Simon was not motivated simply to avoid the noise, the cessation of Asher's crying, like the onset of smiling and laughing, probably reinforced his behavior.

True, Asher's distress often elicited Simon's attention, but, even if it prompted a brief intervention, it did not sustain their interaction. In contrast, Simon's spontaneous interest and Asher's positive feedback formed a solid basis for social exchanges. Simon was interested in Asher from the start, much as he was attracted to babies before becoming a brother. Simon derived considerable pleasure from simply watching Asher, very possibly because he found him cute. But Simon was rarely satisfied with just watching Asher—or, for that matter, other babies. Simon typically wanted more, and he based his standards on our social exchanges with Asher, standards that changed from proximity to attention to positive affect and at last to extended interactions.

Chapter 9
Conversations and Games

Simon's initial interest in attracting Asher's attention ensured that he learned how to interact effectively with his brother. Concurrently, Asher's positive feedback—the delighted smiles and exuberant laughter—were powerful forces that shaped Simon's behavior. Simon constantly attempted to elicit Asher's smiles and was gleeful when he succeeded. Perhaps more critical, Asher's pleasure sustained Simon's interactions, and Asher's laughter eventually transformed the interactions into play. Other factors fostered social exchanges between the boys and transformed brief snippets—such as Simon's verbal greetings and playful tugs—into conversations and games. Thus, Simon and Asher became more and more involved with each other, and involvement is certainly a prerequisite to forming any relationship.

Baby Talk

Women and men in all cultures characteristically adapt their speech and language when talking to an infant (Snow and Ferguson 1977; M. Papousek et al. 1985, Trehub 1990). Such speech, called *motherese* or *baby talk,* involves modifications in the phonology, syntax, semantics, pragmatics, and prosody of regular language. Baby talk is simpler in form and content than adult-directed speech; for example, it is slower paced and includes short utterances with many repetitions. It also includes a variety of devices that either recruit or maintain the infant's attention. Adults repeatedly greet a baby, use the infant's name, and interject expressions such as "Look" or "Hey"; less obviously, they pose many questions whose rising contours and tags, such as "Eh?" or "Hmm?" possibly control attention. But the most striking feature of baby talk is its pattern of intonation and stress, which includes a distinctive set of melodic contours characterized by high modulated pitch. Indeed the pitch-contour of baby talk often supersedes its meaning. Thus melodic contours are unrelated to semantic and linguistic categories, and adults use prototypical pitch contours in contentless utterances or melodies (Grieser and Kuhl 1988, M. Papousek 1987).

Baby talk may serve several functions that can be grouped into two broad categories: expressive-affective and communication-clarification (Brown 1977, Garnica 1977, L. Murray and Trevarthen 1986, H. Papousek and Papousek 1987, Snow 1977b, Stern et al. 1983). More specifically, baby talk may enable an adult to express or share affect, to specify the infant as listener, to regulate the infant's attention or state, to sustain proto-conversational interactions, or to provide an environment that fosters the infant's cognitive, social, and linguistic competence. Note that the functions of baby talk are actually its effects, so they do not account for origins or causes. Descriptions of function may seemingly attribute intentionality to the adult, but such attributions should be understood figuratively; if we say, for example, that adults use baby talk to regulate the infant's state, we do not mean that they do so purposefully or even consciously.

Probably the most coherent account of baby talk classifies it as an intuitive parenting behavior (H. Papousek and Papousek 1987, M. Papousek et al. 1985). Such behaviors are evidently carried out unintentionally, with latencies above those of simple reflexes but below those of conscious, rational decisions. Adults are often not aware of intuitive parenting behaviors and sometimes deny or misinterpret them. But even individuals who do become aware of them still find them hard to control. For example, adults cannot fully reproduce baby talk, although they can intentionally evoke aspects of it, when they are not actually interacting with an infant (Fernald and Simon 1984, Jacobson et al. 1983, L. Murray and Trevarthen 1986). According to Papousek and Papousek, intuitive parenting behaviors probably have deep phylogenetic roots since they are presumably universal across age, sex, and culture. Evolutionary changes in infants' competence were supposedly accompanied by complementary changes in caregiver-infant interaction, with the adaptive significance that, even unknowingly, adults foster their baby's social, emotional, perceptual, cognitive, and linguistic development. Across diverse cultures adults and children respond similarly to babies, who seem to elicit positive responsiveness and nurturance even from children as young as 2 years old (Whiting and Edwards 1988).

An intuitive-parenting explanation of baby talk probably accounts for speech to young infants better than speech to old infants (M. Papousek et al. 1985) and perhaps for its prosodic and phonological features better than its linguistic features. Indeed adults' baby talk changes as the infant grows, apparently in tandem with the infant's emerging linguistic competence (Sherrod et al. 1977, 1978, Snow 1977a, Trehub 1990, Tomasello and Mannle 1985). Mothers' utterances to their baby become simpler from early infancy until the second half of the first year but more complex thereafter. And although nonlinguistic aspects of baby talk may be more important than linguistic content early on, mothers eventually adapt their speech to their infant's language comprehension, production, and conversational, turn-taking skills.

Children's Baby Talk
Preschoolers also modify their speech when they talk to younger children, to baby brothers or sisters, to baby dolls, or to partners pretending to be a baby (Dunn and Kendrick 1982b, P. Miller and Garvey 1984, Sachs and Devin 1976, Shatz and Gelman 1973, Tomasello and Mannle 1985). They not only speak in a high-pitched voice with exaggerated intonation but also adopt other baby-talk features: expressive features (such as an affectionate tone, endearments, rhymes, and playful repetitions) as well as clarification features (such as short utterances, simple syntax, attention-getting devices, and directives).

But children's speech to infants is by no means identical to adults' (P. Miller and Garvey 1984, Sachs and Devin 1976, Stevenson et al. 1988, Tomasello and Mannle 1985, Vandell and Wilson 1987). It is particularly telling that children's baby talk does not seem to differ between real and pretend situations. That is, preschoolers can evoke aspects of baby talk, but they are not as responsive as adults to the many eliciting cues. Children also speak to babies less and ask fewer questions. And preschoolers have trouble maintaining continuous, reciprocal conversations since, unlike mothers, they do not scaffold the baby's participation in a dialogue or in play. (To scaffold is to provide a framework, typically through attention-controlling devices, conversational repairs, and similar behaviors, that supports a baby's role in a social exchange [Bruner and Sherwood, 1976, Ratner and Bruner, 1978].)

Experience with a baby brother or sister does not seem to affect baby talk (Shatz and Gelman 1973, Tomasello and Mannle 1985). Preschoolers with a younger sibling and only children speak similarly to an unfamiliar infant, and firstborns similarly address their baby brother or sister and an unknown baby. Firstborns also do not adjust the linguistic complexity of their speech to a young sibling during the baby's second year. Nonetheless, children's baby talk to a brother or sister is influenced by pragmatic and emotional factors (Dunn and

Kendrick 1982b). Preschoolers are highly directive with younger siblings and use words most often to control the infant's behavior during prohibitions and play. Clarification adjustments appear fairly common and arguably reflect the firstborn's desire to communicate with a less competent speaker. But affective adjustments and the use of questions are related to nonverbal indications of affectionate interest.

We are still far from understanding either the origins or the development of a preschooler's baby talk to a younger brother or sister. The generalizations from the literature are based on little data. No studies have examined children's baby talk to prelinguistic infants, and only one examined longitudinal change (Tomasello and Mannle 1985). Thus, even the most obvious question remains unanswered: How might a preschooler acquire baby talk? Most probably, acquisition of skilled baby talk is multiply determined by a combination of biological and experiential factors. Similarities between the baby talk of adults and children are consistent with a biological interpretation, but differences suggest that experience may play a role. Children may be biologically predisposed to respond to infants in species specific ways (H. Papousek and Papousek 1987, M. Papousek et al. 1985). Alternatively, young children could learn baby talk by imitating how adults talk to them, by imitating adults' speech to babies, or by gradually learning that baby talk positively engages infants.

Simon's Brotherese

Before Asher was born, Simon, like many other children his age, was interested in babies (Berman et al. 1977). We often noticed this after we told Simon that Bev was pregnant, a time when our own sensitivity to infants was heightened (3,4,21). Jerusalem has countless children who spend a lot of time outdoors, and we frequently pointed out young babies to Simon on walks or in the parks. Simon would approach them, greet them by gently putting his palm on their cheek, and talk to them in a high-pitched modulated voice, but his interactions with unfamiliar babies typically ended at that.

Given that Simon spoke baby talk before he became a brother—to Charles, to his cousin Michael, and to other infants—it is not surprising that he used it the first time he met Asher (4,0,3). Early on Simon changed his tone of voice and used simple repetitive sentences.

> Father: (to Asher) That's the way.
> Simon: (high soft voice) That's the way! That's the way! That's the way! That's the way!
> Father: (to Simon) That's nice. That's nice.
> Simon: That's the way (taped 4,0,7).

Yet Simon's early speech to Asher was limited and somewhat artificial, reminiscent of baby talk in pretend play; however, it did change in the ensuing months.

Consider the excerpt just cited. Simon imitated my speech to Asher but expanded it appropriately by repeating the phrase over and over. Then I expressed my approval of his interaction, and Simon continued his repetition of the phrase. A similar sequence occurred on other occasions.

Father: (adjusting Asher in his infant seat and talking in a normal tone of voice) There, that's better.

Simon: (in baby talk) There, that's better, Asher. That's better, Asher.

Mother: (to Simon) That's really nice talking.

Simon: (to Asher) There, that's better Asher. That's better (4,2,10).

Dunn and Kendrick (1982b) argued that imitation plays a minimal role in shaping the content of preschoolers' baby talk, but their observations were probably too short to identify imitated utterances, especially delayed imitations. Besides, they overlooked a potentially important source of modeled baby talk: fathers (Golinkoff and Ames 1979, M. Papousek et al. 1985). And all children in their study interacted with a 14-month-old brother or sister, so it is impossible to rule out imitation as an influence on children's speech to younger babies.

Delayed imitation did play an important role in shaping the content of Simon's baby talk to Asher. Several times during the first week of Asher's life, Simon used the endearment "cherry-tomato nose" (taped 4,0,7). My sister-in-law had coined the phrase to refer aptly to Simon's button nose when he was a baby. Four years later Bev still occasionally used the expression as an endearment for Simon, and she readily extended it to Asher, who had an identical button nose. But Simon did not use the expression immediately after Bev; rather, "cherry-tomato nose" was delayed imitation of her endearment for him or possibly of her endearment for Asher.

Simon also borrowed other phrases from Bev or me, which he typically said to Asher in a high-pitched modulated voice. He not only adapted the content of our speech to Asher in similar contexts but also maintained the structure, including repetitions and questions.

Simon: What do you say baby? What do you say? What do you say baby? (similar to Father) (4,0,8).

Simon: Aren't you a cute baby? Aren't you cute? What a cute cherry-tomato nose (similar to Mother) (4,0,8).

Simon: Don't cry. You're all right. Don't cry. You're at home (similar to Father) (4,1,4).

Simon: Don't worry, Asher. Don't worry. Don't worry, Asher (similar to Father) (4,2,5).

Simon also used a variety of standard greetings and phrases, often including Asher's name and invariably said in a tone of voice appropriate for a baby.

Asher: (sneezes)
Simon: Bless you, Asher (4,2,5).

Simon: (kissing Asher in greeting after entering the room) Hi there. You're a cutie (father's expression of endearment) (4,2,7).

Simon: (having just accidentally poked Asher while helping put on his sweater) Sorry, Asher (4,2,14).

Simon: (typical morning greeting) Did you have a good sleep, Asher? (similar to father's usual morning greeting to Simon) (4,3,0).

Simon's speech to Asher was not limited to a catalogue of imitated and conventional phrases. Indeed Simon generated his own content and even modified imitated greetings. My salutation, "Hi, Asher. I'm your Daddy," became Simon's, "Hi, Asher. I'm your brother" (4,0,28). Eventually he also incorporated Bev's greeting, "Look Asher, here's your big brother," to end up with, "Hi Asher. I'm your big brother" (4,2,26).

By the time Asher was 10 weeks old, Simon's interactional style was quite sophisticated (4,2,9). He used grammatically simple sentences that included many questions and repetitions. He spoke slowly in a modulated high-pitched tone and adopted an expression typical of adults talking to a baby—raised eyebrow, exaggerated smile, and head bobbing that is particularly effective in eliciting an infant's attention (H. Papousek and Papousek 1987). Simon's whole demeanor changed when he spoke to Asher, a reaction I often observed in Bev and myself; Simon might be abrasively confrontational with me one moment but then turn to Asher, immediately become calm, and interact sweetly.

The following two short excerpts, good examples of prototypical baby talk, illustrate that Simon eventually mastered motherese and made it brotherese.

Simon: (trying to get Asher to smile by stroking the side of his mouth) Show your daddy how you smile. Are you

> going to show your daddy how you smile? . . . (re-
> peated several times) (4,2,15).

Asher: (fretting)
Simon: What's wrong, Asher? What's wrong? Tell us what's
          wrong, so we can help (4,3,21).

What might have accounted for the notable improvement in Simon's baby talk over the early months of Asher's life? Certainly he
received no direct instruction in voice modulation and pacing, in facial expressions and head movements, or in simplifying grammar,
repeating phrases, using Asher's name, asking questions, and so on.
Some of these features might have originally reflected Simon's biologically determined response to babies (H. Papousek and Papousek
1987), yet Simon observed literally hundreds of interactions with
Asher, to say nothing about the thousands of interactions in which
he participated when he was younger, and he might have mimicked
features of baby talk just as he imitated the content. He also might
have generalized the grammatical forms of imitated phrases. Regardless of the origin of features of Simon's brotherese, our praise of his
particularly pleasant interactions with Asher may have influenced
him somewhat. But Simon's improvement was more likely fostered
by Asher's response to his speech, a powerful reward given Simon's
desire to attract Asher's attention.

Scaffolding Conversations between Simon and Asher

Like most other parents, Bev and I conducted what were essentially
one-sided conversations with our baby, either supplying lines for him
or accepting nonverbal sounds, like burps, sneezes, or coos, and
other behaviors, like glances, smiles, or kicks, as substitutes (Snow
1977a). But Simon did not sustain conversations with Asher, especially when the baby was very young. Simon apparently could not
scaffold Asher's participation, not surprising since preschoolers generally have trouble supporting interactions with siblings who are
even as old as 6 months and more (Stevenson et al. 1988, Tomasello
and Mannle 1985, Vandell and Wilson 1987).

As a result, Simon's earliest interactions with Asher were typically
short, not progressing much beyond stock greetings, imitated
phrases, single expressions of concern, and the like. These exchanges
with Asher lengthened in the ensuing months for a number of reasons: Asher started to vocalize, which lessened the need for Simon
to scaffold conversations; Simon learned what amused Asher and ac-

quired a number of scripts for interacting with him; and Bev or I often supported the social exchanges between the boys.

Coos and Squeaks Are Easy to Imitate
By as early as 2 months, babies acquire a variety of nonreflexive, non-distress sounds—some vowels, syllabic consonants, and throaty vocalizations—which they add to their repertoire of cries and frets (Oller 1980, Stark 1980). They begin to produce coos, chortles, and laughs during the next two months, especially when they are confronted by a smiling, bobbing face. From 4 to 6 months they not only extend their repertoire with an even wider variety of sounds—raspberries, squeaks, growls, yells, and marginal babbling—but also begin to manipulate and expand vocal sequences playfully, apparently for the simple pleasure of doing so. Even if early vocalizations are not produced intentionally or exclusively within social interaction, they do communicate the baby's state or mood and encourage a social partner to continue an ongoing exchange. They are also easy to mimic, so they afford a particularly good chance to conduct a dialogue with a young baby.

Before Asher was 1 month old, Simon not only took delight in Asher's vocalizations, especially if they seemed to be a response to Simon's behavior, but also attributed meaning to them. Asher once vocalized when Simon was making faces at him, which obviously pleased Simon, who said that Asher had laughed (4,0,27). What could be more gratifying to a preschooler than amusing a baby brother with funny faces? Within a month Simon elicited Asher's squeals more and more readily. Simon was inevitably delighted when Asher vocalized to him and, as in the case with Asher's smile, proudly reported exactly how he made him squeal (4,1,22). Simon was also charmed by Asher's spontaneous sounds; Simon thought they were cute—according to him they made Asher sound like a kitten (4,1,21)—which may be why Simon imitated them.

As young infants gain experience with family members, they may learn that it is more rewarding to socialize with an adult than with an older brother or sister. This would explain why 14-month-olds start far fewer conversations with their preschool sibling than with their mother (Dunn and Kendrick 1982b). But Asher, who spontaneously vocalized more and more, did initiate prelinguistic social exchanges with Simon. Although 8-week-olds do not communicate intentionally, Asher often squeaked seemingly to greet someone who was not attending to him. Simon, for one, certainly responded to Asher as if this were true. One evening at supper Asher was in his usual spot next to Simon. Every time Asher squeaked, Simon interrupted his meal to reciprocate the apparent greeting. "Hello, Asher," he pleasantly said in brotherese (4,1,25). In effect he returned a conversational volley initiated by Asher, a contingent response that conceivably reinforced Asher's squeaks. Sometimes, though, Simon ignored Asher's calls. And if so, Bev or I interceded on Asher's behalf, just as we did when we drew Simon's attention to Asher's smile or to a negative change in Asher's mood (4,1,29).

By Asher's second month, Simon responded to a variety of his brother's vocalizations, including frets, by imitating them. He occasionally did so automatically, even when occupied and apparently not attending to Asher (4,1,28). Simon may not have started to mimic Asher's sounds on his own; he may have copied Bev or me since we both consistently imitated Asher. Indeed Simon often mimicked Asher, just as he often tried to elicit a smile, when someone else did (4,2,12).

Given that Asher vocalized to Simon and that Simon often responded, the exchanges between the boys inevitably lengthened. Simon once approached Asher in his infant seat to talk to him. Asher responded with squeaks and coos, and Simon copied each type of sound. The boys took several turns, back and forth, before Simon giggled and withdrew (4,1,27). Parents commonly play such vocal-matching games with their infant (H. Papousek and Papousek 1987). We were not exceptions, so Simon possibly discovered the game by watching us or other adults interact with Asher. Regardless, he often played the game during the ensuing months, invariably with pleasure. The game had a force of its own. Simon's social interaction with Asher increased Asher's vocalizing, which in turn sustained Simon's conversation (cf. Bloom 1984 for a review of the effects of contingent vocal exchanges on young babies).

Simon eventually realized that he imitated Asher and raised the topic one day. While I was playing with Simon, I was also talking to Asher and imitating his vocalizations. As often happened in such circumstances, Simon also began to imitate Asher, but then Simon shared an insight with me.

> Simon: You know, sometimes when Asher says something, I say the same thing.
> Father: Why do you do that?
> Simon: . . . Because sometimes Asher laughs when I do . . . I squalkeds (*sic*) Asher.
> Father: What's that.
> Simon: It's an expression that means to make him smile (4,2,11).

Simon believed that his imitation amused Asher, apparently reason enough for doing it. Asher's enjoyment and Simon's pleasure from it fostered an interactional game they played for many months to come.

What Does He Mean?
A few days after the boys' first long dialogue, Simon raised a topic that would normally obviate conversation: he said he did not understand Asher. Asher was staring at Simon and calling, apparently bidding for his attention. Simon, who was very tired, sat quietly and did not respond. Bev told Simon that Asher was looking at him and saying something. "But I don't know what he wants," Simon replied in frustration. "Asher is just saying that he loves his brother," Bev interpreted. Her encouragement worked; Simon said a few simple phrases to Asher and then started imitating him, which led to an exchange back and forth several times (4,1,30). Several of the elements I have already mentioned appeared in this situation: Asher's social bid, Simon's ignoring Asher, Bev's interceding by drawing Simon's attention to Asher, and eventually Simon's imitative dialogue with his brother. But a new element emerged: Simon's frustration that he did not understand Asher. As would often happen during the ensuing weeks, Simon wanted to interpret Asher's vocalizations as language.

Asher's vocalizations were easily construed as communication; indeed, we frequently referred to them as such, and Simon seemed to accept the idea readily.

Simon: Asher?
Asher: Aah ehh.
Mother: I think he's talking to you. What's he saying? Does he want to tell you something?
Simon: (high soft voice) Yyyesss!
Mother: What?
Simon: What do you want to tell me Asher? What? (taped 4,2,14).

But Simon was struck by the obvious puzzle of Asher's speech. Simon was once watching me change Asher, who was staring at Simon and cooing. "He's calling you," I interceded. "It's hard to tell who a baby is calling," Simon replied (4,2,14). Despite the difficulty understanding Asher, Simon eventually referred to Asher's vocalizations as talking and even started to count Asher's "words." When Asher vocalized later the same day, Simon told me, "He said his first word" (4,2,14). Over the next few days, Simon continued the tally.

Father: (asks Asher a question)
Asher: (vocalizes)
Simon: He said no. He just said his first . . . second word.
Father: What was his first word?
Simon: Aah. That's nice.
Father: It will be quite a while before Asher says his first word (4,2,15).

Asher: (vocalizes)
Simon: He's beginning to talk.
Mother: Asher won't talk for a while. He won't say his first word until he is about 1 year old.
Simon: But he said, "Aah . . ."
Father: It just sounds like he's saying something . . .
Simon: Yeah.
Father: . . . but he really is only making cooing noises like a little kitten.
Simon: (adopting his baby kitten voice) Like a little furry cute kitten (taped 4,2,18).

During the next few months, Simon still referred to Asher's sounds as talking, but he distinguished between types of vocalizations and even instructed his grandmother in the difference. She once asked him whether Asher was crying or talking. "He's talking," Simon explained seriously. "When he goes, 'Aah' and stops, he's talking. When he goes, 'Aaaaah . . .,' he's crying" (4,4,15). Yet Simon remained troubled that we did not understand Asher. Once when Asher was calling, Simon asked who knew what he said. I suggested that although we did not really know what Asher meant, we could tell if he was happy or sad. "But what is he saying now?" asked Simon (4,4,20). Simon continued to search for proof that Asher's vocalizations were meaningful. Finally Asher uttered something that Simon found truly interpretable: "Mm, mm, mam . . ." And Simon said that when Asher says "mam," he means Mommy (4,5,4).

Even if Simon did not really understand Asher's speech, Asher could still have understood Simon's—or so Simon thought. Asher once rested his hand on a book that Simon was looking through. Simon told Asher not to touch the book, but Asher did not move. "If you don't take your hand away, I'll have to," Simon said, apparently imitating Bev or me and presumably expecting Asher to understand (4,2,16). A couple of weeks later Simon pulled Asher's feet, causing Asher to slide down from where he was leaning. Asher looked uncomfortable, so I propped him back up and admonished Simon to stop. Asher then extended his feet and touched Simon. "If you kick me," Simon warned Asher, "I'll slide you." Simon reiterated the warning when Asher extended his feet again, and the third time carried out his threat by pulling Asher again. "Asher is just a baby," I told Simon, "so you can't tell him if he does one thing you'll do another." Yet Simon insisted that he had warned Asher. "You can't warn a baby," I replied. "Besides, Asher doesn't understand English." Simon's subsequent laughter suggested that he knew I was right (4,3,4).

About six weeks later, Simon thought he had discovered evidence that Asher understood a command to be quiet. Simon was watching television, and Asher was in his stroller, next to Simon's chair.

Asher: Ah, ah, ah . . .
Simon: (forcefully) Quiet!
Asher: (becomes quiet)
Simon: (to parents in other room) He understands.
Father: What?
Simon: Asher understood "quiet."
Father: He really doesn't.
Simon: (after recounting the incident) . . . so Asher
         understands.
Father: Asher really doesn't understand yet, but he will one
         day.

A few minutes later,

Asher: Aah . . . aah . . .
Simon: Quiet, Asher . . . quiet, Asher . . . quiet, Asher . . .
Asher: (becomes quiet)
Simon: (tells Father again) (4,4,21).

What Do You Say After, "Hi, Cute Asher"?
Since young babies neither produce nor understand speech, conversations with them do not have to be comprehensible. Indeed adults often sacrifice meaning to use prototypical pitch contours (Grieser and Kuhl 1988, M. Papousek 1987). After "Hi," even "buzzle, guzzle, wuzzle" will do. Bev and I did use nonsense words with Asher, mainly when playing conventional games or singing but probably also in other circumstances. Yet even if Simon imitated contentless speech as a style of interaction, he usually did not imitate specific nonsense words; rather he invented equivalents to "kootchy-coo" and said them with the appropriate intonation and affect. Simon found an effective strategy in contentless speech for sustaining interactions with Asher. Since Simon was not adept enough to carry on

one-sided conversations, he conveniently dispensed with the content when talking to Asher and simply carried on the interaction, regardless of meaning.

When Asher was 6 days old, Bev and I encouraged Simon to "read" to him and suggested *Pat the Bunny* (Kunhardt 1942). Simon showed Asher the pictures, enthusiastically reciting the first few pages essentially verbatim in baby talk. But he then began to interject the occasional nonsense word: "Paul is smelling the flowers. Now yoouu smell the flowers. *Eeeh*. . . . Now Judy's looking at the bear. Now yoouu look at the bear. Look at the bear! Judy is petting Daddy's face. But it's here. Now you touch it here. *Deee!* . . . Judy could put her hands through Mommy's ring. Now you put your hand in Mommy's . . . turn the page. *Dee dee, baby. Dee dee. Whoooo!* . . . Good bye" (taped 4,0,9).

I heard Simon use nonsense words on other occasions, such as when he greeted his brother—"Ho, little bouncy. Look up," or "Hi Asher! We're a cherry-tomato family, and you're the buddy guddy" (taped 4,0,19; taped 4,1,26). And like me, Simon often sang meaningless songs to Asher. Simon's contentless speech and nonsense lyrics typically sounded like an 8-month-old's babbling: short strings of repetitive syllables with variations on a phonological theme, such as a rhyme or a common first letter. They were not imitations of the sounds Asher made at the time but apparently Simon's impressions of prototypical babbling: "Whoa whoa whoo whoo" or "Gaya gu gu ga ga gaya gu gu" (taped 4,2,14). But Simon went beyond simple babbling and frequently included the common attention-getting device of calling Asher's name: "Go go ga ga ga gee, Asher. Ga gee (giggles) Aasherr" (taped 4,2,25) or (singing) "Yoo hoo, Asher. Ah ah, Asher" (taped 4,4,20).

I usually heard Simon embed nonsense speech in meaningful segments of conversation when showing something to Asher, as in his recitation of *Pat the Bunny*, or when physically interacting with him, but Simon's contentless speech often predominated when the boys were alone. In the following, Simon used long nonsense sequences based on phonological similarity as well as other elements of baby talk, including high-pitched melodic contours, addressing the baby by name, questions, repetitions, and endearments.

> Simon: He's soooo cuddly. Who buttoned it, Asher? Asher?
> Who buttoned it? That? Asher can't see him because
> he took a rocket ship. Is that interesting to you? (singing in a soft high voice) Doo be doo. Dee dee dee dee
> boo de doo. Who who who who who who. Shoo shoo

shoo shoo shoo shoo. Goo goo goo goo goo goo. Shh
shh shh shh. I'll sit him down here. To be do, to be
do, to be do. Oh oh oh oh oh oh oh oh oh oh. Oh
Asher, Asher. Oh Asher. Oh Asher. Hi, Asher. What?
You're a marshmallow today, Asher (taped 4,3,9).

Simon never used such extended sequences of word play when I—
or, as far as I know, anyone else—was present. Perhaps Simon was
self-conscious, just as some adults are embarrassed about interacting
with a baby. Whatever the reason, I never observed Asher's reaction
to Simon's longer bouts of nonsense speech. I assume Asher was as
attentive to it as he would be to regular speech, or even more so, since
highly repetitive yet somewhat variable baby talk is extremely ap-
pealing to prelinguistic infants (H. Papousek and Papousek 1987).
Thus, Simon discovered an effective strategy, which was consistent
with his own conversational abilities, for achieving his general goal
of eliciting and maintaining Asher's attention.

Amusing Asher

Before Asher was born, Simon already had some experience amusing
a young baby, and he developed the skill during Asher's first months
of life. Specifically, Simon honed three strategies—showing toys,
singing, and playing conventional games—each of which sustained
his interaction with Asher. Early on Simon occasionally showed
Asher a toy for a few seconds, usually by holding it in front of Asher
and shaking it a bit—a tactic he had learned by instruction. Once,
Simon was overenthusiastic about showing toys and poked them in
Asher's face, but he immediately complied when we told him to be
gentler (4,0,22).

An adult who shows something to a baby typically carries on a one-
sided conversation, first attracting the baby's attention and then commenting on the object. Although Simon occasionally combined singing with showing—as when he improvised a fish song while holding
up a toy fish (4,1,29)—he did not usually say much at first. Yet he
eventually became adept at both introducing something to Asher—
before showing a musical toy, he might ask, "Do you want to hear
some sweet music?" (4,2,17)—and at commenting—while showing a
cookie, he might say, "Look Asher. It's brown. It's brown. Yes. It's
brown" (4,3,3).

The following excerpt was taped when the boys were alone. Simon,
entertaining Asher by showing him a teddy bear, conducted a
one-sided conversation that included attention-seeking phrases, con-

tentless speech, and singing. And he had discovered another conversational strategy: commenting on the bear by simply cataloguing its features.

> Simon: I'll play a tune on this squeaky thing (makes squeaking noises). Isn't that nice, Asher? How about a little bear? So you could hug and cuddle him. Here. See a bear. Woo woo woo woo woo woo. Ssss, ssss. (starts singing) Now here's the bear, Asher. Here's the bear, Asher, aah . . . Look here. He's right beside you! Look. And he has a rain [badge], a heart nose, a tongue, and a great big smile. Two eyes, with eyelashes and eyebrows, and ears and hands and a tummy and feet (4,3,9).

Simon adopted a baby's perspective on show-and-tell objects. He protected Asher from things that a baby presumably would find frightening, like Disney's *Fantasia* (4,2,0) and a picture of a fire (4,5,2). Rather, he chose things that a baby would presumably like—usually toys but not always. I once amused Simon by honking each time he squeezed my nose. "Asher," Simon said, sharing the fun, "your Daddy's a Honker [a "Sesame Street" character]" (4,3,2).

Simon also entertained Asher by singing, which was noteworthy because I virtually never heard Simon sing at other times. He may have imitated me, since I sang to him every night at bedtime and to Asher quite often. But my repertoire included children's songs and folk tunes from the sixties, while Simon usually invented lyrics—either nonsense or sung conversation, as in the following: "I'll take you in my room to play. If you don't like it on your stomach, I'll turn you over. I'll give you your suss [pacifier] . . ." (4,3,2). Simon also adapted songs in other ways; he almost always used baby talk and occasionally replaced lyrics with Asher's name, as when he sang "Asher, Asher, little Asher," to the tune of the alphabet song (4,2,24). Simon often jumped up and down while he sang, a spectacle that, by 2 months, transfixed Asher (4,2,17). Thus, Simon discovered that singing and dancing were effective ways of holding Asher's attention and sustaining an exchange.

When Bev or I played with Asher, we used a variety of conventional games, like hiding games, exercise games, and pat-a-cake. Early on Simon copied one of my versions of a hiding game. He alternately blocked and unblocked Asher's view, each time mocking puzzlement or surprise. "Where's Asher? There's Asher," he said with exaggerated intonation. "Where's Asher? There's Asher. Where's

Asher. There's Asher. . . ." (4,1,27). Simon obviously enjoyed the game, and, after a few rounds the next day, his delight apparently prompted him to kiss his baby brother. "I gave him an orange-juice kiss," Simon reported. "Where's Asher?" he resumed a bit later, but this time he continued, "There's tickle Asher. Here's another orange-juice kiss" (4,1,28).

Although Simon learned the game by imitation, he soon introduced his own variations, just as he had done with short, soothing phrases. The changes were initially small, like the addition of "tickle" to "There's Asher" in the last example (4,1,28). Two days later Simon transformed "There's Asher" to "Here's Asher." He also switched from holding his hands in front of Asher's face to covering it with a napkin. But when I told him we do not cover a baby's face like that, he immediately removed the napkin and resumed the game, holding the napkin away from Asher's face (4,1,30). Eventually Simon made fairly extensive and completely original changes to my game.

> Simon: (with appropriate tone of voice and gestures) Where's Asher? Here's Asher. . . . Where's Asher's arm? Here's Asher's arm. . . . Where's Asher's hand? Here's Asher's hand. . . . Where's Asher (*sic*) hand? There's Asher hand. . . . Where's Asher cheek? There's Asher cheek . . . (4,2,10).

At about the same time, he also merged two hiding games.

> Simon: (with the appropriate gestures and intonation) Where's Asher? Here's Asher. Where's Asher? Here's peek-a-boo Asher. Where's Asher? Here's peek-a-boo Asher . . . peek-a-boo, peek-a-boo (4,2,4).

Simon did not try to play peek-a-boo conventionally until much later. Bev played a game—looking away from Asher and, after a short delay, looking back—which I copied. By the time Asher was about 3 months old, he responded to it by smiling broadly, especially when Bev played. Although Simon periodically watched us play peek-a-boo, he did not try it himself until Asher was almost 4 months old. And when he did, Asher did not respond, perhaps because Simon did not play enthusiastically enough and because he had trouble with the timing, critical for peek-a-boo (4,3,28). A few weeks later Simon watched Bev playing with Asher, who smiled each time she silently looked away and back. As often happened, Simon wanted a turn. He tried his own version, crouching out of sight and jumping back as he, enthusiastically this time, said, "peek-a-boo." Although Simon's timing was still off, Asher responded with a few smiles (4,4,20). Simon had acquired yet another strategy for amusing Asher and sustaining an interaction with him.

Simon learned physical games that were appropriate for a baby, again mainly by watching Bev or me play with Asher. But as in the case of burping Asher too forcefully or covering Asher's face with a napkin, Simon often had to learn the limits of a game from instruction. He once imitated a clapping game that Bev had just completed with Asher. Although Simon used too much force at first, he heeded Bev's suggestion not to clap Asher's hands so hard and resumed more gently (4,0,27). Simon also copied an exercise game that I used to play with Asher placed face up in my lap. I moved Asher's limbs back and forth, marking time with a nonsense phrase—"oosta goosta roosta, oosta goosta roosta"—that I imitated from Bev and that she had imitated from her mother. I once played the game next to Simon, who was intrigued, presumably by Asher's response to the fun. Predictably Simon wanted to try, so I put Asher face up on the couch, and Simon exercised his limbs, marking time as I had with "oosta goosta roosta, oosta goosta roosta . . ." (4,1,25).

Simon also imitated our games with Asher, after a delay and sometimes a considerable delay. It seemed as if Simon learned interactional scripts by watching us and then used them at appropriate times. For instance, he probably learned that counting could accompany exercises by observing me, so, moving Asher's arms, he might say, "One, two, reach for the sky. One, two, touch your toes . . ." (4,3,2). More often Simon's exercise game was to swing Asher's hand, perhaps in time to music or to improvised lyrics, such as "Yeah. Yeah. Yeah. I'm playing with his arm . . . (4,1,8; 4,1,12). Exercising, either on its own or accompanied by contentless speech, counting, or singing, was yet another strategy for sustaining interactions with Asher.

Touching Asher was not restricted to physical games. From the outset, virtually all of Simon's interactions included some physical contact. The first time Simon watched Asher nurse, Simon talked to him while gently stroking his hair and ears (4,0,3). At other times Simon patted Asher's head, stroked his cheeks, touched his lips, chucked his chin, tweaked his nose, held his hands, hugged him, and often, so often, kissed him. Like baby talk, physical contact maintains an infant's interest in social exchange (Stack and Muir 1990), so Simon may have learned that various types of touching elicited Asher's attention. Regardless, as Asher developed, he responded to exercise games with increasing enthusiasm, which clearly encouraged Simon to use them—a positive feedback loop that likely engendered rough-and-tumble play.

Parents Can Help

Although Simon and Asher did spend some time by themselves, they were usually together with Bev or me. At such times we scaffolded their social exchanges within a rhythm of family interaction—for example, by directing Simon's attention to Asher's signals and needs, modulating Simon's behavior, and keeping the conversation on track. To illustrate, I present, at length, one of many taped interactions.

Simon:	(singing) Whoa whoa whoo whoo.
Mother:	Come on. Sing a song. Come on. Come on. What do you think he'd like to do? (attempting to substitute nonsense lyrics with something intelligible and trying to get Simon to think about Asher's preference)
Simon:	Exercise.
Mother:	OK. Good idea. (supporting Simon's choice)
Simon:	You exercise his arms. OK?
Mother:	Well, you do the legs first. Then you can do the arms. (encouraging Simon's interaction with Asher)
Simon:	Up one two.
Mother:	Take it easy. OK? Good. (modulating Simon's behavior)
Simon:	Up one two.
Mother:	Stretch up. (elaborating on Simon's game)
Simon:	Stretch up.
Mother:	(laughs, which encourages Simon)
Father:	He's smiling at you. (highlighting Asher's response)
Simon:	Yeah.
Asher:	Aggh.
Mother:	Now I'm sure your brother would like to do something with his feet. (mediating Asher's negative feedback)
Simon:	(high soft voice) Make a butterfly with them. And keep them together. Flap flap flap flap. Now over your arms please, Asher. (giggles) He pushed my penis. (giggles)
Mother:	You've got to watch his arms and his legs.
Simon:	(high voice) One two. One two. One two. One two. One two. One two. Daddy, guess what?
Father:	What?
Simon:	Asher push . . . pushed my penis.
Father:	Oh.
Simon:	(giggles) Funny! . . .
Mother:	Why don't you just sit here? (getting things on track)

Simon: Oh hi, Asher. Come, look at me, Asher. (sings) Oh,
           Asher. He looks very sweet and cute, cute. Someday
           he'll come to daaaycare. For Asher. One day we'll
           take him to daaaycare.
Father: (laughs) Is he smiling now? (highlighting Asher's
           response)
Simon: (still singing) Sooometime, Asher. (to parents) He
           smiled two times at me!
Father: Mm hmm. (laughs) I think he loves you. (interpreting
           Asher's behavior)
Mother: I know why. (laughs)
Simon: (giggles) I'll put something soft on his face.
Father: What?
Simon: Just one cotton ball.
Father: Mm hmm.
Mother: (laughs) Look! (highlighting Asher's response)
Simon: (high soft voice) Doesn't that feel good Asher?
           Doesn't that feel good?
Father: Yeah. He likes that. (highlighting and interpreting
           Asher's response)
Simon: Doesn't that feel good?
Asher: Aggh.
Father: (laughs, which encourages Simon)
Simon: (giggles) Hard to keep track of him. Hey little thing,
           doesn't that feel good? Huh? Well it smells good.
Father: Hmm.
Simon: Completely.
Father: (to Asher) That smell?
Asher: Aah.
Father: Smells nice. (interprets Asher's response) . . .
Simon: Oh oh! Here, Asher, Asher, Asher.
Father: Now don't get all the puffs in his face please. OK?
           Cause that may bother him a bit. You could just
           stroke his face with it sort of . . . No like that. (modu-
           lating Simon's behavior)
Simon: I'm keeping him calm.
Mother: (laughs)
Father: Yeah, you're keeping him calm.
Simon: (high soft voice) Hi, Asher. Isn't that good? I'll put
           the cotton here in case he starts to cry (taped 4,2,14).

Presumably Simon benefited from such extended interactions, certainly by practicing what he already knew, but perhaps also by learn-

ing appropriate limits for his own behavior, by becoming more attuned to Asher's signals, and by discovering what succeeded and what failed to amuse Asher. Besides learning skills that would enable him to interact with Asher on his own, Simon discovered the pleasure to be derived from social exchanges with his baby brother.

From Interest to Interactions

Exchanges between Simon and Asher grew more and more complex over the early months of Asher's life. Simon acquired various skills and strategies that facilitated interactions with his baby brother, and Asher simultaneously developed a number of behaviors that fostered Simon's interactions with him. Two subjects are central to the changes I observed: Simon's baby talk and his ability to scaffold interactions with Asher.

Baby talk, with its apparently universal characteristics, is reasonably described as a species-specific pattern, yet even species-specific behaviors are influenced by experience. Thus baby talk probably develops from biological capacities, such as language skills and responsiveness to babies, from species-typical experiences, such as hearing baby talk as a young child and observing others use it, and from individual experiences, such as interacting successfully with a particular baby. When Asher was born, Simon's baby talk was rudimentary and somewhat stilted, but it improved over the early months of Asher's life and eventually included a variety of common features: attention-controlling devices, short utterances, simplified grammar, endearments, and contentless speech. Simon not only coordinated the features within utterances but coordinated his baby talk with appropriate facial expressions and head movements.

Preschoolers use baby talk with older infants who already have some linguistic competence and, perhaps more relevant here, with pretend or imaginary babies (Dunn and Kendrick 1982b, P. Miller and Garvey 1984, Sachs and Devin 1976, Shatz and Gelman 1973, Tomasello and Mannle 1985). Thus, it is not surprising that Simon directed baby talk to a linguistically naive newborn. But preschoolers' baby talk apparently does not change over their sibling's second year, and young children's baby talk to dolls or to make-believe babies would presumably not change with experience either. Yet Simon's baby talk did improve over the first months of Asher's life, probably because of changes in Asher's competence—not in his linguistic competence, which was negligible at the time, but in his social competence as an infant (his ability to attend, to smile, to coo, and so on). Just as Asher's smile reinforced Simon's chin tweaking, Asher's responses undoubtedly reinforced Simon's baby talk, especially the extensive use of improvised singing and contentless speech. Simon was motivated to attract Asher's attention and he undoubtedly discovered that baby talk was a good way to do it.

Bev and I also probably shaped Simon's baby talk by praising him when he sweetly spoke to Asher. But we influenced Simon more by providing models. When one of us interacted with Asher, Simon asked to try what we were doing, which, at the very least, gave him a chance to practice baby talk. Simon also imitated our imitations, copying Asher when we did. The imitation game was an effective strategy for extending interactions with Asher. By responding contingently to Asher's sounds, Simon prompted Asher to vocalize more and learned that Asher could participate in a conversation. Finally, Simon imitated both the form and the content of our baby talk, which may account for his acquisition of certain features such as posing questions and addressing Asher by name. Simon's imitations were frequently delayed and were not necessarily rote; he gradually adapted our phrases, some of them directed to him, to suit his desire to interact with Asher. As a result Simon's imitations would have been overlooked in a traditional study, so it is not surprising that others have minimized the importance of mimicry in preschoolers' baby talk (Dunn and Kendrick 1982b, Shatz and Gelman 1973).

Previous writers have noted how poorly preschoolers scaffold a baby's participation in conversations or play (Stevenson et al. 1988, Tomasello and Mannle 1985). Yet several external supports, including Asher himself, scaffolded Simon's interactions with Asher. The most powerful influence on an individual's interaction with a social partner may be the partner's behavior, an apparent truism that also applies when the partner is a baby. In a sense, an infant is more competent than inexperienced parents (to say nothing of preschoolers) at bringing parents near and at eliciting beneficial behavior (R. Q. Bell 1974, M. Lewis and Rosenblum 1974, H. Papousek and Papousek 1987).

Babies also influence interactions with preschoolers (Dunn and Kendrick 1982a, Lamb 1978c, Melson, Fogel, and Mistry 1986, Whiting and Edwards 1988). Asher was no exception. His developing skills helped to extend social exchanges with Simon: Asher's social bids initiated interactions; his vocalizations contributed content to conversations, if not meaning; and his response to Simon's imitations contributed dialogical structure. Asher's interest and enjoyment generally reinforced Simon's behavior; his pleasure signaled that Simon was reaching him. In a sense, Asher unwittingly scaffolded conversations, even when Simon could not.

Eventually Simon acquired strategies and scripts that he used to interact with Asher. Besides baby talk, essentially a species-specific strategy for recruiting and maintaining an infant's attention, Simon sang to Asher, showed him things, exercised his limbs, and played conventional games. Simon learned ways to scaffold Asher's participation and, to the extent that we helped Simon enact his scripts, we supported his scaffolding. Simon often learned by imitation, but his initial attempts were usually stilted; he needed practice to improve. And although he gradually expanded his repertoire of interactional games, he adopted some far more often than others—for example, exercises more than peek-a-boo—so Asher became familiar with Simon's favorites. Simon probably chose what worked best for him. Regardless, the boys' interactions with each other became increasingly coordinated. Presumably Asher was also learning, unknowingly, what worked with Simon (Vandell et al. 1981).

This chapter and the previous one illustrate how early interest on the part of a firstborn might develop into a positive relationship later (Dunn and Kendrick 1982a). Simon's interest in Asher was expressed as a desire for more and more involvement: to have Asher near, to have Asher face him, for Asher to look at him, for Asher to smile at him, to make Asher laugh, and so on. With each goal Simon placed himself in a position to practice ever improving skills for interacting with his brother. Skillful baby talk and conventional games increased Simon's effectiveness, which enhanced Asher's participation, which, in turn, added to Simon's pleasure. Participation and pleasure were solid foundations for the positive relationship that continued to develop between the boys.

Chapter 10

The Foundations of a Sibling Relationship

Becoming a brother or sister is an extended transition that involves a complex set of processes. Children who adapt to the transition begin forging a relationship with the new baby and emotionally adjust to the changes that inevitably accompany the arrival of a family member—changes in everyday routines, in family relationships, and in self-concept. Simon's transition to big brother was no exception. During the course of a year, he confronted a variety of cognitive, social, and emotional issues concerning both aspects of adaptation.

Although I have identified these issues, my study necessarily ignored possible differences among children and their families. Hence, my research does not generalize statistically to any population, even to the population of 4-year-old firstborn boys, but it can generalize analytically to theory (Yin 1984). Simon's transition highlights psychological processes that are relevant to any preschooler who becomes a big brother or sister, and Simon's early relationship with Asher suggests a general model of any relationship between a young child and a new brother or sister.

A Model of the Early Sibling Relationship

According to family systems theory, family members and subsystems both influence and are influenced by other members, other subsystems, and the total family system (Belsky 1981; Feiring and Lewis 1978). I have already illustrated the implications of this general statement with system diagrams, including a simplified diagram of a four-member family. Here I add details that transform the simplified diagram from a general theory to a domain-specific model of the early sibling relationship. (The simplified diagram is reproduced and unfolded in figure 10.1, and the expanded model is presented in figure 10.2.)

The proposed model is meant to account for the early interactions and emerging relationship between a child and a new brother or sister. The central explanatory constructs include the child's self-

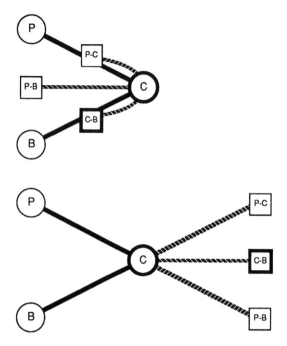

Figure 10.1
System diagrams of a four-member family (P = parents; C = child/sibling; B = baby/sibling). The top diagram includes only those elements most relevant to a discussion of the child and the child-baby relationship; the bottom diagram is an unfolded version of the top one.

concept, interactive skills, and motivation. But the model highlights that these aspects of the child are affected by family members and by family relationships. The child is influenced by interactions with a baby whose appearance and behavior elicit and shape the child's behavior. Parents also influence their children's relationship by providing information, by their behavior, by sustaining a relationship with the child, and by establishing a relationship with the baby. Although the child's long-standing relationship with each parent may change as a result of the new baby, the child is influenced by patterns of interaction established in the past and by patterns that emerge in the present. The child is also affected by each parent's relationship with the baby, since the situation and content of parent-baby interactions are at once potentially models and threats.

The model illustrated in figure 10.2 serves several functions. It provides an integrative framework for summarizing Simon's early relationship with Asher. I have already discussed details of parts of the

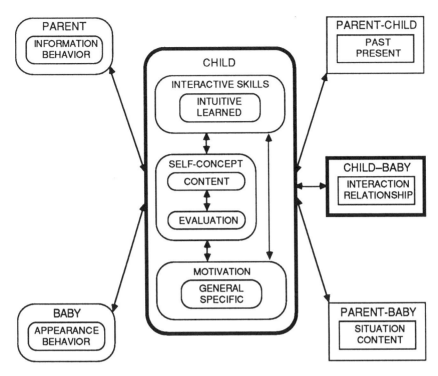

Figure 10.2
A framework for considering the child and the child-baby relationship within the context of the family.

model, especially the child's self-concept, interactive skills, and motivation. Yet the model is still useful since it reveals interconnections among these and other aspects of Simon's experience. The model also helps explain Simon's emotional adjustment to becoming a brother by highlighting potential sources of stress and support. Even if Asher's arrival did not radically alter the structure of Simon's week or significantly disrupt Simon's interactions with others, Simon still had to cope with the transition to a four-member family.

The model incorporates general developmental processes and can be used to account for a young child's relationship with anyone, not just with a new sibling. The model can also help explain differences in children's adaptation to a baby brother or sister, so it is presented not merely as an interpretation of Simon's adaptation to Asher, but as a framework for considering any preschooler's adaptation to a new sibling. More important, the model is a general invitation and guide to further research on young children and their baby brothers and sisters.

The Firstborn Child

The proposed model focuses specifically on a young child's self-concept, interactive skills, and motivation to interact with a new brother or sister.

Self-Concept

Psychologists who have studied the firstborn's reaction to the birth of a sibling have typically focused on the situational demands of family change and have characterized the transition either as traumatic or less dramatically as stressful. Yet the transition to sibling status can also be characterized as an instance of role acquisition. Thus, the child's identity or self-concept figures centrally in the proposed model. When I started this study, I suspected that self-concept issues, specifically self-knowledge, would be important. Self-knowledge is presumably enhanced by social comparison—the process of identifying both similarities and differences between self and others (Harter 1983)—and a baby brother or sister is an obvious target for such comparisons (Dunn and Kendrick 1982a). Dimensions that are already important to a preschooler—gender, size, ability, and privilege—gain new significance not only after a sibling is born but even before, when the child is expecting the baby. Talking about such dimensions surely contributes to a preschooler's self-awareness.

But I soon realized that several self-concept issues were best understood in terms of personal narratives (Mancuso and Sarbin 1983, Gergen and Gergen 1983), an important way to describe a child's identity, which includes knowledge of roles and relationships, as well as a personal story with a past, present, and future. A baby brother or sister certainly influences these aspects of the firstborn's self-concept. The arrival of a new sibling highlights developmental change and developmental trajectories, which may encourage firstborns to ask about the past and consider the future and thereby construct a personal history. A new baby also raises biological questions, which may prompt young children to consider the apparent mysteries of reproduction. As a result they may begin to construct not only general narratives but also personal ones: a general biological explanation of conception, gestation, and birth, as well as an account that includes personal details; or a general social narrative—for example, that people usually get married before having babies—as well as a personal one—that specifies, say, when and where Mommy met Daddy.

A new brother or sister also forces firstborns to revise existing self-narratives that involve the family. A second child changes the family system from a triad to a tetrad and highlights the divisions between parents and children, between males and females, or between other subsystems. The new baby heralds changes in both family roles and everyday routines (Cowan et al. 1976, LaRossa 1983, Walz and Rich 1983). Before becoming a sibling, preschoolers might foresee some changes in family organization—for example, that their parents would redistribute child care and household tasks—but probably would not foresee others—for example, that their parents would encourage them to be more independent. Even if young children did predict such changes, they could not possibly understand the social and emotional implications of family reorganization until it actually happened. Eventually firstborns have to revise their self-narratives, which necessarily include information like who cooks the meals, who reads them bedtime stories, and who takes them to the playground, to reflect changes in the structure of their family, family roles, and everyday routines.

Narratives about family roles and everyday routines also presumably include scripts for interacting with others in specific situations. Such scripts support not only children's behavior but also their predictions about family members (Nelson 1981). Changes that invalidate the scripts would probably disrupt young children and would therefore be resisted, at least until the scripts were appropriately revised and maybe even until the narratives about relationships that included the scripts were also revised. For example, a child trying to preserve a narrative about a three-member family might initially exclude a new brother or sister from a family outing, but eventually the narrative would involve a four-member family, and the child would then naturally include the baby. Or a preschooler trying to preserve a previously established script for bathtime games might resist any attempts to hurry the bath, but eventually the child might revise the bathtime script and accept the change.

Since the mere presence of a baby brother or sister nominally defines a firstborn as an older sibling, firstborns are forced by the baby's arrival, or perhaps even by their mother's pregnancy, to construct an identity that includes their new role. In representing the role of older brother or sister, young children probably incorporate relevant information and scripts into existing self-narratives and construct new self-narratives that encompass the baby. They initially learn about the role from a variety of sources, including parents, friends, books, and the media (Murphy 1988). But some of the information that they receive may be misleading. Before the baby is born, the helping myth fosters expectations that preschoolers will care for the baby, probably unrealistic expectations beyond their competence. It might be more realistic to tell them that they will be able to help their parents a little, watch what their parents do, and learn. The playmate myth promotes expectations that the preschooler will play with the baby, again unrealistic expectations, at least for the baby's first year or so. Here, it might be more realistic to tell them that they will be able to entertain the baby a little by showing things, singing songs, talking, making funny faces, and so on. Still, even inadvertently unrealistic information may give young children concrete ideas about what a big brother or sister does, and if firstborns simply believe that they have a role to play with the baby, they may be interested enough to be involved and carve out an actual role for themselves.

Young children also learn about the role of big brother or sister by participating in and observing other relationships, especially those within the family. Of course, they will eventually learn about the role directly, by interacting with the baby, but they can also learn by talking about the baby—their role partner—and by observing their parents interact with him or her. Independent of the baby, children probably get their first ideas about complementary aspects of the sibling role—like helping, protecting, and teaching—from their own relationships with parents, teachers, babysitters, and older children. They probably get their first ideas about reciprocal aspects—like playing, sharing, and loving—from the same relationships and from their relationships with friends (Kramer 1989).

Self-evaluations, which may be explicit or implicit, also figure in the proposed model. Self-evaluations about roles and social interaction are particularly relevant. For example, Simon's first predictions about protecting the baby contained implicit positive evaluations of his ability; in contrast, Simon's queries about how to prevent the baby from touching the stove were based on explicit negative evaluations. Like other aspects of children's self-concept, self-evaluations can be influenced by a variety of sources. Parents may provide relevant information, even if it is unrealistic, as when they promote positive self-evaluations about helping care for the baby. Parents may also highlight positive and negative aspects of children's interactions with the baby. For example, they may point out how much the firstborn makes the baby laugh or how poorly the firstborn holds the baby. Most important, young children are probably sensitive to some of the baby's feedback about the adequacy of their interactions. Even if children do not respond to all the baby's cues, they probably interpret the positive ones as signs of successful interactions, which would certainly account for the pride associated with making a baby smile or laugh.

In sum, preschoolers who are expecting a new brother or sister must undertake psychological work related to restructuring the self-concept. They must revise existing narratives about the self and others and revamp ideas about family relationships. They must also construct new self-narratives and define new social roles, even while still developing a concept of the baby.

Restructuring the self-concept is stressful (Epstein 1973, 1980). But a variety of environmental and personal factors may account for individual differences in the amount of stress that young children experience and in their reactions to it. Environmental factors may reduce the stress associated with restructuring the self-concept. For example, preschoolers who do not have to renegotiate existing relationships will not be distracted from the psychological task of defining a new social role, and children whose parents appropriately moderate maturity demands may not find such demands troublesome. Generally if daily routines and existing relationships are maintained after the birth of a sibling, fewer aspects of the self-concept have to be reformulated, presumably diminishing the overall threat of the transition.

Independent of environmental factors, children's cognitive, social, and affective readiness are also important. Very young firstborns who are just becoming aware of themselves, their relationships, and family roles would seemingly not have to restructure their self-concept to navigate the role transition to big brother or sister. In a sense, they would simply grow up with the role. It is therefore not surprising that toddlers are usually not upset by the birth of a sibling (Lasko 1954, Nuttall and Nuttall 1975).

For older firstborns, changes in self-concept that are consistent with ongoing psychological processes will be less stressful than changes that demand new skills. Firstborns who are ready to meet situational demands for independence by virtue of their age or ability may even welcome the need to adopt the role of big boy or big girl. Children who are proficient at pretend play may find it easy to adopt new social roles. And preschoolers who are aware of the coordination of roles or of other people's perspectives may find it easy to reformulate narratives about family relationships. Finally, both securely attached firstborns, whose self-narratives include ideas and feelings based on a long history of responsive parenting (Bretherton 1985), and children who otherwise have extensive, flexible narratives may be psychologically prepared to accommodate to new situations.

Interactive Skills
A model of the early sibling relationship must account for the origins and development of children's interactive skills—both general skills for any social encounter and specific ones for interacting with babies.

I have distinguished between intuitive skills, which are presumably biologically based (H. Papousek and Papousek 1987), and learned skills, but the distinction is admittedly artificial, since learning undoubtedly plays a role in the acquisition of any interactive skill.

Preschoolers' intuitive skills for interacting with a new sibling are probably evoked by the baby's infantile appearance and behavior. Yet intuitive skills are also shaped by experience. Parents can, for example, instruct or show young children how to attract a baby's attention and how to soothe the baby. Preschoolers may also imitate interactive behaviors that parents or other social partners direct to them or to the baby. But it is perhaps a truism that the most powerful influence on an individual's interaction with another is the other person's behavior, a truism even when that person is a baby or a toddler (Dunn and Kendrick 1982a, Lamb 1978a, Melson, Fogel, and Mistry 1986, Whiting and Edwards 1988). Children's interactive skills will be shaped by the baby's behavior, perhaps mainly by positive responses—like smiling, laughing, vocalizing, and increased attention—but also by negative responses—like crying, fretting, and loss of interest.

Children's interactive skills obviously influence the baby's behavior during social encounters, and, by influencing interactions, interactive skills presumably shape the child-baby relationship. Indeed, babies who have an older sibling and those who spend time with preschoolers acquire slightly more passive interactional styles than babies who are only children and those who spend time with other infants (Vandell et al. 1981). But children's interactive skills also affect parents, parent-child interactions, and the parent-baby relationship. For example, a socially unskilled preschooler will occasionally be clumsy with the baby or interact inappropriately. If parents interpret the behavior as malicious, they may chastise or punish the firstborn; if they interpret the behavior as unskilled, they may instruct or guide. In either case, parents may also change their interactions with the baby, may increase their surveillance of both children, and may limit the preschooler's access to the new brother or sister.

Motivation
Firstborns' attitudes will influence both the amount and the quality of their interaction with a new sibling. It is a mistake to assume that preschoolers will necessarily be jealous of the baby. Motivation is multifaceted, with positive and negative components that may change as the two children develop. General interest, disinterest, or rejection will determine how much firstborns approach, ignore, or avoid the baby. Specific feelings that change from situation to situa-

tion will determine if firstborns are benevolent, malevolent, or both. And on any occasion, children's behavior toward the baby will be determined by a variety of motivations and emotions. Hoping to gain approval, children may show off a newly acquired skill; being curious, they may poke the baby's eyes and mouth; or wanting to continue an activity, they may ignore the baby's distress.

A variety of factors shape firstborns' motivation. Children's self-narratives, including role definitions, may motivate certain types of interaction with a new brother or sister. Preschoolers may want to play with or help take care of the baby simply because they assume that is what a big brother or sister does. In turn, children's motivation may influence their self-concept. Preschoolers may incorporate their jealousy and rivalry into their personal definition of the sibling role, or they may include loving the baby as part of their personal history.

Preschoolers may be generally motivated to interact with babies or with babies of a particular sex, but their general motivation to interact with a new brother or sister can also be affected by parents. Before the baby arrives, parents usually try to promote firstborns' acceptance of the sibling in a number of ways: for example, by encouraging the firstborns to feel fetal movement, by letting them help prepare for the baby, or by bringing them to antenatal check-ups to listen to the fetal heartbeat (Walz and Rich 1983). Afterward a positive attitude toward a new brother or sister may be fostered by discussions of the baby as a person who experiences feelings—like love, anger, and pain—and desires—like hunger and thirst (Dunn and Kendrick 1982a). Later a negative attitude may result if parents intrude into their children's disputes with prohibitions (Kendrick and Dunn 1983).

But whether or not preschoolers are generally interested in interacting with a baby brother or sister, they are probably motivated by the baby's cues on specific occasions. A baby's social bids and crying can directly recruit young children's attention, and feedback from the baby—like continuing attention, smiling, and laughing—can sustain their interactions. Parents may directly influence preschoolers' motivation on specific occasions by encouraging interactions—perhaps suggesting a game of pat-a-cake with the baby—and by discouraging them—perhaps because the baby is sleeping. Finally, parents may indirectly influence children's motivation to interact with a baby brother or sister. For example, young children may become interested in the baby the moment they observe a parent's interest and they may want to try the game the parent is playing.

The Firstborn Child and the Baby

Preschoolers initiate social exchanges with a baby brother or sister for various reasons. They may be intrinsically motivated to interact with the baby, they may be encouraged by parents, or they may simply respond to the baby's social bids. Their interactive skills may also motivate involvement; possessing a skill, especially a newly acquired one, may be reason enough to use it. And once the interaction has started, it may continue for other reasons: because the children have a few appropriate skills, because they want to practice a new one, because the baby is sufficiently responsive, or because a parent provides necessary support.

Regardless, firstborns potentially have many opportunities to rehearse skills for soothing, amusing, or otherwise interacting with the baby. By successfully interacting with the baby, children acquire information not only about themselves and their own abilities but also about the baby and about their relationship. They may consequently elaborate their existing self-narratives and revise their role definition, and, most important, they may acquire positive self-evaluations. Such changes in self-concept presumably increase their motivation to interact with the baby, especially in similar situations using similar skills. In time, as firstborns and second borns develop a variety of appropriate skills, their interactions will last longer and become more sophisticated. They will accumulate day-to-day experiences and incorporate each other into their own psychological space, into their own self-narratives. Then their relationship changes from a series of interactions, which vary situationally, to a complex fabric of feelings, ideas, and memories, which transcends situations.

Acquisition of the Sibling Role

The transition to big brother or sister is an instance of role acquisition. The proposed model, which focuses on role representation, role enactment, and motivation, is certainly consistent with this view. But can the model accommodate the changes implied by a role transition? Simon's transition to the role of big brother shows that it can. Interestingly, the process took many months and apparently involved anticipatory, formal, informal, and personal phases, the same phases that have been identified for the acquisition of other roles (Mercer 1981; Thornton and Nardi 1975).

Bev's pregnancy served as the anticipatory phase during which Simon began to adapt socially and psychologically. Simon accepted the reality of the unborn baby, especially after he felt it move. Hence, he nominally adopted his new role very early and began thinking of himself as a big brother even before Asher was born. At the time, Simon also gained practical experience with babies, thereby acquiring a number of rudimentary skills that would be useful when interacting with his new brother, and he speculated about fulfilling his role, as when he asked for advice about protecting the baby.

Simon also sought information about other topics relevant to the transition. He wondered about biological and practical aspects of pregnancy and delivery, which helped him understand his new role partner. His discussions of arrangements for the baby helped him understand his own role and possible changes in family roles. Such information also may have helped him cope with stress that he experienced before the baby was born (Deutsch et al. 1988).

Asher's arrival initiated the formal phase of Simon's adaptation to the role of big brother. Understanding the role partner is an important aspect of acquiring a reciprocal or complementary role. Simon began to identify Asher by watching him and asking questions about him. Bev and I facilitated the process mainly by highlighting Asher's characteristics and by comparing Asher to Simon as a baby. Initially Simon's enactment of his new role was strongly determined by prescribed expectations that he learned mainly from Bev and me but also from other experts, like his grandparents, and from books, like *101 Things to Do with a Baby* (Ormerod 1984). Bev and I controlled Simon's access to Asher, suggested what Simon could and could not do with him, and monitored their interactions. Thus, at the time, Simon lacked the knowledge, the freedom, and the skill to enact his new role fully.

Gradually Simon moved to an informal phase, during which he developed his own way of dealing with his role. We all learned more about Asher as a baby and about Simon's ability to interact with his brother. And even if Simon originally mimicked us or explicitly followed our instructions, he eventually rejected some models and adapted others, apparently evaluating the extent to which particular models were appropriate for him and Asher. Thus, Simon fully expected to help care for Asher but rarely did so after Asher's first week; he discovered that bathing and diapering were beyond his ability and not all that much fun. We initially encouraged Simon to "read" to Asher, but Simon virtually never did so on his own; artificial interactions based on reading were also not really fun. In contrast, Simon imitated conventional games and eventually adapted them as he discovered what amused Asher.

I doubt that Simon fully achieved the personal phase of role acquisition during the study, yet he clearly accepted Asher as the baby in the family. And although Simon likely did not often think about where he had been and where he was going, he did relinquish some aspects of his previous roles that competed with his new one. Even before he became a brother, he adamantly insisted that he was big, not little, and afterward, he apparently used pretense to work through losing the roles of baby and little boy. Simon began to develop a real sense of his own identity within the role of big brother—as protector and playmate, for example. And he started to establish an individual enactment style that Bev and I generally accepted; actually, as Asher grew, the two boys developed their own style of interaction, which included playful roughhousing, not-so-playful arguing, and a variety of other features common to sibling relationships.

Simon and Asher's relationship continues to develop. They play together, joke at supper, fight over television shows, and share their games. They love and help each other; they also hit and frustrate each other—and more, much more. Separately they have each constructed a place for the other. Together they have constructed a place in our family. I watch them and learn. Most of all, I delight in what they have.

Appendix A
Qualitative Methods

My qualitative data consist of over 750 pages of notes and language protocols, including a log of my own observations of Simon's actions and comments, audiotaped conversations and interviews, and audiotaped interactions between Simon and Asher.

Log Entries

I started keeping a daily log about five months before Asher was born (3,7,8). I recorded everything I saw Simon do or heard him say that was remotely related to becoming a brother. Before Asher was born, I was interested in Simon's knowledge of conception, prenatal development, and childbirth, his understanding of babies, family relationships, and family constellations, his expectations for changes in family life and for Bev's stay in the hospital, his helping prepare for the baby, his interactions with babies, and his self-concept. Afterward I was also interested in his understanding of our family, his acceptance of Asher, and his interactions with Asher.

For the most part, I did not raise topics relevant to my study because I wanted to learn about Simon's spontaneous behavior and concerns during normal daily life, but I was quite willing to talk as a father to a son about anything that he brought up. In a few instances, I obtained information from Bev or from Simon's daycare teachers, but mostly I recorded my own observations. Thus, although Bev and I spent similar amounts of time with Simon during this period, I am overrepresented, relative to her, in my account of his transition to brotherhood.

Audiotaped Conversations

I originally planned to interview Simon from time to time about topics that I thought were important, but our conversations were very stilted when I tried. Still, I successfully began natural conversations

Table A.1
Coding Scheme for Qualitative Material

Category	Examples of Codes	Examples of Subcodes
Situation	caregiving baby	nurse, carry
	pretend play	as baby, as family
Issue	arrangements for the baby	room, clothes
	biology	conception, birth
Person concept (Self/Baby)[a]	abilities	reach, talk
	preferences	type of food, play
Social comparison	self-other (e.g., Simon-Baby)	person concept codes
	two others (e.g., Asher-Father)	person concept codes
Behavior	distress	dependency, withdrawal
	taking Baby's place	bed, toy
Emotions	empathy	cry, hurt
	feelings	happy, jealous

Direct effects		
Simon → Baby	caregive	burp, feed
	imitate	action, vocalization
Baby → Simon	distress	cry, fret
	positive affect	laugh, smile
Simon → Parent[b]	imitate	activity, talk
	invite near	involved, uninvolved
Parent → Simon	caregiving	dress, hold
	discuss: issues (as above), person concept (as above), social comparison (as above)	
Indirect effects		
Simon → (Parent ⇄ Baby)	bridge	noticing baby, play
	interfere	caregiving, location
Parent → (Simon ⇄ Baby)	instruct	aggression, soothing
	model	imitate baby, talk to baby

a. Baby could refer to any infant, although most of the time it referred to Asher.
b. Coding for parent was applied separately for Mother and Father.

that I could audiotape about topics already on Simon's mind. I also had a few chances to tape conversations that Simon started himself. I taped fourteen such conversations, each 10 to 30 minutes long.

Audiotaped Interviews

I had planned to obtain information with a number of semistructured interviews but had trouble adopting an interviewer mode with Simon. I therefore supervised an undergraduate student on a research project that involved thirteen sessions with Simon: five before Asher was born and eight afterward. The sessions lasted between 1 and 2 hours each and were all taped. They included a few structured interviews, described in appropriate chapters, but mainly open-ended conversations during games and stories that were chosen to highlight topics relevant to the case study.

Audiotaped Interactions

I taped ten interactions between Asher and Simon, each lasting between 10 and 30 minutes. In some cases, I was with the boys, so the tapes supplemented other information in my log. In other cases, the boys were alone, so the tapes provided data about interactions that were not influenced by my presence.

Coding Categories

A qualitative analysis rests on the coding scheme applied to the data (table A.1). In a sense, the coding scheme is the finding. I initially developed the computer-based scheme for my logged observations, which included the most varied material. Each log entry was identified by date, number, and relevant background material. It was then multiply classified according to a two-tiered system involving codes and subcodes on as many of the categories in table A.1 as were appropriate. I did not develop the coding scheme a priori; rather it evolved when I repeatedly coded the qualitative material and verified the codes. I was then able to code the audiotaped conversations without changing the categories, which validated the scheme.

When I started coding the taped interviews and interactions, it became obvious that there was virtually no information to be gained by coding the material completely. As eventually happens in qualitative research, no new categories emerged from the data (Glaser and Strauss 1965). Thus I approached the interviews and interactions globally, with reference to specific topics or questions I had already identified during the detailed coding of the log entries and the taped conversations.

Appendix B
Daily Diaries

I kept daily diaries of Simon's activities for seven consecutive days during the three months before Asher's arrival—October (3,9,19–25), November (3,10,15–21), and December (3,11,20–26)—and during four of the five months afterward—January (4,0,21–27), February (4,1,17–23), April (4,3,16–22), and May (4,4,28–5,4). Throughout the day I kept notes on sheets that were divided into 15-minute segments. The unit of description was an activity—breakfast, play, singing songs, and so on—and I included as much detail as possible about the location and the individuals involved. In most cases I kept notes throughout the day, reconstructing periods of time I did not directly observe Simon with help from people who were involved.

The raw records were transcribed into a database program in the format illustrated in table B.1. For each of the 2,057 entries, the following items were coded: (1) date; (2) dc = whether Simon attended daycare that day; (3) day of the week; (4) h = hour in which the activity started; (5) # = order of the entry during the hour; (6) activity; (7) typ = type of activity; (8) loc = location of the activity; (9) dur = duration of the activity (minutes); (10) p# = number of people interacting with Simon; and (11–16) level of interaction with M = mother, F = father, A = Asher, Ch = other children, Ba = babies besides Asher, and Ad = adults besides parents.

What Simon Did

Table B.2 lists the types of activities coded for each diary entry. I collapsed some of the codes and used the following broad categories to analyze Simon's activities: care (bedtime and care), conflict (misbehavior and discipline), daycare, hang around (hang around and socialize), help (baby care and household help), mealtime, play, stories/songs, religious services, sleep (quiet in bed or asleep), talk, travel, and television. In a sense, the codes describe the roles that Simon fulfilled in his daily life.

Table B.1
Example of Daily Diary Raw Data

date	dc	day	h	#	activity	typ[a]	loc[b]	dur (minutes)	#p	M	F	A	Ch	Ba	Ad
10/14	0	su	18	a	S vacuumed living room rug. M and F in and out of room.	hh	ho[b]	30	0	1[c]	1	0	0	0	0
10/14	0	su	18	b	S plays by self. Calls M or F occasionally to look at toys.	pl	ho	30	0	1	1	0	0	0	0
10/14	0	su	19	a	PGM and PGF come by. They, M, and F talk together and with S.	ha	ho	30	4	2	2	0	0	0	2
10/14	0	su	19	b	PGM reads S story until babysitter arrives.	re	ho	15	1	0	0	0	0	0	4
10/14	0	su	19	c	Babysitter reads stories.	re	ho	15	1	0	0	0	0	0	4
5/26	0	su	18	a	M and S in S's room.	ha	ho	10	1	3	0	0	0	0	0
5/26	0	su	18	b	M and S look at magazines.	re	ho	5	1	4	0	0	0	0	0
5/26	0	su	18	c	S plays; M reads paper.	pl	ho	10	0	1	0	0	0	0	0
5/26	0	su	18	d	"Muppets"; M and F read paper.	tv	ho	30	0	1	1	0	0	0	0
5/26	0	su	18	e	"Fraggle Rock." M and F read paper/watch.	tv	ho	15	0	1	1	0	0	0	0
5/26	0	su	18	f	"Fraggle Rock." S, M, and F.	tv	ho	15	2	2	2	0	0	0	0
5/26	0	su	19	a	S to bathroom self.	ca	ho	5	0	0	0	0	0	0	0
5/26	0	su	19	b	M reads stories.	re	ho	25	1	4	0	0	0	0	0

Note: S = Simon, M = mother, F = father, PGM = paternal grandmother, PGF = paternal grandfather, Ba = any baby other than Asher, Ch = any child, Ad = any adult other than parents.
a. See table B.2 for codes of types of activities.
b. ho = home.
c. See table 5.2 for definitions of levels of involvement.

Table B.2
Codes and Definitions for Types of Activities in the Daily Diary

Activity Type	Definition	Example
bc = baby care	directly involved with caring for a baby	helps change diapers, gives a bottle
bt = bedtime	bedtime rituals	hugs and kisses, walking to bed
ca = care	receiving care or self care	dressing, brushing teeth, getting ready for daycare
d = discipline	being disciplined	
dc = daycare	all time at daycare	
ha = hang around	undirected activity, doing nothing in particular	
hh = household	household chores, shopping	washing dishes, taking out garbage, grocery shopping
ib = in bed	in bed but not asleep, in bed less then 20 minutes	
mb = misbehave	acting out, consistently not complying	
mt = meal time	sitting down to eat	
pl = play	play	coloring, games, swimming, fantasy play, bicycling
re = stories/songs	books, newspapers, songs	
rs = religious services	attending the service	
so = socialize	greeting or seeking out others	greeting grandparents
sl = sleep	in bed and quiet for a minimum of 20 minutes	
tk = talk	direct conversation	phone conversation
tr = travel	driving or walking somewhere	
tv = television	watching television	

A Typical Week

I first examined the distribution of Simon's time during a typical week by calculating the average duration per week for each activity, collapsing across the seven weeks. The data are presented in table B.3. The time devoted to each activity is presented as a proportion of three values: the total time in a week (168 hours), the total time that Simon was neither sleeping nor falling asleep at home (although including naptime at daycare), and the total time that Simon was awake and not involved in daycare activities.

Of 168 hours per week, Simon was falling asleep or asleep for about 73 hours at home plus another 5 to 10 hours for naptime at daycare. He spent on average approximately 38 hours a week on daycare activities. He attended a university-based center that offered high-quality programming with an emphasis on social-emotional development. For practical reasons and because changes at home would only minimally affect Simon's daycare schedule, I kept no record of his daycare routine, but it should be understood that Simon participated at daycare in many of the listed activities—specifically play,

Table B.3
Mean Duration Per Week of Each Type of Activity

Activity	Hours per Week	Percentage[a] of		
		Total Time	Waking Time[b]	Waking (nondaycare)
Sleep	73.3	44		
Daycare	37.9	23	40	
Play	15.4	9	16	27
Television	7.1	4	7	12
Mealtime	6.7	4	7	12
Care	6.5	4	7	11
Hang around	5.2	3	5	9
Travel	4.9	3	5	9
Help	4.2	2	4	7
Stories/songs	4.1	2	4	7
Religious services	1.2	1	1	2
Talk	0.8	0	1	1
Conflict	0.7	0	1	1

a. Percentages do not sum to 100 because of rounding.
b. Time at daycare includes naptime.

care, mealtime, travel, help, stories/songs, hang around, talk, and conflict.

Simon was awake and not involved in daycare activities for about 57 hours a week. What he did during this time is our main concern. A young child's work is clearly play, a point strongly made even without play time at daycare. Simon spent almost half his nondaycare waking time in one type of amusement or another: playing (27 percent), watching television (12 percent), and listening to stories or songs (7 percent).

I could also include help (7 percent) as an amusement activity. Like most other preschoolers, Simon frequently became involved in household tasks or shopping and less often performed a chore on his own. Simon helped mostly with food preparation (55 times in the 49 sampled days) but also with the dishwasher (11), washing machine (10), and vacuum cleaner (10) and with tidying up (10), watering plants (7), and making beds (6). Occasionally his participation was more of a hindrance, as when he dropped a dish or spilled the watering can, but he was often really helpful, as when he made his bed or vacuumed his room. Regardless of the outcome, helping certainly appeared to be play for Simon.

Simon spent a quarter of his nondaycare waking time in basic caretaking routines (13 percent) and mealtime (12 percent). Activities such as these must be fit into a child's schedule one way or another, although there is some flexibility in the amount of time devoted to

Table B.4
Mean Duration Per Week at Each Locale

| | | Percentage[a] of | | |
Locale	Hours per Week	Total Time	Waking Time	Waking (nondaycare)[b]
Home	112.9	67	42	70
Daycare	38.7 (0.8[c])	23	41	2
Visiting	5.3	3	6	9
Outdoors	3.9	2	4	7
Car	3.2	2	3	5
Synagogue	2.4	1	3	4
Public building	1.8	1	2	3

a. Percentages do not sum to 100 because of rounding.
b. Nondaycare refers to activities, not to the locale.
c. Duration of nondaycare activities that took place at daycare.

each. And Simon spent almost a tenth of nondaycare waking time both traveling (9 percent), which always involved an adult, and just hanging around (9 percent).

Where Simon Spent His Time

Table B.4 presents the duration of time per week at each of seven locales: home, daycare center, someone else's home, outdoors (including an indoor pool), car, synagogue (but not necessarily attending the service), and public buildings (including shops and the Y). Of the 168 hours in a week, Simon spent approximately 67 percent at home, 23 percent at daycare, and the remaining 10 percent in other locales. Of his waking time, he spent equal proportions—about 40 percent—at home and at daycare. He was at home for about 70 percent of the waking time in which he was not participating in daycare activities, with the largest portion of the remaining time spent visiting or outdoors.

Appendix C
Behavioral Ratings of Adjustment

Traditionally, psychologists have used behavioral checklists to assess preschoolers' adjustment or maladjustment. Three such checklists were completed on a regular basis: one by Bev and me and two by Simon's teachers.

Home Behavioral Rating Scale (HBRS)

Laurie Gottlieb and I (Gottlieb and Mendelson 1990) modified previous scales (Nadelman and Begun 1982, Vernon et al. 1966) to develop a forty-eight-item questionnaire that assesses a young child's behavioral adjustment. The items were generated a priori with reference to six subscales (see table C.1, left column): (a) Reaction to Separation, (b) Withdrawal, (c) Anger/Hostility, (d) Insecurity, (e) Dependence, and (f) Independence. Each of the subscales consisted of eight items that had obvious face validity, and the first five subscales could be combined as a measure of distress.

Biweekly Bev and I each independently rated the frequency with which Simon exhibited the forty-eight behaviors during the previous two weeks (3,6,21–4,3,28). Each item was presented with an analog scale similar to the following:

never _____ always

We indicated our judgments by slashing a 105-mm line between the extremes labeled never and always. For scoring purposes, the line was divided into 21 5-mm bins—numbered 0 for never to 20 for always—and the item was rated in terms of the bin in which the slash occurred. The item score was then expressed as a proportion of the line length [(bin number)/20], which varied from 0 for never to 1 for always, and the scale score was the mean of the eight items. To assess changes over time, I obtained single ratings for each four-week period by averaging the ratings of adjacent two-week periods.

Table C.1
Subscales and Items From the Behavioral Rating Scales

Home Version (HBRS)	Daycare Version (DBRS and DBCS)
A. Reaction to separation	
1.[a] MAKE A FUSS ABOUT GOING TO BED AT NIGHT	Make a fuss about lying down for nap
6. Get upset when you left him alone for a few minutes	Cry or make a fuss about being left at daycare
12. TRY HARD TO GET YOUR ATTENTION	TRY TO GET YOUR ATTENTION
18. FOLLOW YOU AROUND THE HOUSE	Follow you around the daycare
24. Cling or want to be held or carried about	Cling or want to be held or carried about
30. Make a fuss when you left him for the day or evening	Ask about his mother or father
36. INTERRUPT YOU WHEN YOU WERE BUSY	NOT GET RIGHT INTO AN ACTIVITY WHEN HE WAS DROPPED OFF AT DAYCARE[b]
42. Make a fuss about going to a playgroup, nursery school, or other activities	GET UPSET WHEN OTHER CHILDREN DID NOT SHARE THEIR TOYS OR LET HIM JOIN THEIR PLAY
B. Withdrawal	
2. Spend time just sitting around and doing nothing	Spend time just sitting around and doing nothing
7. NOT FIND IT EASY TO GET SIMON INTERESTED IN DOING THINGS[b]	NOT FIND IT EASY TO GET SIMON INTERESTED IN DOING THINGS[b]
13. Have trouble concentrating on an activity	Have trouble concentrating on an activity
19. Seem listless or tire easily	Seem listless or tire easily
25. Shy or fearful around strangers	Shy or fearful around strangers
31. Appear unhappy, sad, or depressed	Appear unhappy, sad, or depressed
37. Prefer playing alone when in a group	PREFER PLAYING ALONE THAN IN A GROUP
43. Not interested in things and games that other children like[b]	NOT INTERESTED IN THINGS AND ACTIVITIES THAT OTHER CHILDREN LIKE[b]
C. Anger/hostility	
8. Have temper tantrums	Fly off the handle or have a temper tantrum
14. Break toys or throw objects	KICK, BITE, PUSH, OR EXPRESS ANGER TOWARD OTHER CHILDREN

Table C.1 (continued)

Home Version (HBRS)	Daycare Version (DBRS and DBCS)
20. CRY EASILY	Cry
26. Hit, kick, or express anger toward you or your spouse	Hit, kick, or express anger toward you or other adults
32. Have difficulty getting along with playmates (not taking turns, fighting, etc.)	HAVE DIFFICULTY TAKING TURNS OR SHARING TOYS
38. Fly off the handle or get easily hurt or insulted	NOT EASILY SOOTHED WHEN HE STARTED TO CRY[b]
44. TALK BACK OR ACT RUDE	Talk back or act rudely to an adult
47. ACT STUBBORNLY OR INSIST ON GETTING HIS WAY	ACT STUBBORNLY OR INSIST ON GETTING HIS WAY
D. *Insecurity*	
3. Use a pacifier or bottle during the day	Reluctant to try a new activity
9. Use a security object such as a blanket or a teddy bear during the day	Suck his thumb or use a security object (e.g., a pacifier, a blanket, etc.)
15. Complain that nobody loved him	Boast
21. Bite his fingernails or suck on his fingers	SEEK APPROVAL FOR SOMETHING THAT HE MADE OR DID
27. ACT SILLY OR SHOW OFF	ACT SILLY OR SHOW OFF
33. Seem worried, anxious, or fearful	Seem worried, anxious, or fearful
39. WHINE	WHINE
45. Wake up during the night or come into your bed	WANT TO SPEND TIME WITH AN ADULT INSTEAD OF PLAYING WITH OTHER CHILDREN
E. *Dependence*	
4. Have toileting accidents during the day	Have toileting accidents while awake
10. Have toileting accidents during the night	Have toileting accidents during nap
16. Talk baby talk or pretend to be a baby	Talk baby talk or pretend to be a baby
22. Ask for the bottle or ask to be breast-fed	Show bad table manners (e.g., eat inappropriately with his hands, throw food, etc.)
28. Want to be cradled or rocked	Play with considerably younger children
34. Show interest in playing with his "baby" toys	Play with toys that were too young for him

Table C.1 (continued)

Home Version (HBRS)	Daycare Version (DBRS and DBCS)
40. Have speech difficulties	BREAK ESTABLISHED DAYCARE RULES
46. Ask for help in areas in which he previously did not need assistance	Ask for help in areas in which he previously did not need assistance
F. *Independence*	
5. Refer to himself as a big boy	Refer to himself as a big boy
11. Try to care for himself (for example, dress, eat, go to the bathroom)	Try to care for himself (for example, dress, eat, go to the bathroom)
17. Listen to what you and your spouse asked	Listen to what you or other adults asked
23. Entertain himself for periods by himself	Offer to share toys or invite other children to join his play
29. Quietly wait until you were ready to attend to him	Find something to do on his own
35. Ask to help you or to assume new responsibilities	Ask to help you or to assume new responsibilities
41. Show that he understood how you felt	Comfort or otherwise show that he understood someone else's feelings
48. Act maturely or grown-up compared to children his age	Act maturely or grown-up compared to children his age

a. Numbers refer to the order of the item in the complete scale.
b. Items were expressed in the positive form, and ratings were reversed for scoring.

Daycare Behavioral Rating Scale (DBRS)

I also developed a daycare version of the HBRS. The DBRS consisted of the same six subscales as the HBRS, but I changed or replaced items that were not relevant to daycare experience (table C.1, right column). About a month after the fall term started, both of Simon's teachers filled out the DBRS almost every two weeks (3,9,11–4,3,29). Both teachers missed the last period in December, when the daycare was closed, and one missed one period in the spring due to an oversight. The response format and scoring of the DBRS were identical to those of the HBRS.

Daycare Behavioral Comparison Scale (DBCS)

Simon's teachers completed an adaptation of the DBRS that enabled them to compare Simon with the other eleven children in his class,

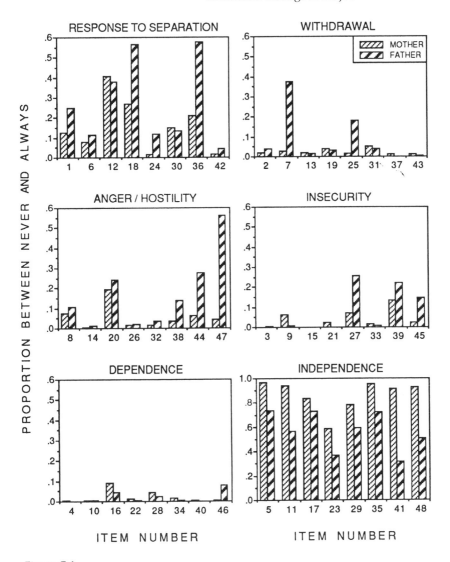

Figure C.1
Mother's and father's frequency ratings, expressed as the mean proportion of the distance from never (0.0) to always (1.0) computed across all weeks for each behavioral item on each of the subscales of the Home Behavioral Rating Scale.

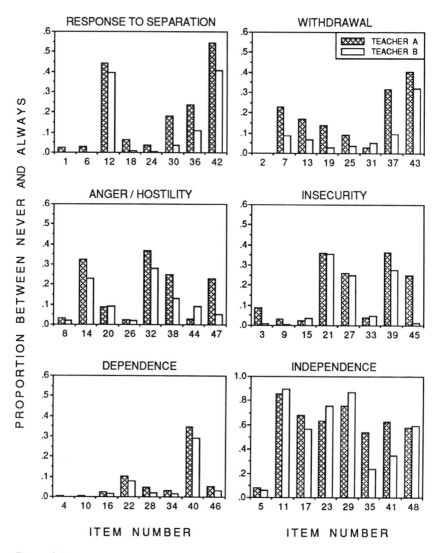

Figure C.2
Frequency ratings by each of Simon's daycare teachers, expressed as the mean proportion of the distance from never (0.0) to always (1.0) computed across all weeks
for each behavioral item on each of the subscales of the Daycare Behavioral Rating
Scale.

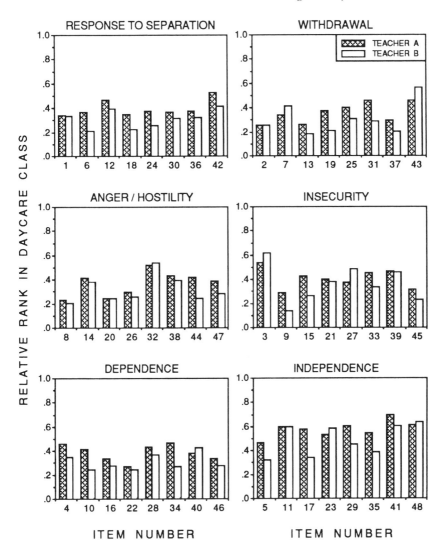

Figure C.3
Relative rankings by each of Simon's daycare teachers, expressed as the mean proportion of the distance from less than all (0.0) to more than all (1.0) computed across all weeks for each behavioral item on each of the subscales of the Daycare Comparison Rating Scale.

children who were all within about six months of his age. The items on the DBCS were the same as those on the DBRS, but the response format differed. Using an analog rating scale, the teachers indicated the frequency relative to his classmates with which Simon exhibited each behavior within the previous two weeks:

less   more
than _____ than
all   all

The teachers completed the DBCS every two weeks, with the two exceptions noted for the DBRS (3,10,9–4,3,29). The scoring of the DBCS was identical to that of the previous scales.

Overall Ratings

I first obtained a general description of Simon by calculating Bev's and my average ratings for each item on the HBRS across the twenty sampled weeks. Each panel in figure C.1 shows the data for the eight items from each subscale. Generally Simon rarely exhibited most of the distress behaviors and typically showed most of the independence behaviors. Either Bev or I rated only ten of the distress behaviors above 0.2 (capitalized items in table C.1, left column) and only three above 0.5. We both rated Simon relatively high on several items of only one subscale—Response to Separation. Simon appeared to be a generally well-adjusted child at home.

I calculated Simon's teachers' average ratings for each item on the DBRS (figure C.2) and on the DBCS (figure C.3) across all the sampled weeks. Simon rarely exhibited most of the distress behaviors and typically showed most of the independence behaviors (figure C.2). Either teacher rated only fourteen of the distress behaviors about 0.2 (capitalized items in table C.1, right column) and only one above 0.5. Both teachers also ranked Simon at or below the class median on virtually all the distress behaviors and at or above the class median on most of the independence behaviors (figure C.3). Simon was a generally well-adjusted child at daycare.

Bibliography

Aboud, F. E., and Ruble, D. N. (1987). Identity constancy in children: Developmental processes and implications. In T. Honess and K. Yardley (eds.), *Self and identity: Perspectives across the lifespan* (pp. 95–146). London: Routledge and Kegan Paul Ltd.

Abramovitch, R., Corter, C., and Lando, B. (1979). Sibling interaction in the home. *Child Development 50*, 997–1003.

Abramovitch, R., Corter, C., and Pepler, D. J. (1980). Observations of mixed-sex sibling dyads. *Child Development 51*, 1268–1271.

Adler, A. (1959). *Understanding human nature* (W. B. Wolfe, trans.). New York: Greenberg. (Original work published 1927.)

Ainsworth, M.D.S. (1969). Object relations, dependency, and attachment: A theoretical review of the mother-infant relationship. *Child Development 40*, 969–1025.

Ainsworth, M. D. S., Blehar, M., Waters, E., and Wall, S. (1978). *Patterns of attachment*. Hillsdale, NJ: Erlbaum.

Althea (Braithwaite). (1973). *The new baby*. London: Souvenir Press.

Anderson, D. R., Alwitt, L. F., Puzgles Lorch, E., and Levin, S. R. (1979). Watching children watch television. In G. A. Hale and M. Lewis (eds.), *Attention and cognitive development* (pp. 331–361). New York: Plenum.

Arnstein, H. S. (1974). *Billy and our new baby*. New York: Behavioral Publications.

Baldwin, A. L. (1947). Changes in parent behavior during pregnancy: An experiment in longitudinal analysis. *Child Development 18*, 29–39.

Baldwin, J. M. (1897). *Social and ethical interpretations in mental development*. New York: Macmillan.

Bank, S. P., and Kahn, M. D. (1982). *The sibling bond*. New York: Basic Books.

Bannister, D., and Agnew, J. (1977). The child's construing of self. In J. Cole (ed.), *Nebraska symposium on motivation*. Lincoln: University of Nebraska Press.

Baskett, L. M., and Johnson, S. M. (1982). The young child's interactions with parents versus siblings: A behavioral analysis. *Child Development 53*, 643–650.

Bateson, G. (1956). The message "This is play." In B. Schaffner (ed.), *Group processes*. New York: Josiah Macy.

Bell, R. Q. (1974). Contributions of human infants to caregiving and social interaction. In M. Lewis and L. A. Rosenblum (eds.), *The effect of the infant on its caregiver* (pp. 1–19). New York: Wiley.

Bell, S. M., and Ainsworth, M. D. S. (1972). Infant crying and maternal responsiveness. *Child Development 43*, 1171–1190.

Belsky, J. (1979). Mother-father-infant interaction: A naturalistic study. *Developmental Psychology 15*, 601–607.

Belsky, J. (1981). Early human experience: A family perspective. *Developmental Psychology 17*, 3–23.

Belsky, J., and Rovine, M. (1984). Social-network contact, family support, and the transition to parenthood. *Journal of Marriage and the Family 46*, 455–462.

Berman, P. W. (1986). Young children's responses to babies: Do they foreshadow differences between maternal and paternal styles? In A. Fogel and G. F. Melson (eds.), *Origins of nurturance: Developmental, biological and cultural perspectives on caregiving* (pp. 25–52). Hillsdale, N.J.: Erlbaum.

Berman, P. W., and Goodman, V. (1984). Age and sex differences in children's responses to babies: Effects of adults' caretaking requests and instructions. *Child Development 55*, 1071–1077.

Berman, P. W., Monda, L. D., and Myerscough, R. P. (1977). Sex differences in young children's responses to an infant: An observation within a day care setting. *Child Development 48*, 711–715.

Bernstein, A. C., and Cowan, P. A. (1975). Children's concepts of how people get babies. *Child Development 46*, 77–91.

Bissex, G. L. (1980). *Gnys at wrk: A child learns to write and read.* Cambridge, Mass.: Harvard University Press.

Bloom, K. (1984). Distinguishing between social reinforcement and social elicitation. *Journal of Experimental Child Psychology 38*, 93–102.

Blum, B. (ed.). (1980). *Psychological aspects of pregnancy, birthing and bonding.* New York: Human Science Press.

Bowlby, J. (1969). *Attachment and loss.* Vol. 1: *Attachment.* New York: Basic Books.

Breen, D. (1975). *The birth of a first child.* London: Tavistock Publications.

Bretherton, I. (1984). Representing the social world in symbolic play: Reality and fantasy. In I. Bretherton (ed.), *Symbolic play: The development of social understanding* (pp. 3–41). New York: Academic Press.

Bretherton, I. (1985). Attachment theory: Retrospect and prospect. In I. Bretherton and E. Waters (eds.), Growing points of attachment theory and research. *Monographs of the Society for Research in Child Development 50*(1–2, serial no. 209), 3–35.

Bretherton, I., and Waters, E. (eds.). (1985). Growing points of attachment theory and research. *Monographs of the Society for Research in Child Development 50* (serial no. 209).

Bromley, D. B. (1986). *The case-study method in psychology and related disciplines.* New York: Wiley.

Bronfenbrenner, U. (1979). *The ecology of human development.* Cambridge, Mass.: Harvard University Press.

Brown, R. (1973). *A first language: The early stages.* Cambridge, Mass.: Harvard University Press.

Brown, R. (1977). Introduction to C. E. Snow and C. A. Ferguson (eds.), *Talking to children: Language input and acquisition* (pp. 1–27). Cambridge: Cambridge University Press.

Bruner, J. S., and Sherwood, V. (1976). Peek-a-boo and the learning of rule structures. In J. S. Bruner, A. Jolly, and K. Silva (eds.), *Play: Its role in evolution and development* (pp. 277–285). Harmondsworth: Penguin.

Bryant, B. K. (1982). Sibling relationships in middle childhood. In M. E. Lamb and B. Sutton-Smith (eds.), *Sibling relationships: Their nature and significance across the lifespan* (pp. 87–122). Hillsdale, N.J.: Erlbaum.

Carey, S. (1983). Cognitive development: The descriptive problem. In M. Gazzaniga (ed.), *Handbook for cognitive neurology.* Hillsdale, N.J.: Erlbaum.

Carey, S. (1985). *Conceptual change in childhood.* Cambridge, Mass.: The MIT Press.

Cicirelli, V. G. (1975). Effects of mother and older sibling on the problem-solving behavior of the older child. *Developmental Psychology 11*, 749–756.

Clarke-Stewart, K. A. (1978). And daddy makes three: The father's impact on mother and young child. *Child Development 49*, 466–478.

Corter, C., Pepler, D., and Abramovitch, R. (1983). The role of the mother in sibling interaction. *Child Development 54*, 1599–1605.

Cowan, C. P., Cowan, P. A., Coie, L., and Coie, J. D. (1976). Becoming a family: The impact of a first child's birth on the couple's relationship. In W. B. Miller and L. F. Newman (eds.), *The first child and family formation* (pp. 296–324). Chapel Hill, N.C.: Carolina Population Center, University of North Carolina.

Crider, C. (1981). Children's conceptions of the body interior. In R. Bibace and M. Walsh (eds.), *New directions for child development: Children's conceptions of health, illness, and bodily functions* (no. 14, pp. 49–65). San Francisco: Jossey-Bass.

Darwin, C. (1877). A biographical sketch of an infant. *Mind 2*, 286–294.

Deutsch, F. M., Ruble, D. N., Fleming, A., Brooks-Gunn, J., and Stangor, C. S. (1988). Information-seeking and maternal self-definition during the transition to motherhood. *Journal of Personality and Social Psychology 55*, 420–431.

Douglas, J. W. B., Lawson, A., Cooper, J. E., and Cooper, E. (1968). Family interaction and the activities of young children. *Journal of Child Psychology and Psychiatry 9*, 157–171.

Dunn, J. (1983). Sibling relationships in early childhood. *Child Development 54*, 787–811.

Dunn, J., and Kendrick, C. (1979). In M. Lewis and L. Rosenblum (eds.), *The child and its family*. New York: Plenum Press.

Dunn, J., and Kendrick, C. (1980). The arrival of a sibling: Changes in patterns of interactions between mother and firstborn-child. *Journal of Child Psychology and Psychiatry 21*, 119–132.

Dunn, J., and Kendrick, C. (1982a). *Siblings: Love, envy, and understanding*. Cambridge, Mass.: Harvard University Press.

Dunn, J., and Kendrick, C. (1982b). The speech of two- and three-year-olds to infant siblings: "Baby talk" and the context of communication. *Journal of Child Language 9*, 579–595.

Dunn, J., Kendrick, C., and MacNamee, R. (1981). The reaction of firstborn children to the birth of a sibling: Mothers' report. *Journal of Child Psychology and Psychiatry 22*, 1–18.

Dunn, J., and Munn, P. (1985). Becoming a family member: Family conflict and the development of social understanding in the second year. *Child Development 56*, 580–492.

Dunn, J., and Munn, P. (1986). Sibling quarrels and maternal interventions: Individual differences in understanding and aggressions. *Journal of Child Psychology and Psychiatry 27*, 583–595.

Eibl-Eibesfeldt, I. (1975). *Ethology: The biology of behavior*. 2d ed. New York: Holt, Rinehart and Winston.

Emde, R. N., Gaensbauer, T. J., and Harmon, R. J. (1976). Emotional expression in infancy: A biobehavioral study. *Psychological Issues 10* (serial no. 37).

Epstein, S. (1973). The self-concept revisited: Or a theory of a theory. *American Psychologist 28*, 404–416.

Epstein, S. (1980). The self-concept: A review and the proposal of an integrated theory of personality. In E. Staub (ed.), *Personality: Basic aspects and current research* (pp. 82–131). Englewood Cliffs, N.J.: Prentice-Hall.

Erikson, E. H. (1968). *Identity: Youth and crisis*. New York: Norton.

Feiring, C., and Lewis, M. (1978). The child as a member of the family system. *Behavioral Science 23*, 225–233.

Feiring, C., Lewis, M., and Jaskir, J. (1983). The birth of a sibling: Its effects on the mother-firstborn child interaction. *Journal of Developmental and Behavioral Pediatrics 4*, 190–195.

Fernald, A., and Simon, T. (1984). Expanded intonation contours in mothers' speech to newborns. *Developmental Psychology 20*, 104–113.

Field, T., and Reite, M. (1984). Children's responses to separation from mother during the birth of another child. *Child Development 55*, 1308–1316.

Fischer, K. W. (1980). A theory of cognitive development: The control and construction of hierarchies of skills. *Psychological Review 87*, 477–531.

Fischer, K. W., Hand, H. H., Watson, M. W., Van Parys, M. M., and Tucker, J. L. (1984). Putting the child into socialization: The development of social categories in preschool children. In L. Katz (ed.), *Current topics in early childhood education* (5:27–72). Norwood N.J.: Ablex.

Freud, S. (1955). Analysis of a phobia in a five-year-old boy. In J. Strackey (ed. and trans.), *The standard edition of the complete psychological works of Sigmund Freud* (vol. 10). London: Hogarth Press. (Original work published 1909.)

Freud, S. (1959). Creative writers and daydreaming. In J. Strackey (ed. and trans.), *The standard edition of the complete psychological works of Sigmund Freud* (vol. 9). London: Hogarth. (Original work published 1908.)

Frodi, A. (1985). When empathy fails: Aversive infant crying and child abuse. In B. M. Lester and C. F. Z. Boukydis (eds.), *Infant crying: Theoretical and research perspectives* (pp. 263–278). New York: Plenum.

Fullard, W., and Reiling, A. M. (1976). An investigation of Lorenz's babyness. *Child Development 47*, 1191–1193.

Furman, W., and Buhrmester, D. (1985). Children's perceptions of the qualities of sibling relationships. *Child Development 56*, 448–461.

Gardner, H. (1980). *Artful scribbles: The significance of children's drawings*. New York: Basic Books.

Garmezy, N., and Rutter, M. (eds.). (1983). *Stress, coping, and development*. New York: McGraw-Hill.

Garnica, O. (1977). Some prosodic and paralinguistic features of speech to young children. In C. E. Snow and C. A. Ferguson (eds.), *Talking to children: Language input and acquisition* (pp. 63–88). Cambridge: Cambridge University Press.

Gelman, R., and Baillargeon, R. (1983). A review of some Piagetian concepts. In P. H. Mussen (series ed.) and J. H. Flavell and E. M. Markman (vol. ed.), *Handbook of child psychology*, vol. 3: *Cognitive development* (pp. 167–230). New York: Wiley.

Gelman, S. A. (1988). The development of induction within natural kind and artifact categories. *Cognitive Psychology 20*, 65–95.

Gergen, K. J., and Gergen, M. M. (1983). Narratives of the self. In T. R. Sarbin and K. E. Scheibe (eds.), *Studies in social identity* (pp. 254–273). New York: Praeger.

Gewirtz, J. L. (1965). The course of infant smiling in four child-rearing environments in Israel. In B. M. Foss (ed.), *Determinants of infant behavior* (3:205–248). London: Methuen.

Gilby, R. L., and Pederson, D. R. (1982). The development of the child's concept of the family. *Canadian Journal of Behavioral Science 14*, 111–121.

Glasberg, R., and Aboud, F. E. (1981). Keeping one's distance from sadness: Children's self-reports of emotional experience. *Developmental Psychology 17*, 195–202.

Glaser, B. G., and Strauss, A. L. (1965). Discovery of substantive theory: A basic strategy underlying qualitative research. *American Behavioral Scientist 8*, 5–12.

Glaser, B. G., and Strauss, A. L. (1971). *The discovery of grounded theory: Strategies for qualitative research*. Chicago: Aldine.

Gloger-Tippelt, G. (1988, April). The development of the mother's conceptions of the child before birth. Paper presented at the International Conference on Infant Studies. Washington, D.C.

Goetting, A. (1986). The developmental tasks of sibship over the life span. *Journal of Marriage and the Family 48*, 703–714.

Goldberg, S. (1977). Social competence in infancy: A model of parent-infant interaction. *Merrill-Palmer Quarterly 23*, 163–177.

Goldman, R. J., and Goldman, J. D. G. (1982). *Children's sexual thinking*. London: Routledge and Kegan Paul.

Goldman, R. J., and Goldman, J. D. G. (1988). *Show me yours! Understanding children's sexuality*. Ringwood, Australia: Penguin Books Australia.

Golinkoff, R. M., and Ames, G. J. (1979). A comparison of fathers' and mothers' speech to their young children. *Child Development 50*, 28–32.

Gottlieb, L. (1975). Maternal attachment in primiparas. *Journal of Obstetrics and Gynecological Nursing 7*, 39–44.

Gottlieb, L. N. (1985). Parental responsiveness and firstborn girls' adaptation to a new sibling. Ph.D. dissertation, McGill University.

Gottlieb, L. N., and Mendelson, M. J. (1990). Parental support and firstborn girls' adaptation to the birth of a sibling. *Journal of Applied Developmental Psychology 11*, 29–48.

Grieser, D. L., and Kuhl, P. K. (1988). Maternal speech to infants in a tonal language: Support for universal prosodic features in motherese. *Developmental Psychology 44*, 133–145.

Grossmann, K., Grossmann, K. E., Spangler, G., Suess, G., and Unzner, L. (1985). Maternal sensitivity and newborns' orientation responses as related to quality of attachment in northern Germany. In I. Bretherton and E. Waters (eds.), Growing points of attachment theory and research. *Monographs of the Society for Research in Child Development 50*(1–2, serial no. 209), 233–256.

Harris, M. (1969). *On understanding infants*. London: Dickens Press.

Harter, S. (1983). Developmental perspectives on the self-system. In P. H. Mussen (series ed.) and E. M. Hetherington (vol. ed.), *Handbook of child psychology*. Vol. 4: *Socialization, personality, and social development* (pp. 275–386). New York: Wiley.

Hinde, R. A., and Stevenson-Hinde, J. (eds.). (1988). *Relationships within families: Mutual influences*. Oxford: Oxford University Press.

Hoban, R. (1973). *Harvey's hideout*. London: Jonathon Cape.

Hoffman, M. (1975). Developmental synthesis of affect and cognition and its implication for altruistic motivation. *Developmental Psychology 11*, 607–622.

Holyoak, K. J. (1985). The pragmatics of analogical transfer. In G. H. Bower (ed.), *The psychology of learning and motivation* (vol. 9). New York: Academic Press.

Holyoak, K. J., Junn, E. N., and Billman, D. O. (1984). Development of analogical problem-solving skill. *Child Development 55*, 2042–2055.

Howe, N., and Ross, H. S. (1990). Socialization, perspective-taking and the sibling relationship. *Developmental Psychology 26*, 160–165.

Huston, A. C. (1983). Sex-typing. In P. H. Mussen (series ed.) and E. M. Hetherington (vol. ed.), *Handbook of child psychology*, Vol. 4: *Socialization, personality, and social development* (pp. 387–467). New York: Wiley.

Huttenlocher, J., and Higgins, E. T. (1978). Issues in the study of symbolic development. In W. A. Collins (ed.), *Minnesota symposium on child psychology* (vol. 2). Hillsdale, N.J.: Erlbaum.

Jacobson, J. L. Boersma, D. C., Fields, R. B., and Olson, K. L. (1983). Paralinguistic features of adult speech to infants and small children. *Child Development 54*, 436–442.

James, W. (1963). *Psychology.* New York: Fawcett. (Original work published 1890.)

Janis, I. L. (1971). *Stress and frustration.* New York: Harcourt Brace Jovanovich.

Kantor, D., and Lehr, W. (1976). *Inside the family.* San Francisco: Jossey-Bass.

Keil, F. C. (1986). The acquisition of natural kind and artifact terms. In W. Demopoulos and A. Marras (eds.), *Language learning and concept acquisition* (pp. 133–153). Norwood N.J.: Ablex.

Keller, A., Ford, L. H., and Meacham, J. A. (1978). Dimensions of self-concept in preschool children. *Developmental Psychology 14*, 483–489.

Keltner, B. R. (1988, May). Family characteristics of resilient preschool children. *Proceedings of the International Family Nursing Conference.* Calgary, Alberta, 232 (abstract).

Kendrick, C., and Dunn, J. (1980). Caring for the second baby: Effects on interaction between mother and firstborn. *Developmental Psychology 16*, 303–311.

Kendrick, C., and Dunn, J. (1983). Sibling quarrels and maternal responses. *Developmental Psychology 19*, 62–90.

Klein, D. M., Jorgensen, S. R., and Miller, B. C. (1978). Research methods and developmental reciprocity in families. In R. M. Lerner and G. B. Spanier (eds.), *Child influences on marital and family interaction: A life-span perspective* (pp. 107–135). London: Academic Press.

Klein, M. (1975). Criminal tendencies in normal children. In S. Lawrence (ed. and trans.), *Love, guilt and reparation and other works—1921–1945.* New York: Delacorte Press. (Original work published 1927.)

Kohlberg, L. A. (1966). A cognitive-developmental analysis of children's sex-role concepts and attitudes. In E. E. Maccoby (ed.), *The development of sex differences.* Stanford: Stanford University Press.

Kramer, L. (1989). The contribution of peers to children's adaptation to becoming a sibling. Ph.D. dissertation, University of Illinois.

Kreppner, K., Paulsen, S., and Schuetze, Y. (1982). Infant and family development: From triads to tetrads. *Human Development 25*, 373–391.

Kunhardt, D. (1942). *Pat the bunny.* New York: Western Publishing.

LaBarbera, J. D., Izard, C. E., Vietze, P., and Parisi, S. A. (1976). Four- and six-month-old infants' visual responses to joy, anger, and neutral expressions. *Child Development 47*, 535–538.

Lamb, M. E. (1978a). Interactions between eighteen-month-olds and their preschool-aged siblings. *Child Development 49*, 51–59.

Lamb, M. E. (1978b). The development of sibling relationships in infancy: A short-term longitudinal study. *Child Development 49*, 1189–1196.

Lamb, M. E., and Easterbrooks, M. A. (1981). Individual differences in parental sensitivity: Origins, components, and consequences. In M. E. Lamb and L. R. Sherrod (eds.), *Infant social cognition: Empirical and theoretical considerations* (pp. 127–154). Hillsdale, N.J.: Erlbaum.

LaRossa, R. (1983). The transition to parenthood and the social reality of time. *Journal of Marriage and the Family 45*, 579–589.

LaRossa, R., and LaRossa, M. M. (1981). *Transition to parenthood: How infants change families.* Beverly Hills, Calif.: Sage.

Lasko, J. K. (1954). Parent behavior toward first and second children. *Genetic Psychology Monographs 49*, 47–137.

Lawson, A., and Ingleby, J. D. (1974). Daily routines of preschool children: Effects of age, birth order, sex and social class, and developmental correlates. *Psychological Medicine 4*, 399–415.

Lazarus, R. S., and Folkman, S. (1984). *Stress, appraisal, and coping.* New York: Springer.

Legg, C., Sherick, I., and Wadland, W. (1974). Reaction of preschool children to the birth of a sibling. *Child Psychiatry and Human Development 5*, 3–39.

Leifer, M. (1980). *Psychological aspects of motherhood: A study of first pregnancy.* New York: Praeger.

Lester, B. M., and Boukydis, C. F. Z. (eds.). (1985). *Infant crying: Theoretical and research perspectives.* New York: Plenum.

Levy, D. M. (1937). Studies in sibling rivalry. *American Orthopsychiatric Association Research Monographs 2*, 1–96.

Lewis, C. (1986). *Becoming a father.* Milton Keynes, England: Open University Press.

Lewis, M., and Brooks, J. (1974). Self, other and fear: Infants' reactions to people. In M. Lewis and L. Rosenblum (eds.), *Fear: The origins of behavior* (vol. 2). New York: Wiley.

Lewis, M., and Brooks-Gunn, J. (1979). *Social cognition and the acquisition of self.* New York: Plenum Press.

Lewis, M., and Rosenblum, L. A. (eds.). (1974). *The effect of the infant on its caregiver.* New York: Wiley.

Light, P. (1979). *The development of social sensitivity.* Cambridge: Cambridge University Press.

Lorenz, K. (1970). *Studies in animal and human behavior* (R. Martin, trans.). London: Methuen. (Original work published 1935.)

Maccoby, E. E. (1988). Gender as a social category. *Developmental Psychology 24*, 755–765.

Maccoby, E. E., and Martin, J. A. (1983). Socialization in the context of the family: Parent-child interaction. In P. H. Mussen (series ed.) and E. M. Hetherington (vol. ed.), *Handbook of child psychology*, vol. 4: *Socialization, personality, and social development* (pp. 1–101). New York: Wiley.

McGraw, M. B. (1935). *Growth: A study of Johnny and Jimmy.* East Norwalk, Conn.: Appleton-Century-Crofts.

McQueen, L. (illus.). (1984). *Xavier's fantastic discovery (Cabbage Patch Kids).* Cleveland, Ga.: Parker Brothers.

Mahalksi, P. A. (1983). The incidence of attachment objects and oral habits at bedtime in two longitudinal samples of children aged 1.5–7 years. *Journal of Child Psychology and Psychiatry 24*, 283–295.

Maier, R. A., Jr., Holmes, D. L., Slaymaker, F. L., and Reich, J. N. (1984). The perceived attractiveness of preterm infants. *Infant Behavior and Development 7*, 403–414.

Mancuso, J. C., and Sarbin, T. R. (1983). The self-narrative in the enactment of roles. In T. R. Sarbin and K. E. Scheibe (eds.), *Studies in social identity* (pp. 233–253). New York: Praeger.

Mandler, J. M. (1983). Representation. In P. H. Mussen (series ed.) and J. H. Flavell and E. M. Markman (vol. eds.), *Handbook of child psychology*, vol 3: *Cognitive Development* (pp. 420–494). New York: Wiley.

Mead, G. H. (1934). *Mind, self, and society.* Chicago: University of Chicago Press.

Melson, G. F., and Fogel, A. (1982). Young children's interest in unfamiliar infants. *Child Development 53*, 693–700.

Melson, G. F., Fogel, A., and Mistry, J. (1986). The study of nurturant interactions: From the infant's perspective. In A. Fogel and G. F. Melson (eds.), *Origins of nurturance: Developmental, biological and cultural perspectives on caregiving* (pp. 69–90). Hillsdale, N.J.: Erlbaum.

Melson, G. F., Fogel, A., and Toda, S. (1986). Children's ideas about infants and their care. *Child Development 57*, 1519–1527.

Mendelson, M. J. (1988a, April). A 4-year-old's interactions with a new sibling. Paper presented at the International Conference on Infant Studies, Washington, D.C. *Infant Behavior and Development 11*, 217 (abstract).

Mendelson, M. J. (1988b, April). The foundations of interaction with a new sibling. Address to the Quebec Developmental Psychologists' Consortium, Montreal, Quebec.

Mendelson, M. J. (1990). Becoming a sibling: A role acquisition framework. Paper presented at the International Conference on Infant Studies, Montreal, Quebec. *Infant Behavior and Development 13*, 154 (abstract).

Mendelson, M. J., Aboud, F. E., and Lanthier, R. (1988). Sibling relationship questionnaire. McGill University, Montreal, Quebec.

Mendelson, M. J., Aboud, F. E., and Vera, A. (1987, June). Self-knowledge and social comparison in preschool children. Poster presented at the Canadian Psychological Association, Vancouver. *Canadian Psychology 28*, 408 (abstract).

Mendelson, M. J., and Gottlieb, L. N. (1987, April). Parents' involvement with first-born girls from before to 1 year after a sibling's birth. Poster presented at the Society for Research in Child Development, Baltimore, Md. *SRCD Abstracts 6*, 183.

Mendelson, M. J., and Gottlieb, L. N. (1988). Early sibling relationship rating scale. McGill University, Montreal, Quebec.

Mendelson, M. J., and Haith, M. M. (1976). The relation between audition and vision in the human newborn. *Monographs of the Society for Research in Child Development 41*(4, serial no. 167).

Mercer, R. T. (1981). A theoretical framework for studying factors that impact on the maternal role. *Nursing Research 30*, 73–77.

Miller, B. C., and Myers-Walls, J. A. (1983). Parenthood: Stresses and coping strategies. In H. I. McCubbin and C. R. Figley (eds.), *Stress and the family*, Vol. 1: *Coping with normative transitions* (pp. 54–73). New York: Brunner/Mazel.

Miller, E. (1974.). *Mousekin's birth*. Englewood Cliffs, N.J.: Prentice-Hall.

Miller, P., and Garvey, C. (1984). Mother-baby role play: Its origins in social support. In I. Bretherton (ed.), *Symbolic play: The development of social understanding* (pp. 101–130). New York: Academic Press.

Murphy, S. O. (1988, April). Newborns and school-age siblings: Children's meanings and parental communications. Poster presented at the International Conference on Infant Studies, Washington, D.C. *Infant Behavior and Development 11*, 232 (abstract).

Murray, A. D. (1979). Infant crying as an elicitor of parental behavior: An examination of two models. *Psychological Bulletin 86*, 191–215.

Murray, A. D. (1985). Aversiveness is in the mind of the beholder: Perception of infant crying by adults. In B. M. Lester and C. F. Z. Boukydis (eds.), *Infant crying: Theoretical and research perspectives* (pp. 217–240). New York: Plenum.

Murray, L., and Trevarthen, C. (1986). The infant's role in mother-infant communications. *Journal of Child Language 13*, 15–29.

Myers-Walls, J. A. (1979). *A role theory approach to the transition into parenthood*. Ph.D. dissertation, Purdue University.

Nadelman, L., and Begun, A. (1982). The effect of the newborn on the older sibling: Mothers' questionnaires. In M. E. Lamb and B. Sutton-Smith (eds.), *Sibling re-*

lationships: Their nature and significance across the lifespan (pp. 13–37). Hillsdale, N.J.: Erlbaum.

Nelson, K. (1981). Social cognition in a script framework. In J. H. Flavell and L. Ross (eds.), *Social cognitive development* (pp. 97–118). New York: Cambridge University Press.

Nelson, K., and Gruendel, J. (1981). Generalized event representation: Basic building blocks of cognitive development. In M. E. Lamb and A. Brown (eds.), *Advances in developmental psychology* (1:131–158). Hillsdale, N.J.: Erlbaum.

Nuttall, R. L., and Nuttall, E. V. (1975). *Family size and spacing in the United States and Puerto Rico.* Washington, D.C.: Center for Population Research, National Institute of Child Health and Development.

Oakley, A. (1980). *Women confined: Towards a sociology of childbirth.* New York: Schocken Books.

Odom, R. D., and Lemond, C. M. (1972). Developmental differences in the perception and production of facial expressions. *Child Development 43*, 359–369.

Olioff, M. I. (1982). An examination of Beck's theory within the context of postpartum depression. Ph.D. dissertation, McGill University.

Oller, D. K. (1980). The emergence of sounds of speech in early infancy. In G. H. Yeni-Komshian, J. F. Kavanagh, and C. A. Ferguson (eds.), *Child Phonology,* Vol. 1: *Production* (pp. 93–112). New York: Academic Press.

Ormerod, J. (1984). *101 things to do with a baby.* Harmondsworth, England: Kestrel Books.

Oster, H. (1981). "Recognition" of emotional expression in infancy? In M. E. Lamb and L. R. Sherrod (eds.), *Infant social cognition: Empirical and theoretical considerations* (pp. 85–126). Hillsdale, N.J.: Erlbaum.

Ostwald, P. (1963). *Soundmaking: The acoustic communication of emotion.* Springfield, Ill.: Charles C. Thomas.

Packer, M. J. (1985). Hermeneutic inquiry in the study of human conduct. *American Psychologist 40*, 1081–1093.

Paley, V. G. (1988). *Bad guys don't have birthdays: Fantasy play at four.* Chicago: University of Chicago Press.

Papousek, H., and Papousek, M. (1987). Intuitive parenting: A dialectic counterpart to the infants' integrative competence. In J. D. Osofsky (ed.), *Handbook of infant development,* 2d ed. (pp. 669–720). New York: Wiley.

Papousek, M. (1987, April). Models and messages in the melodies of maternal speech in tonal and nontonal languages. Paper presented at the Society for Research in Child Development, Baltimore, Md. *SRCD Abstracts 6*, 407.

Papousek, M., Papousek, H., and Bornstein, M. H. (1985). The naturalistic vocal environment of young infants: On the significance of homogeneity and variability in parental speech. In T. M. Field and N. A. Fox (eds.), *Social perception in infants* (pp. 269–297). Norwood, N.J.: Ablex.

Pederson, D. R., and Gilby, R. L. (1986). Children's concepts of the family. In R. D. Ashmore and D. M. Brodzinsky (eds.), *Thinking about the family: Views of parents and children.* Hillsdale, N.J.: Erlbaum.

Peller, L. E. (1954). Libidinal phases, ego development, and play. *Psychoanalytic Study of the Child 9*, 178–198.

Pelletier-Stiefel, J., Pepler, D., Crozier, K., Stanhope, L., Corter, C., and Abramovitch, R. (1986). Nurturance in the home: A longitudinal study of sibling interaction. In A. Fogel and G. F. Melson (eds.), *Origins of nurturance: Developmental, biological and cultural perspectives on caregiving* (pp. 3–24). Hillsdale, N.J.: Erlbaum.

Pepler, D. J., Corter, C., and Abramovitch, R. (1982). Social relations among children: Comparison of sibling and peer interaction. In K. Rubin and H. Ross (eds.), *Peer relationships and social skills in childhood* (pp. 209–228). New York: Springer-Verlag.

Piaget, J. (1962). *Play, dreams and imitation in childhood* (C. Gattegno and F. M. Hodgson, trans.). New York: Norton. (Original work published 1951.)

Piaget, J. (1963). *The origins of intelligence in children* (M. Cook, trans.). New York: Norton. (Original work published 1952.)

Pipp, S., Fischer, K. W., and Jennings, S. (1987). Acquisition of self- and mother-knowledge in infancy. *Developmental Psychology 23,* 86–96.

Power, T. G., Hildebrandt, K. A., and Fitzgerald, H. E. (1982). Adults' responses to infants varying in facial expression and perceived attractiveness. *Infant Behavior and Development 5,* 33–44.

Ratner, N., and Bruner, J. S. (1978). Games, social exchange, and the acquisition of language. *Journal of Child Language 5,* 1–15.

Ricks, M. H. (1985). The social transmission of parental behavior: Attachment across generations. In I. Bretherton and E. Waters (eds.), Growing points of attachment theory and research. *Monographs of the Society for Research in Child Development 50*(1–2, serial no. 209), 211–232.

Roche, P. K. (1979). *Good-bye, Arnold!* New York: Dial Press.

Rubin, K. H., and Gordon, S. (1987, June). Relations between young children's experiences of stressful life events and their socio-emotional behaviors. Paper presented at the Canadian Psychological Association, Vancouver, B.C. *Canadian Psychology 28,* 523 (abstract).

Rubin, K. H., Fein, G. G., and Vandenberg, B. (1983). Play. In P. H. Mussen (series ed.) and E. M. Hetherington (vol. ed.), *Handbook of child psychology,* Vol 4: *Socialization, personality, and social development* (pp. 693–774). New York: Wiley.

Rubin, R. (1967). Attainment of the maternal role. Part 1: Processes. *Nursing Research 14,* 237–245.

Rubin, R. (1975). Maternal tasks in pregnancy. *Maternal-Child Nursing Journal 4,* 143–153.

Sachs, J., and Devin, J. (1976). Young children's use of age-appropriate speech styles in social interaction and role-playing. *Journal of Child Language 3,* 81–98.

Samuels, H. R. (1980). The effect of an older sibling on infant locomotor exploration of a new environment. *Child Development 51,* 607–609.

Sarbin, T. R., and Scheibe, K. E. (eds.). (1983). *Studies in social identity.* New York: Praeger.

Saxe, G. B., Guberman, S. R., and Gearhart, M. (1987). Social processes in early number development. *Monographs of the Society for Research in Child Development 52*(2, serial no. 214).

Schank, R. C., and Abelson, R. P. (1977). *Scripts, plans, goals and understanding.* Hillsdale, N.J.: Erlbaum.

Shatz, M., and Gelman, R. (1973). The development of communication skills: Modifications in the speech of young children as a function of listener. *Monographs of the Society for Research in Child Development 38*(5, serial no. 152).

Shaw, M. E., and Costanzo, P. R. (1982). *Theories of social psychology.* 2d ed. New York: McGraw-Hill.

Shereshefsky, P. M., and Yarrow, L. J. (eds.). (1973). *Psychological aspects of a first pregnancy and early postnatal adaptation.* New York: Raven Press.

Shereshefsky, P. M., Liebenberg, B., and Lockman, R. F. (1973). In P. M.

Shereshefsky and L. J. Yarrow (eds.), *Psychological aspects of a first pregnancy and early postnatal adaptation* (pp. 165–180). New York: Raven Press.

Sherrod, K. B., Crawley, S., Petersen, G., and Bennett, P. (1978). Maternal language to prelinguistic infants: Semantic aspects. *Infant Behavior and Development 1*, 335–345.

Sherrod, K. B., Friedman, S., Crawley, S., Drake, D., and Devieux, J. (1977). Maternal language to prelinguistic infants: Syntactic Aspects. *Child Development 48*, 1662–1665.

Shultz, T. R. (1982). Rules of causal attribution. *Monographs of the Society for Research in Child Development 47*(1, serial no. 194).

Snow, C. E. (1977a). The development of conversation between mothers and babies. *Journal of Child Language 4*, 1–22.

Snow, C. E. (1977b). Mothers' speech research: From input to interaction. In C. E. Snow and C. A. Ferguson (eds.), *Talking to children: Language input and acquisition* (pp. 31–49). Cambridge: Cambridge University Press.

Snow, C. E., and Ferguson, C. A. (eds.). (1977). *Talking to children: Language input and acquisition.* Cambridge: Cambridge University Press.

Spock, B., and Rothenberg, M. B. (1985). *Dr. Spock's baby and child care.* New York: Pocket Books.

Stack, D. M., and Muir, D. W. (1990). Tactile stimulation as a component of social interchange: New interpretations for the still-face effect. *British Journal of Developmental Psychology*, in press.

Stark, R. E. (1980). Stages of speech development in the first year of life. In G. H. Yeni-Komshian, J. F. Kavanagh, and C. A. Ferguson (eds.), *Child Phonology*, Vol. 1: *Production* (pp. 73–92). New York: Academic Press.

Steiner, G. A. (1963). *The people look at television.* New York: Knopf.

Stern, D. N., Spieker, S., Barnett, R. K., and MacKain, K. (1983). The prosody of maternal speech: Infant age and context related changes. *Journal of Child Language 10*, 1–15.

Sternglanz, S. H., Gray, J. L., and Murakami, M. (1977). Adult preferences for infantile facial features: An ethological approach. *Animal Behavior 25*, 108–115.

Stevenson, M. B., Leavitt, L. A., Thompson, R. H., and Roach, M. A. (1988). A social relations model analysis of parent and child play. *Developmental Psychology 24*, 101–108.

Stewart, A. J. (1982). The course of individual adaptation to life changes. *Journal of Personality and Social Psychology 42*, 110–113.

Stewart, A. J., Sokol, M., Healy, J. M., and Chester, N. L. (1986). Longitudinal studies of psychological consequences of life changes in children and adults. *Journal of Personality and Social Psychology 50*, 143–151.

Stewart, R. B. (1983). Sibling attachment relationships: Child-infant interactions in the strange situation. *Developmental Psychology 19*, 192–199.

Stewart, R. B., and Marvin, R. S. (1984). Sibling relations: The role of conceptual perspective-taking in the ontogeny of sibling caregiving. *Child Development 55*, 1322–1332.

Stewart, R. B., Mobley, L. A., Van Tuyl, S. S., and Salvador, M. A. (1987). The firstborn's adjustment to the birth of a sibling: A longitudinal assessment. *Child Development 58*, 341–355.

Stewart, R. B., Paulson-Benson, J. D., Farren, D. E., and Murray, R. L. (1983). Sibling interaction: The role of the older child as teacher for the younger. *Merrill-Palmer Quarterly 29*, 47–68.

Stubblefield, R. L. (1955). Children's emotional problems aggravated by family moves. *American Journal of Orthopsychiatry 25,* 120–126.

Taylor, M. K., and Kogan, K. L. (1973). Effects of the birth of a sibling on mother-child interactions. *Child Psychiatry and Human Development 4,* 53–58.

Thomas, A., Birch, H. C., Chess, S., and Robbins, L. C. (1961). Individuality in responses of children to similar environmental situations. *American Journal of Psychiatry 117,* 798–803.

Thompson, S. K., and Bentler, P. M. (1971). The priority of cues in sex discrimination by children and adults. *Developmental Psychology 5,* 181–185.

Thornton, R., and Nardi, P. M. (1975). The dynamics of role acquisition. *American Journal of Sociology 80,* 870–885.

Tomasello, M., and Mannle, S. (1985). Pragmatics of sibling speech to one-year-olds. *Child Development 56,* 911–917.

Tomkins, S. (1963). *Affect, imagery and consciousness,* Vol. 2: *Negative affects.* London: Tavistock.

Trause, M. A. (1978). Birth in the hospital: The effect on the sibling. *Birth and the Family Journal 5,* 207–210.

Trause, M. A., Voos, D., Rudd, C., Klaus, M., Kennell, J., and Boslett, M. (1981). Separation for childbirth: The effect on the sibling. *Child Psychiatry and Human Development 12,* 32–39.

Trehub, S. E. (1990). The perception of musical patterns by human infants: The provision of similar patterns by their parents. In W. C. Stebbins and M. Berkley (eds.), *Comparative perception.* New York: Wiley Interscience.

Trivers, R. L. (1974). Parent-offspring conflict. *American Zoologist 14,* 249–264.

Vandell, D. L., Wilson, K. S., and Whalen, W. T. (1981). Birth-order and social-experience differences in infant-peer interaction. *Developmental Psychology 17,* 438–445.

Vandell, D. L., and Wilson, K. S. (1987). Infants' interactions with mother, sibling, and peer: Contrasts and relations between interaction systems. *Child Development 58,* 176–186.

Vernon, D. T. A., Schulman, J. L., and Foley, J. M. (1966). Changes in children's behavior after hospitalization. *American Journal of Disease in Children 111,* 581–593.

Vessey, J. A. (1988). Comparison of two teaching methods on children's knowledge of their internal bodies. *Nursing Research 37,* 262–267.

Volterra, V. (1984). Waiting for the birth of a sibling: The verbal fantasies of a 2-year-old boy. In I. Bretherton (ed.), *Symbolic play: The development of social understanding* (pp. 219–248). New York: Academic Press.

Vygotsky, L. S. (1967). Play and its role in the mental development of the child. *Soviet Psychology 12,* 62–67.

Walz, B. L., and Rich, O. J. (1983). Maternal tasks of taking-on a second child in the postpartum period. *Maternal-Child Nursing Journal 12,* 185–216.

Watson, M. W., and Amgott-Kwan, T. (1983). Transitions in children's understanding of parental roles. *Developmental Psychology, 19,* 659–666.

Whiting, B. B., and Edwards, C. P. (1988). *Children of different worlds: The formation of social behavior.* Cambridge, Mass.: Harvard University Press.

Wilson, E. O. (1975). *Sociobiology: The new synthesis.* Cambridge, Mass.: Belknap Press.

Yin, R. K. (1984). *Case study research: Design and methods.* Beverly Hills, Calif.: Sage Publications.

Index